STAR WARS

THE **HIGH REPUBLIC**

TRAIL OF SHADOWS

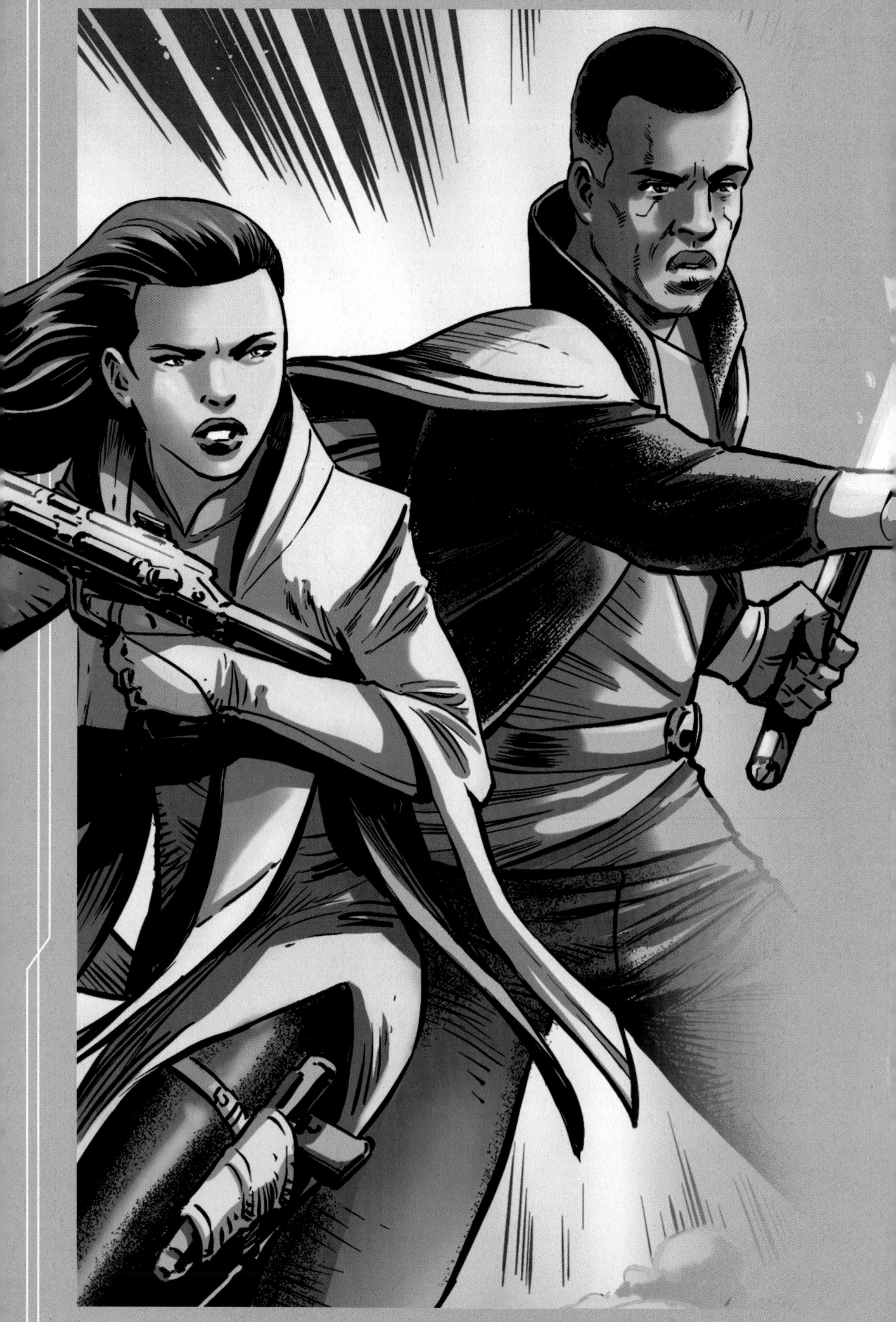

STAR WARS
THE HIGH REPUBLIC

TRAIL OF SHADOWS

Writer
DANIEL JOSÉ OLDER

Artist
DAVE WACHTER

Color Artists
GIADA MARCHISIO with **IAN HERRING** (#3)

Letterer
VC's **JOE SABINO**

Cover Art
PHIL NOTO

Timeline Design
CARLOS LAO

Editors
TOM GRONEMAN & **DANNY KHAZEM**

Supervising Editor
MARK PANICCIA

Collection Editor	JENNIFER GRÜNWALD
Assistant Editor	DANIEL KIRCHHOFFER
Assistant Managing Editor	MAIA LOY
Associate Manager, Talent Relations	LISA MONTALBANO
VP Production & Special Projects	JEFF YOUNGQUIST
Book Designer	ADAM DEL RE
SVP Print, Sales & Marketing	DAVID GABRIEL
Editor in Chief	C.B. CEBULSKI

For Lucasfilm:

Senior Editor	ROBERT SIMPSON
Creative Director	MICHAEL SIGLAIN
Art Director	TROY ALDERS
Lucasfilm Story Group	MATT MARTIN
	PABLO HIDALGO
	EMILY SHKOUKANI
	JASON D. STEIN
Creative Art Manager	PHIL SZOSTAK

STAR WARS: THE HIGH REPUBLIC — TRAIL OF SHADOWS. Contains material originally published in magazine form as STAR WARS: THE HIGH REPUBLIC — TRAIL OF SHADOWS (2021) #1-5. First printing 2022. ISBN 978-1-302-93298-5. Published by MARVEL WORLDWIDE, INC., a subsidiary of MARVEL ENTERTAINMENT, LLC. OFFICE OF PUBLICATION: 1290 Avenue of the Americas, New York, NY 10104. **Printed in Canada.** KEVIN FEIGE, Chief Creative Officer; DAN BUCKLEY, President, Marvel Entertainment; JOE QUESADA, EVP & Creative Director; DAVID BOGART, Associate Publisher & SVP of Talent Affairs; TOM BREVOORT, VP, Executive Editor; NICK LOWE, Executive Editor, VP of Content, Digital Publishing; DAVID GABRIEL, VP of Print & Digital Publishing; MARK ANNUNZIATO, VP of Planning & Forecasting; JEFF YOUNGQUIST, VP of Production & Special Projects; ALEX MORALES, Director of Publishing Operations; DAN EDINGTON, Director of Editorial Operations; RICKEY PURDIN, Director of Talent Relations; JENNIFER GRÜNWALD, Director of Production & Special Projects; SUSAN CRESPI, Production Manager; STAN LEE, Chairman Emeritus. For information regarding advertising in Marvel Comics or on Marvel.com, please contact Vit DeBellis, Custom Solutions & Integrated Advertising Manager, at vdebellis@marvel.com. For Marvel subscription inquiries, please call 888-511-5480. **Manufactured between 1/28/2022 and 3/1/2022 by SOLISCO PRINTERS, SCOTT, QC, CANADA.**

10 9 8 7 6 5 4 3 2 1

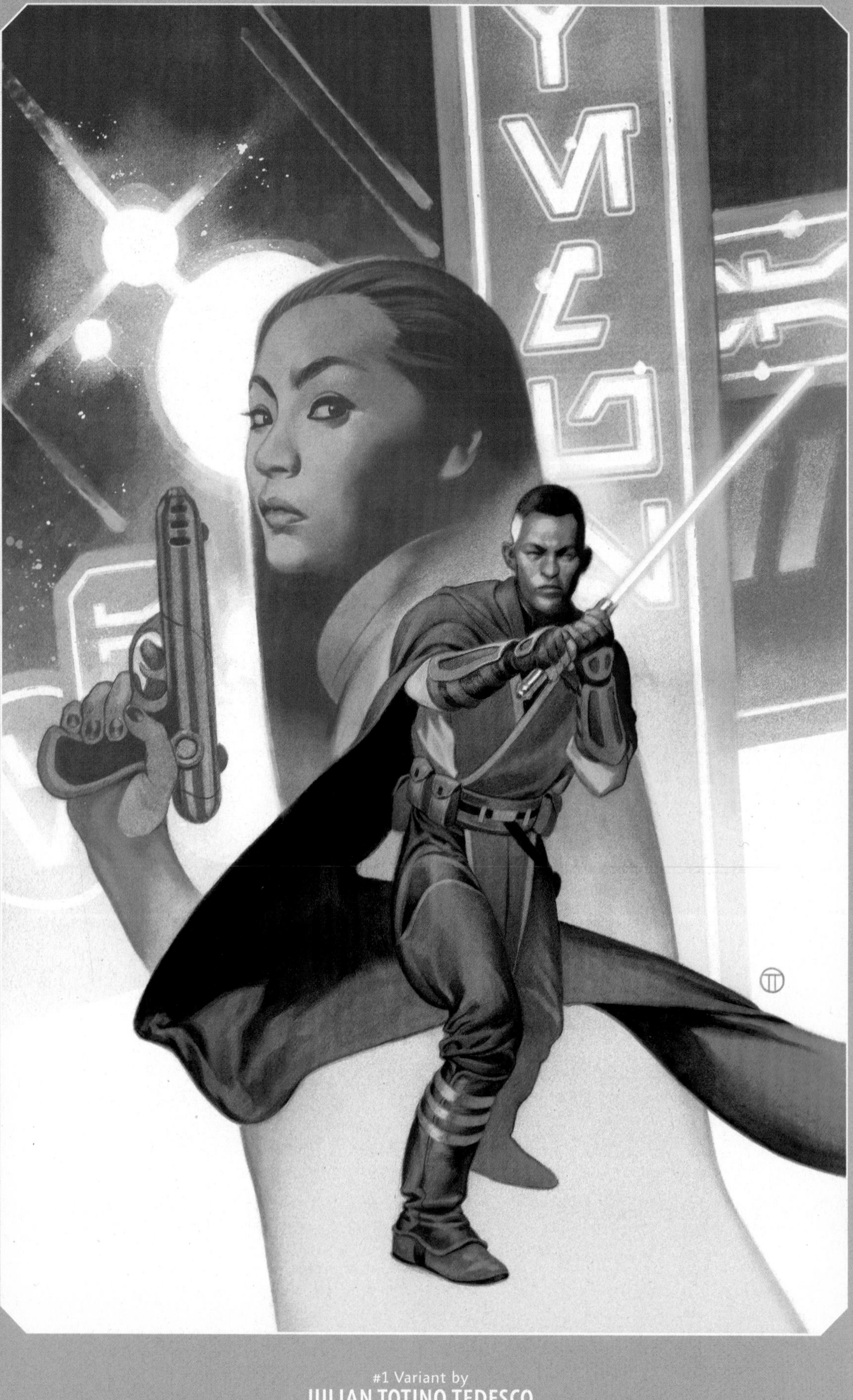

#1 Variant by
JULIAN TOTINO TEDESCO

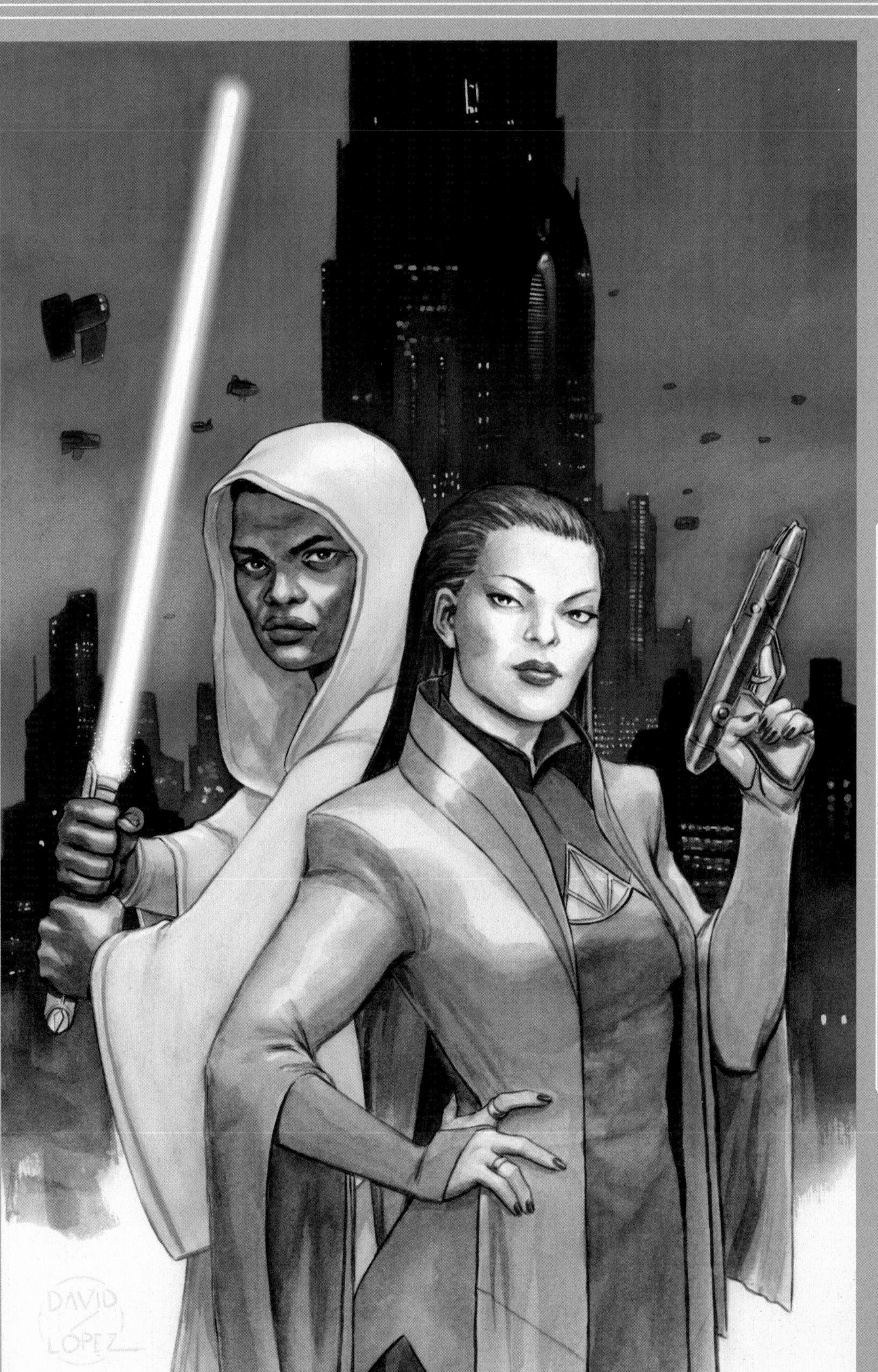
DAVID
LOPEZ

1 | TRAIL OF SHADOWS

TIMELINE

THE HIGH REPUBLIC

FALL OF THE JEDI

THE
PHANTOM
MENACE

ATTACK OF
THE CLONES

THE CLONE
WARS

REVENGE OF
THE SITH

REIGN OF THE EMPIRE

THE
BAD BATCH

SOLO:
A STAR WARS
STORY

REBELS

ROGUE ONE:
A STAR WARS
STORY

A NEW HOPE

THE EMPIRE
STRIKES BACK

RETURN OF
THE JEDI

AGE OF REBELLION

THE NEW REPUBLIC

THE
MANDALORIAN

RESISTANCE

THE FORCE
AWAKENS

THE LAST JEDI

THE RISE OF
SKYWALKER

RISE OF THE FIRST ORDER

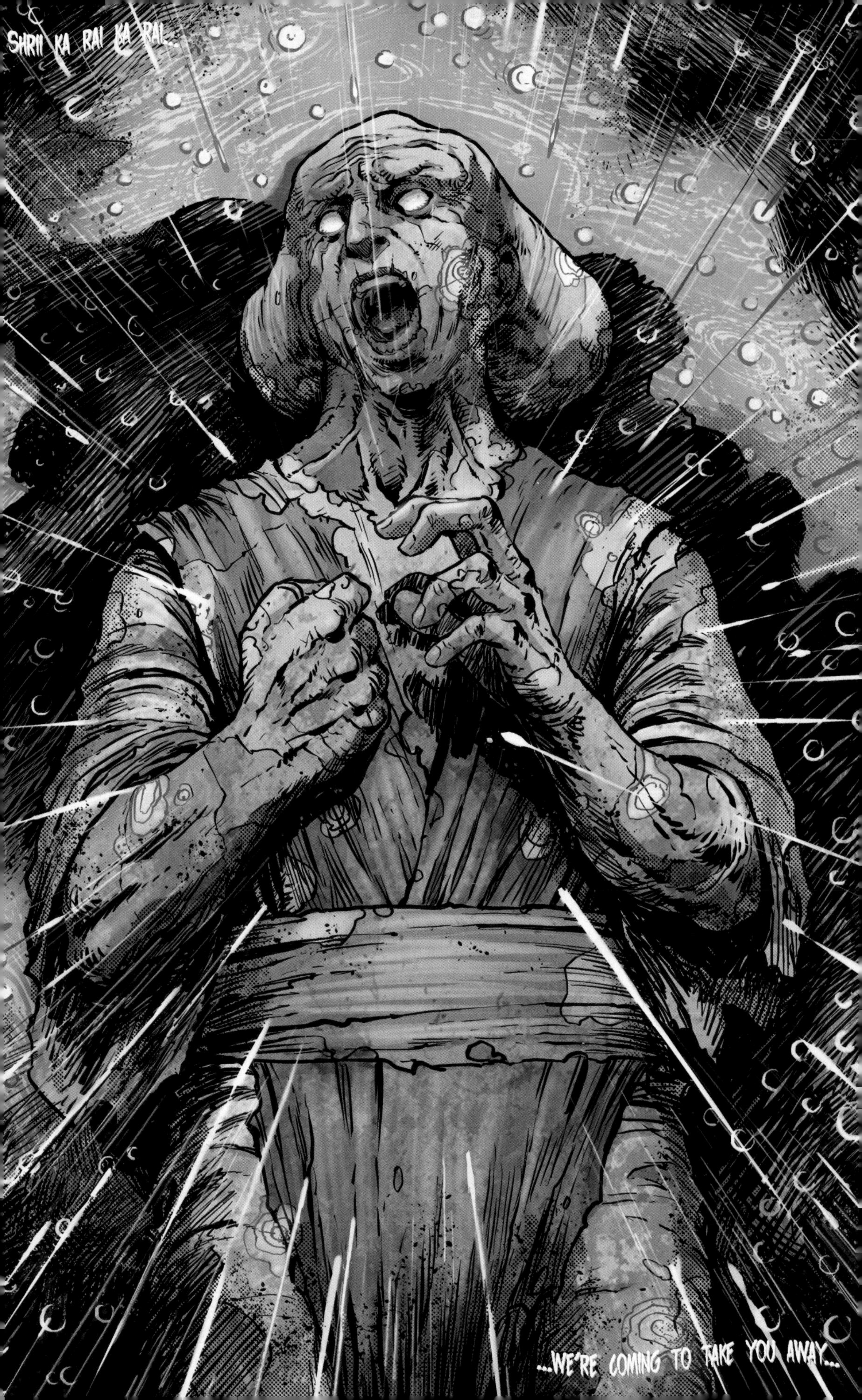
SHRII KA RAI KA RAI...
...WE'RE COMING TO TAKE YOU AWAY...

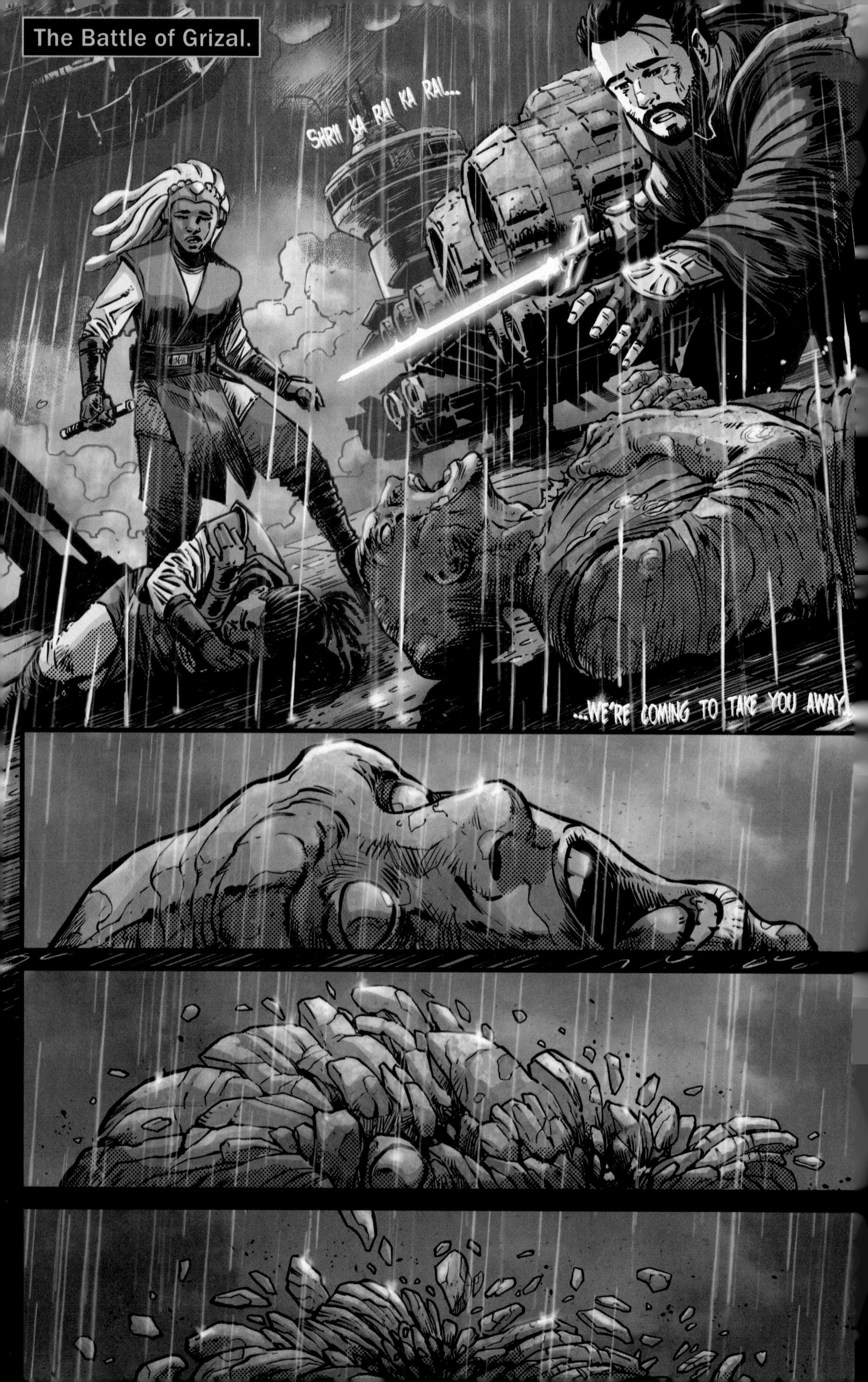
The Battle of Grizal.
SHRII KA RAI KA RAI...
...WE'RE COMING TO TAKE YOU AWAY.

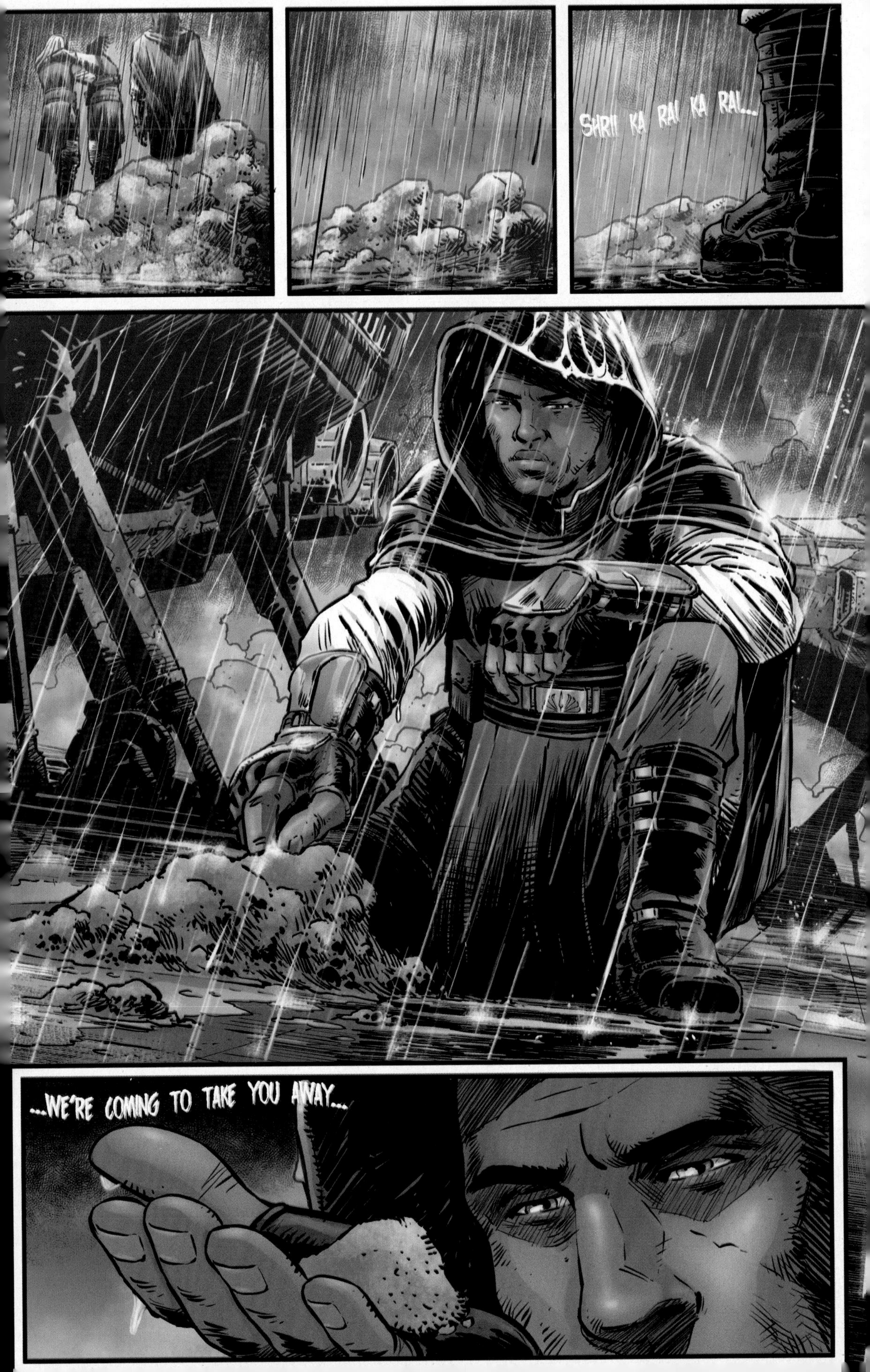
SHRII KA RAI KA RAI...
...WE'RE COMING TO TAKE YOU AWAY...

Jedi Temple.
Coruscant.

WHY IS IT YOU KEEP SINGING THAT OLD NURSERY RHYME, STELLAN?

HM? OH...I HADN'T NOTICED I WAS... WHAT SONG IS IT?

OLD VIDYARVRIKT USED TO SING IT TO US WHEN WE WERE YOUNGLINGS AND WOULDN'T GO TO SLEEP. TRYING TO TERRORIZE US INTO BEING WELL BEHAVED, I IMAGINE.

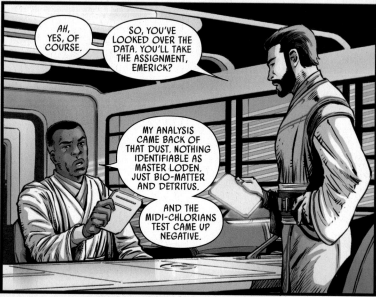

AH, YES, OF COURSE.

SO, YOU'VE LOOKED OVER THE DATA. YOU'LL TAKE THE ASSIGNMENT, EMERICK?

MY ANALYSIS CAME BACK OF THAT DUST. NOTHING IDENTIFIABLE AS MASTER LODEN. JUST BIO-MATTER AND DETRITUS.

AND THE MIDI-CHLORIANS TEST CAME UP NEGATIVE.

I KNOW WHAT I SAW.

INDEERA SAW IT TOO. AND BELL...

I UNDERSTAND. BUT THERE'S VERY LITTLE TO GO ON HERE. THERE ARE NO FOOTPRINTS OR TRACKS. THERE'S NO HOLO-FOOTAGE, NO CONCLUSIVE CAUSE OF DEATH...

AND NO ONE CAN AGREE ON WHAT IT *LOOKED LIKE* OR EVEN IF THERE WAS AN *IT* AT ALL. *PADAWAN ZETTIFAR* IS STILL HAVING TROUBLE MAKING SENSE OF WHAT HAPPENED.

EMERICK, I DON'T KNOW HOW ELSE TO PUT IT TO YOU. I'VE NEVER SEEN OR FELT ANYTHING LIKE THIS IN MY LIFE. WHATEVER HAPPENED OUT THERE ON GRIZAL, IT SENT TWO OF OUR JEDI TO THE SHOCK WARD AND A THIRD IS SIMPLY GONE.

AND I'M STILL HAVING *NIGHTMARES* ABOUT IT.

ONE MINUTE WE HAD THE NIHIL ON THE RUN...

I'VE NEVER SEEN STELLAN LIKE THIS.

AND THE NEXT, ELZAR WAS NOSE-DIVING OUT OF THE SKY, BELL WAS IN SHOCK AND *MASTER LODEN*... WELL...

GRANTED, HE HAS A LOT ON HIS PLATE AS THE NEWEST AND ONE OF THE YOUNGEST MEMBERS OF THE JEDI COUNCIL.

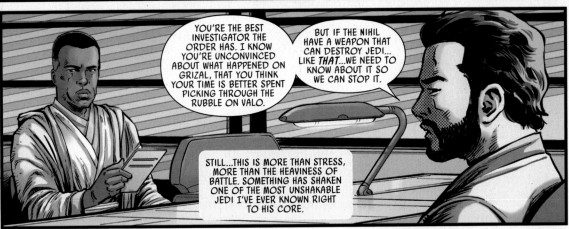

YOU'RE THE BEST INVESTIGATOR THE ORDER HAS. I KNOW YOU'RE UNCONVINCED ABOUT WHAT HAPPENED ON GRIZAL, THAT YOU THINK YOUR TIME IS BETTER SPENT PICKING THROUGH THE RUBBLE ON VALO.

BUT IF THE NIHIL HAVE A WEAPON THAT CAN DESTROY JEDI... LIKE *THAT*...WE NEED TO KNOW ABOUT IT SO WE CAN STOP IT.

STILL...THIS IS MORE THAN STRESS, MORE THAN THE HEAVINESS OF BATTLE. SOMETHING HAS SHAKEN ONE OF THE MOST UNSHAKABLE JEDI I'VE EVER KNOWN RIGHT TO HIS CORE.

ALL I ASK YOU IS THAT YOU LOOK INTO IT. MY FORMER PADAWAN VERNESTRA AND MASTER KANTAM CAME UPON A SMALL NIHIL BASE ON VRANT TARNUM IMMEDIATELY BEFORE THE ATTACK.

THE RAIDERS CAPTURED ON VALO WHO WERE STATIONED THERE SPEAK ABOUT IT WITH A CERTAIN... REVERENCE. HARD TO EXPLAIN. START THERE. TAKE A TEAM OF TROOPERS. THEY'RE ALREADY AT THE BARRACKS, READY TO GO.

SEE WHAT YOU CAN FIND.

THIS IS DESPERATION.

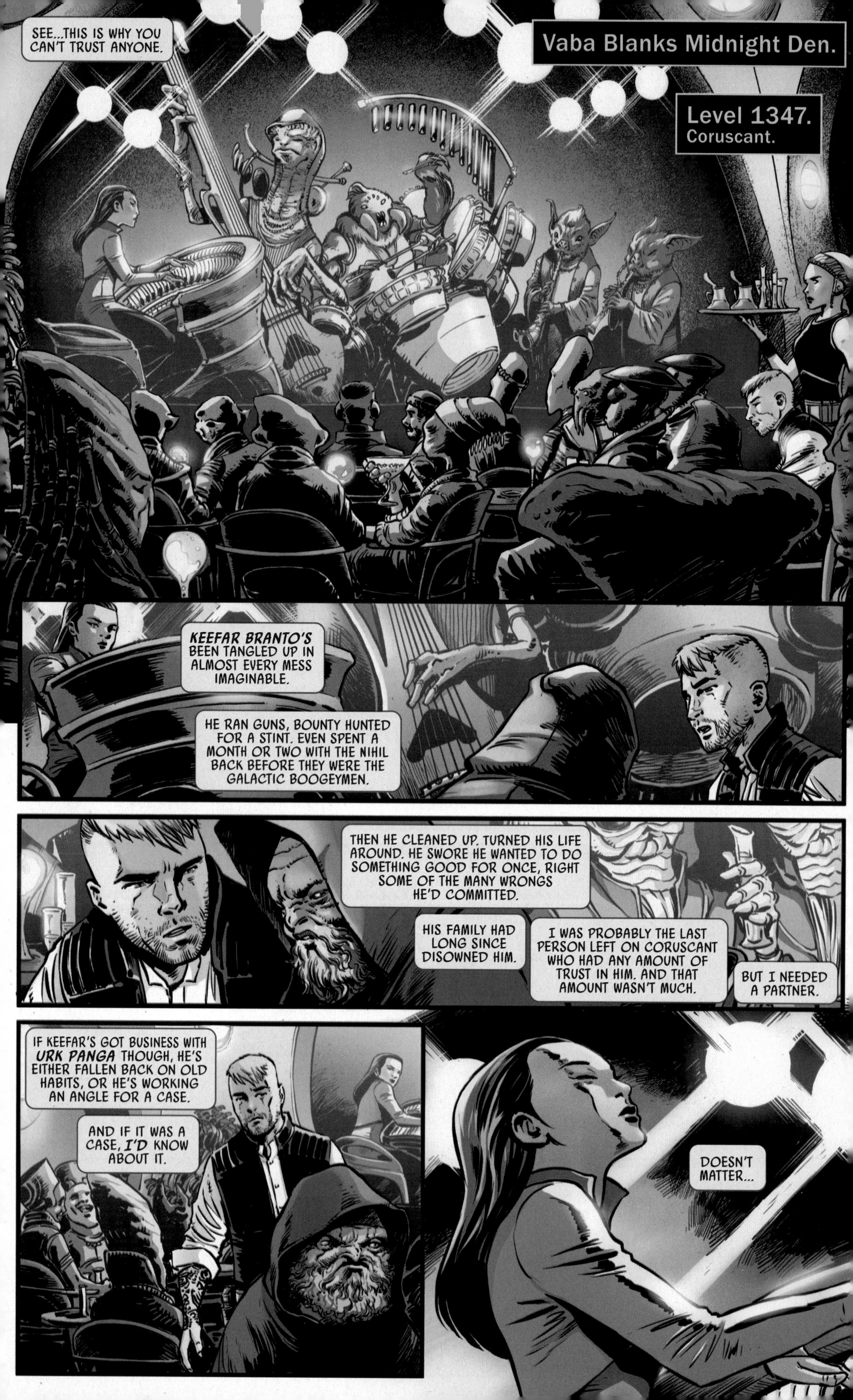

SEE...THIS IS WHY YOU CAN'T TRUST ANYONE.
Vaba Blanks Midnight Den.
Level 1347. Coruscant.
KEEFAR BRANTO'S BEEN TANGLED UP IN ALMOST EVERY MESS IMAGINABLE.
HE RAN GUNS, BOUNTY HUNTED FOR A STINT. EVEN SPENT A MONTH OR TWO WITH THE NIHIL BACK BEFORE THEY WERE THE GALACTIC BOOGEYMEN.
THEN HE CLEANED UP. TURNED HIS LIFE AROUND. HE SWORE HE WANTED TO DO SOMETHING GOOD FOR ONCE, RIGHT SOME OF THE MANY WRONGS HE'D COMMITTED.
HIS FAMILY HAD LONG SINCE DISOWNED HIM.
I WAS PROBABLY THE LAST PERSON LEFT ON CORUSCANT WHO HAD ANY AMOUNT OF TRUST IN HIM. AND THAT AMOUNT WASN'T MUCH.
BUT I NEEDED A PARTNER.
IF KEEFAR'S GOT BUSINESS WITH URK PANGA THOUGH, HE'S EITHER FALLEN BACK ON OLD HABITS, OR HE'S WORKING AN ANGLE FOR A CASE.
AND IF IT WAS A CASE, I'D KNOW ABOUT IT.
DOESN'T MATTER...

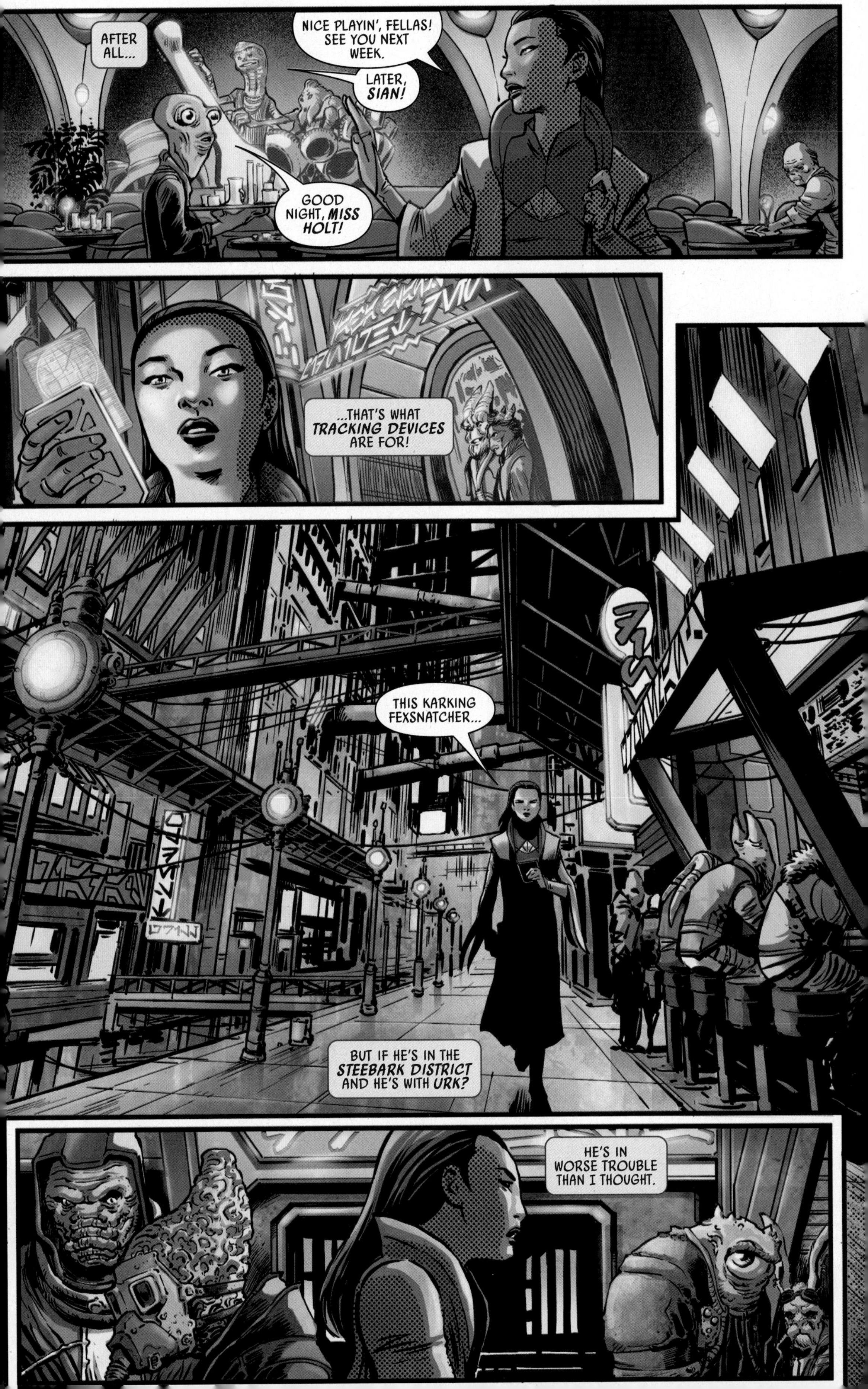
AFTER ALL...
NICE PLAYIN', FELLAS! SEE YOU NEXT WEEK.
LATER, SIAN!
GOOD NIGHT, MISS HOLT!
...THAT'S WHAT TRACKING DEVICES ARE FOR!
THIS KARKING FEXSNATCHER...
BUT IF HE'S IN THE STEEBARK DISTRICT AND HE'S WITH URK?
HE'S IN WORSE TROUBLE THAN I THOUGHT.

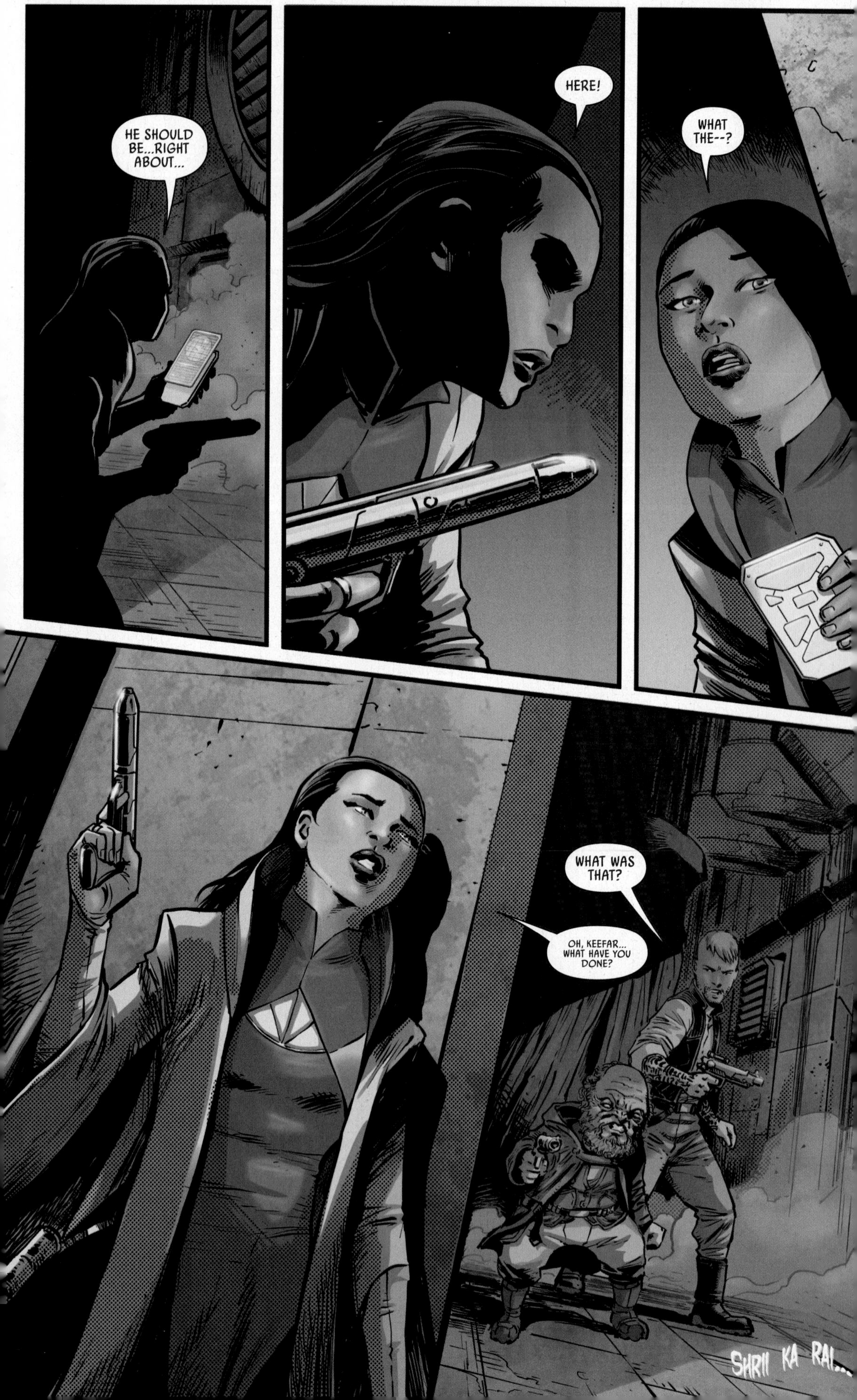
HE SHOULD BE...RIGHT ABOUT...
HERE!
WHAT THE--?
WHAT WAS THAT?
OH, KEEFAR... WHAT HAVE YOU DONE?
SHRII KA RAI...

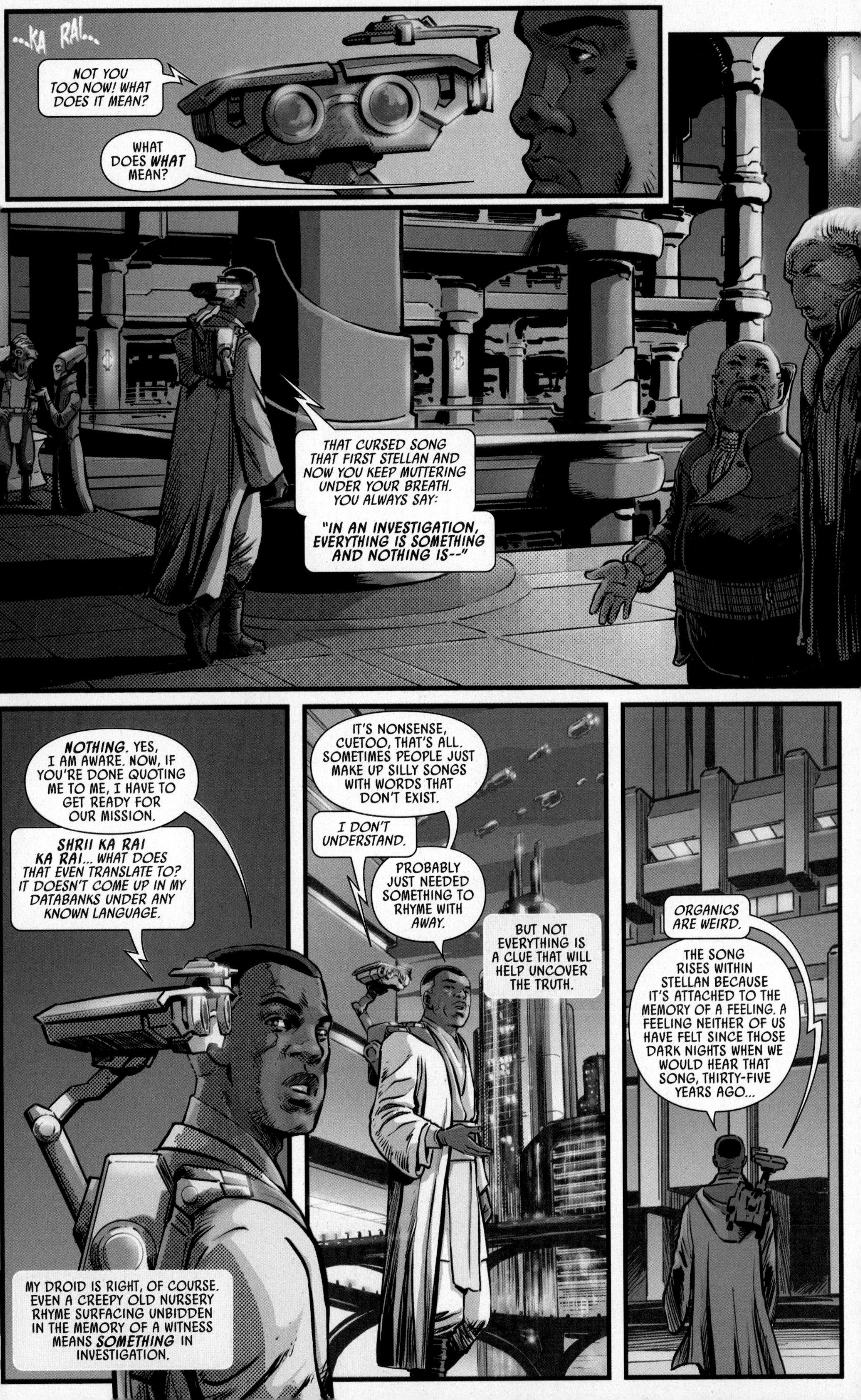

...KA RAI...
NOT YOU TOO NOW! WHAT DOES IT MEAN?
WHAT DOES WHAT MEAN?
THAT CURSED SONG THAT FIRST STELLAN AND NOW YOU KEEP MUTTERING UNDER YOUR BREATH. YOU ALWAYS SAY:
"IN AN INVESTIGATION, EVERYTHING IS SOMETHING AND NOTHING IS--"
NOTHING. YES, I AM AWARE. NOW, IF YOU'RE DONE QUOTING ME TO ME, I HAVE TO GET READY FOR OUR MISSION.
SHRII KA RAI KA RAI... WHAT DOES THAT EVEN TRANSLATE TO? IT DOESN'T COME UP IN MY DATABANKS UNDER ANY KNOWN LANGUAGE.
MY DROID IS RIGHT, OF COURSE. EVEN A CREEPY OLD NURSERY RHYME SURFACING UNBIDDEN IN THE MEMORY OF A WITNESS MEANS SOMETHING IN INVESTIGATION.
IT'S NONSENSE, CUETOO, THAT'S ALL. SOMETIMES PEOPLE JUST MAKE UP SILLY SONGS WITH WORDS THAT DON'T EXIST.
I DON'T UNDERSTAND.
PROBABLY JUST NEEDED SOMETHING TO RHYME WITH AWAY.
BUT NOT EVERYTHING IS A CLUE THAT WILL HELP UNCOVER THE TRUTH.
ORGANICS ARE WEIRD.
THE SONG RISES WITHIN STELLAN BECAUSE IT'S ATTACHED TO THE MEMORY OF A FEELING. A FEELING NEITHER OF US HAVE FELT SINCE THOSE DARK NIGHTS WHEN WE WOULD HEAR THAT SONG, THIRTY-FIVE YEARS AGO...

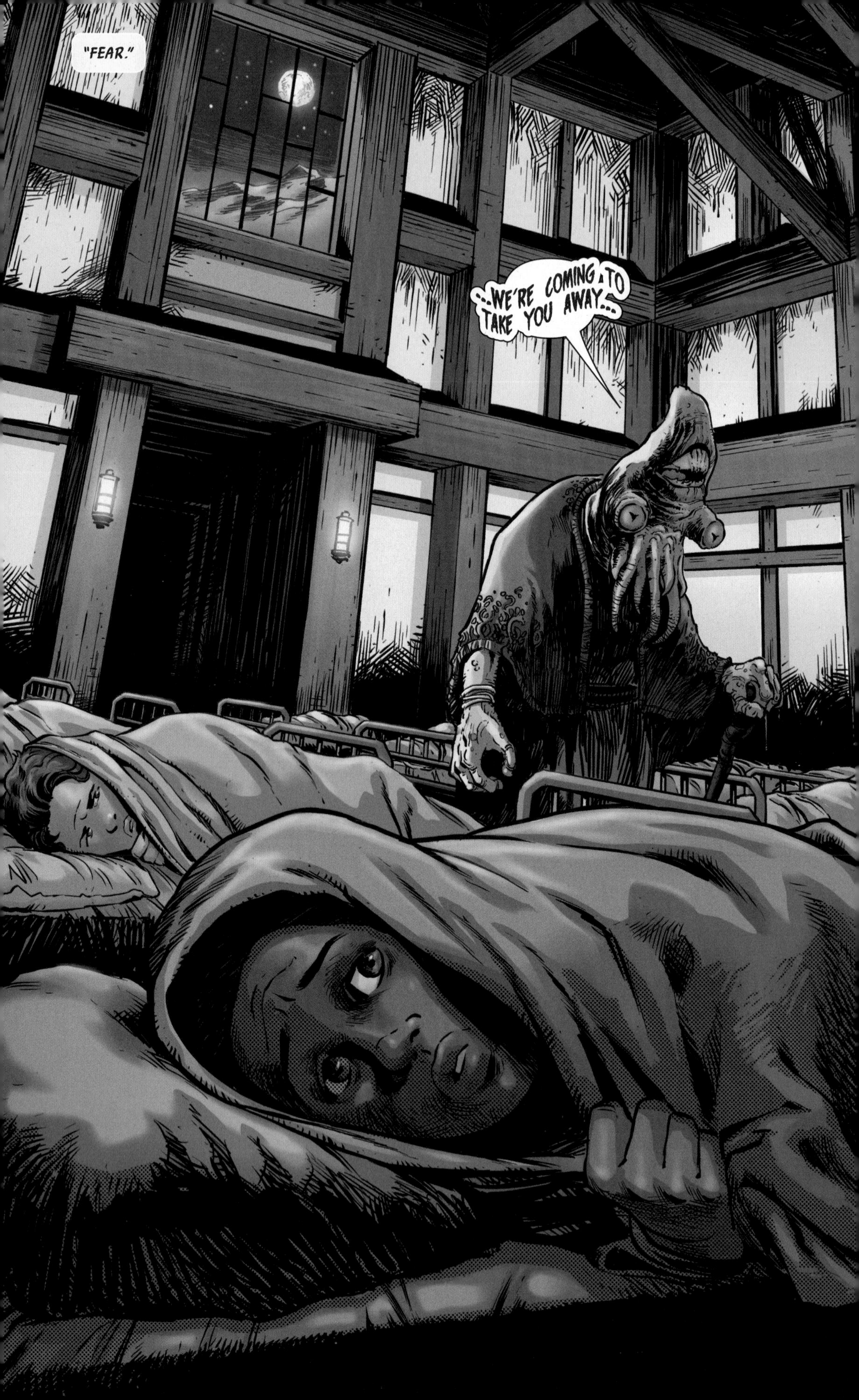
"FEAR."
...WE'RE COMING TO TAKE YOU AWAY...

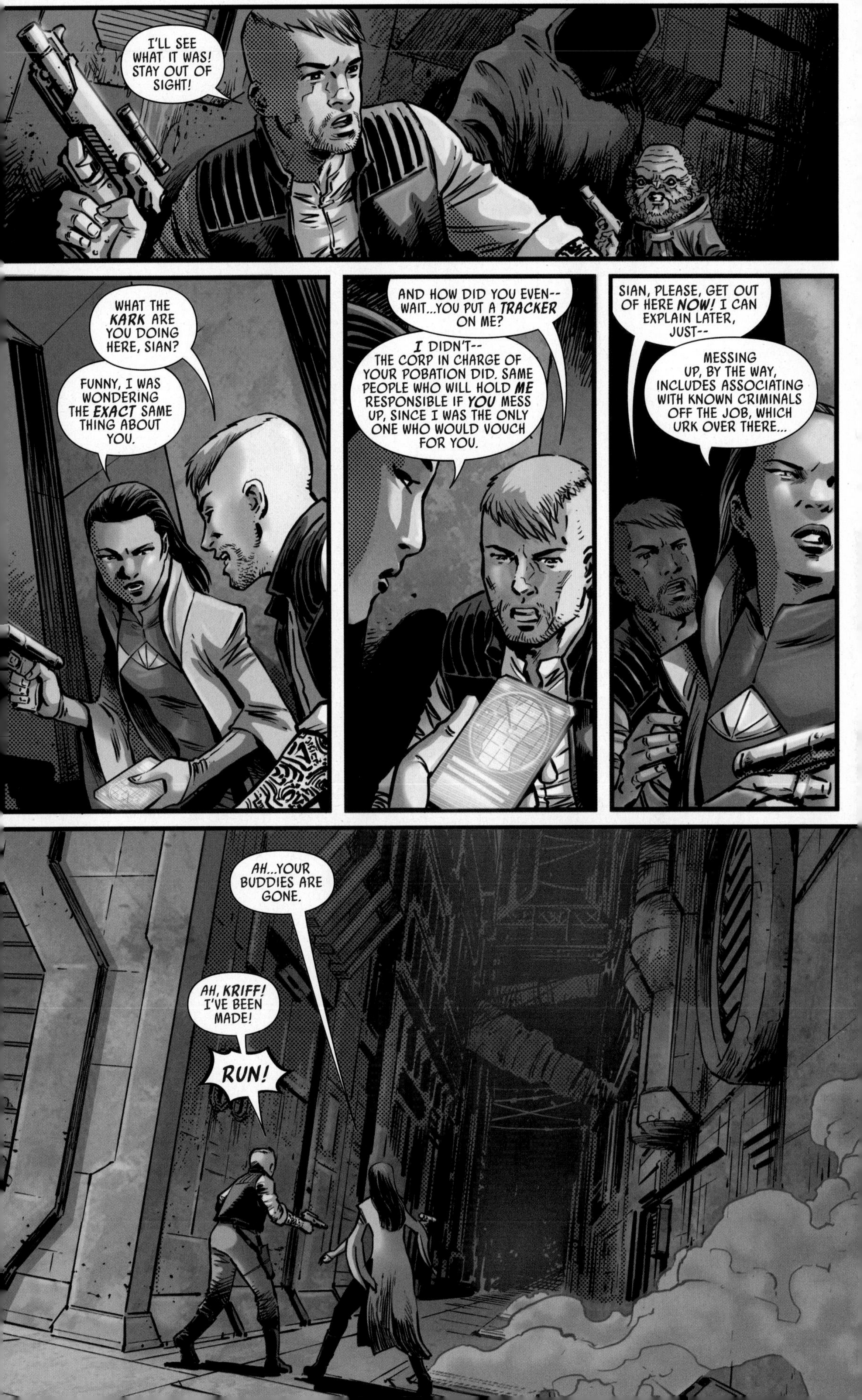
I'LL SEE WHAT IT WAS! STAY OUT OF SIGHT!
WHAT THE KARK ARE YOU DOING HERE, SIAN?
FUNNY, I WAS WONDERING THE EXACT SAME THING ABOUT YOU.
AND HOW DID YOU EVEN-- WAIT...YOU PUT A TRACKER ON ME?
I DIDN'T-- THE CORP IN CHARGE OF YOUR POBATION DID. SAME PEOPLE WHO WILL HOLD ME RESPONSIBLE IF YOU MESS UP, SINCE I WAS THE ONLY ONE WHO WOULD VOUCH FOR YOU.
SIAN, PLEASE, GET OUT OF HERE NOW! I CAN EXPLAIN LATER, JUST--
MESSING UP, BY THE WAY, INCLUDES ASSOCIATING WITH KNOWN CRIMINALS OFF THE JOB, WHICH URK OVER THERE...
AH...YOUR BUDDIES ARE GONE.
AH, KRIFF! I'VE BEEN MADE!
RUN!

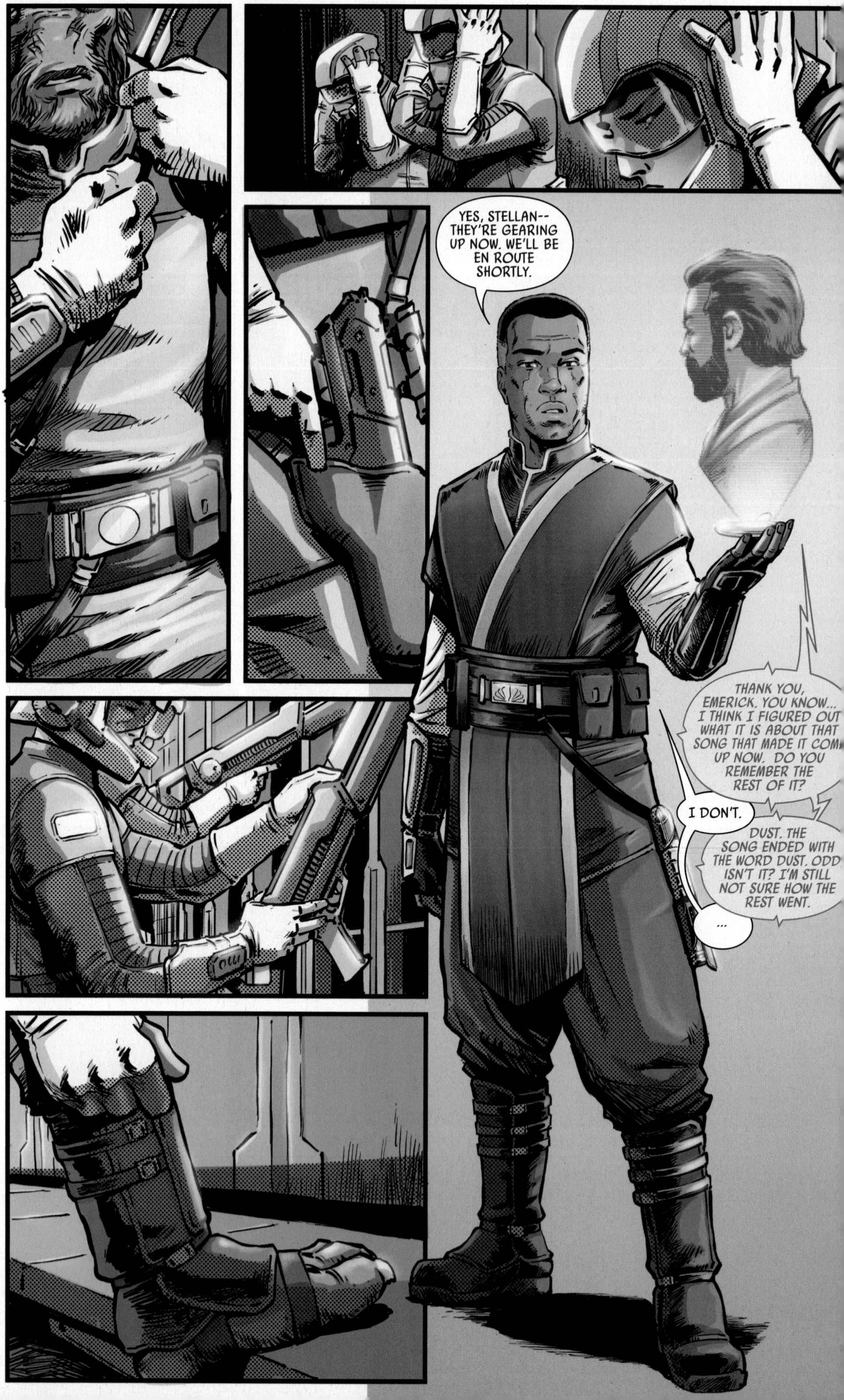
YES, STELLAN-- THEY'RE GEARING UP NOW. WE'LL BE EN ROUTE SHORTLY.
THANK YOU, EMERICK. YOU KNOW... I THINK I FIGURED OUT WHAT IT IS ABOUT THAT SONG THAT MADE IT COME UP NOW. DO YOU REMEMBER THE REST OF IT?
I DON'T.
DUST. THE SONG ENDED WITH THE WORD DUST. ODD ISN'T IT? I'M STILL NOT SURE HOW THE REST WENT.
...

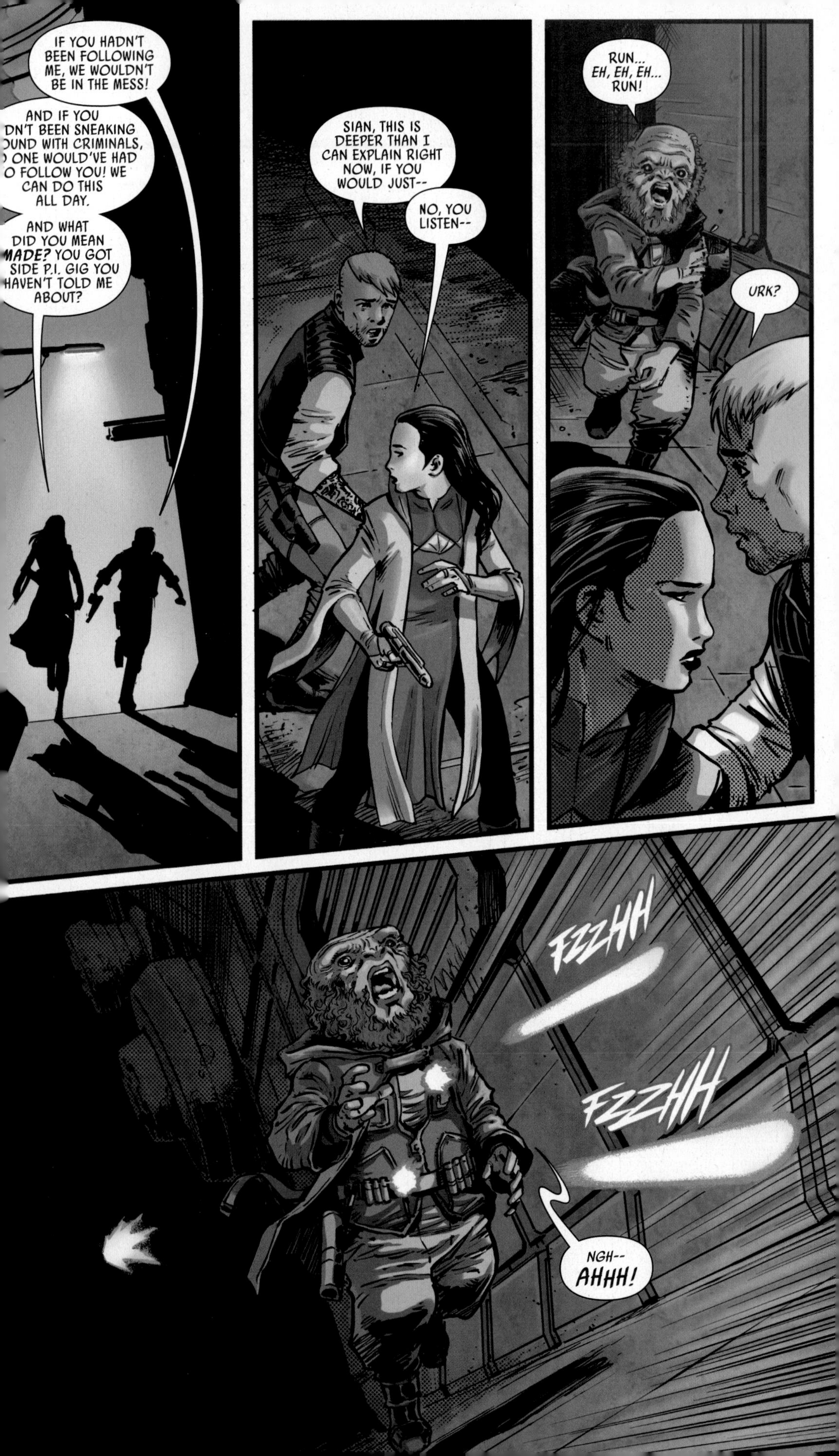

IF YOU HADN'T BEEN FOLLOWING ME, WE WOULDN'T BE IN THE MESS!
AND IF YOU DN'T BEEN SNEAKING OUND WITH CRIMINALS, O ONE WOULD'VE HAD O FOLLOW YOU! WE CAN DO THIS ALL DAY.
AND WHAT DID YOU MEAN MADE? YOU GOT SIDE P.I. GIG YOU HAVEN'T TOLD ME ABOUT?
SIAN, THIS IS DEEPER THAN I CAN EXPLAIN RIGHT NOW, IF YOU WOULD JUST--
NO, YOU LISTEN--
RUN... EH, EH, EH... RUN!
URK?
FZZHH
FZZHH
NGH-- AHHH!

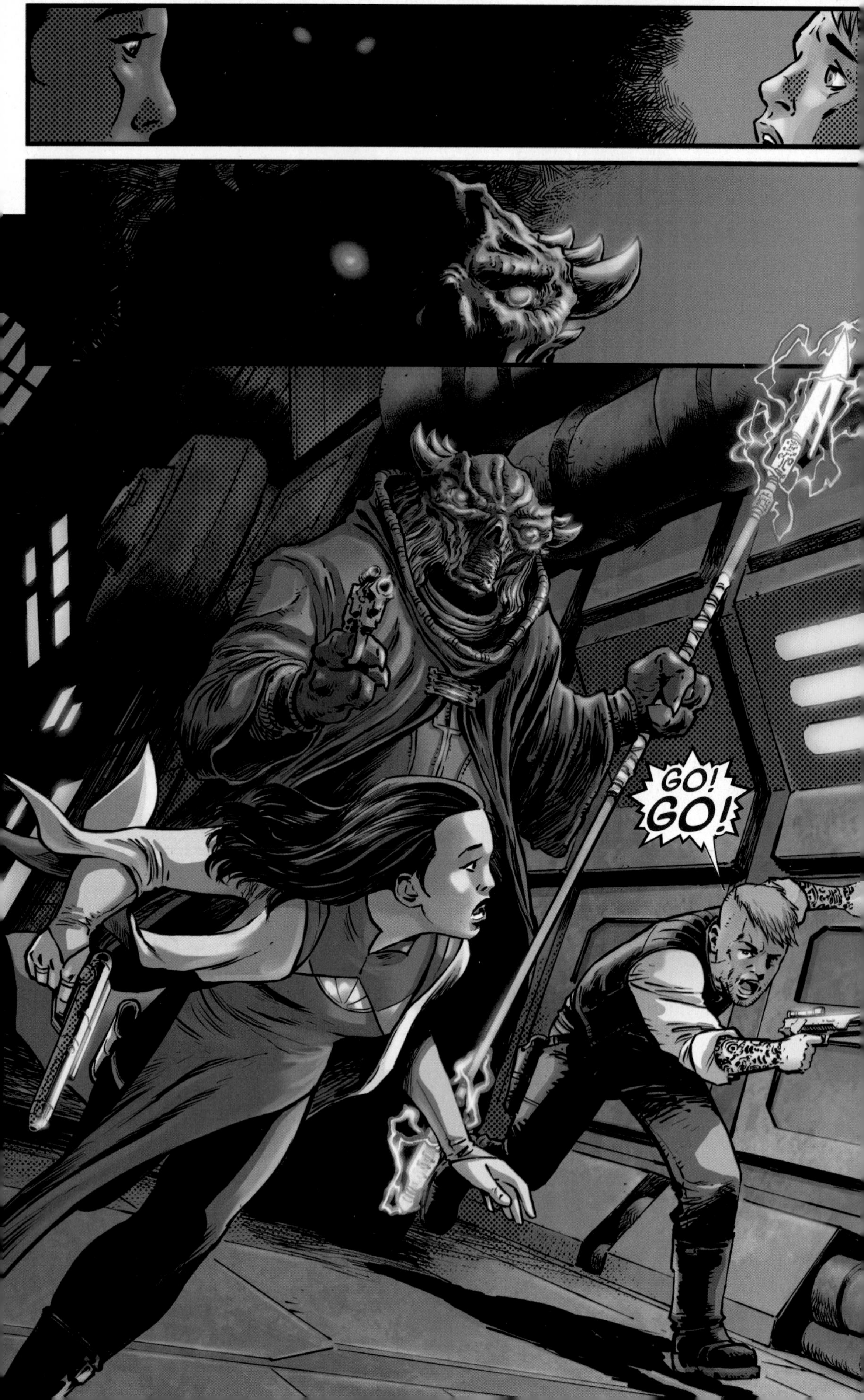
GO! GO!

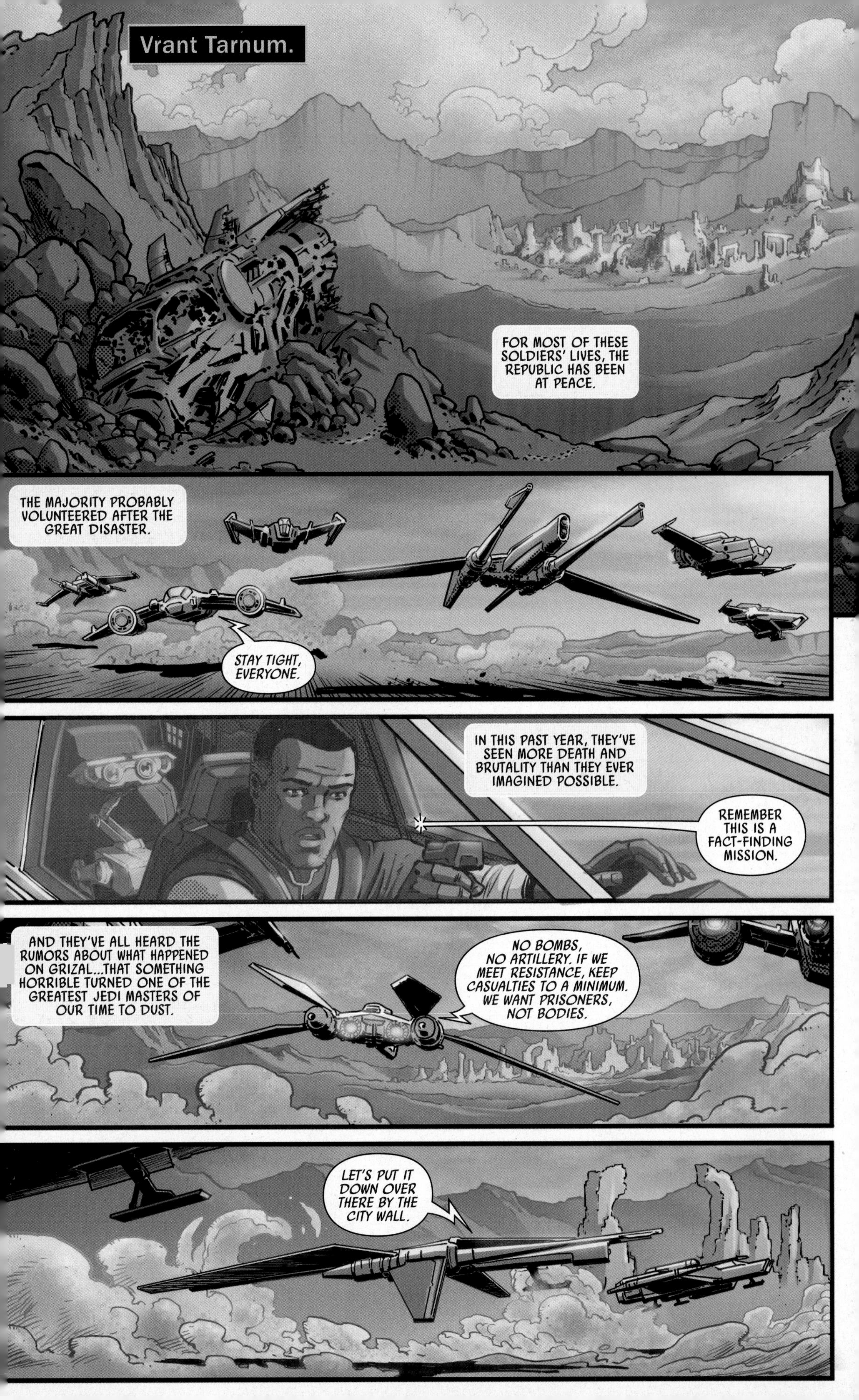
Vrant Tarnum.
FOR MOST OF THESE SOLDIERS' LIVES, THE REPUBLIC HAS BEEN AT PEACE.
THE MAJORITY PROBABLY VOLUNTEERED AFTER THE GREAT DISASTER.
STAY TIGHT, EVERYONE.
IN THIS PAST YEAR, THEY'VE SEEN MORE DEATH AND BRUTALITY THAN THEY EVER IMAGINED POSSIBLE.
REMEMBER THIS IS A FACT-FINDING MISSION.
AND THEY'VE ALL HEARD THE RUMORS ABOUT WHAT HAPPENED ON GRIZAL...THAT SOMETHING HORRIBLE TURNED ONE OF THE GREATEST JEDI MASTERS OF OUR TIME TO DUST.
NO BOMBS, NO ARTILLERY. IF WE MEET RESISTANCE, KEEP CASUALTIES TO A MINIMUM. WE WANT PRISONERS, NOT BODIES.
LET'S PUT IT DOWN OVER THERE BY THE CITY WALL.

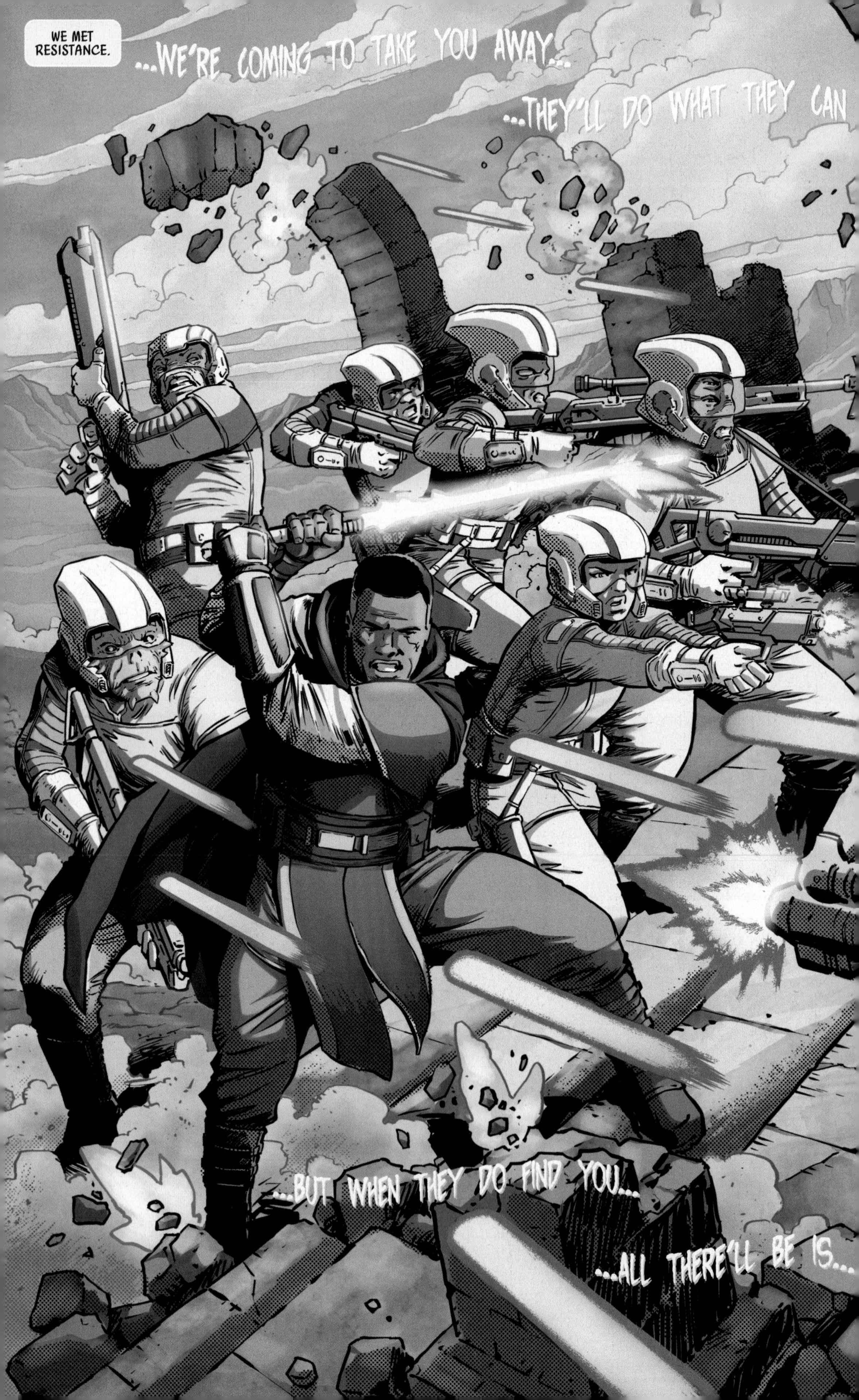
WE MET RESISTANCE.
...WE'RE COMING TO TAKE YOU AWAY...
...THEY'LL DO WHAT THEY CAN
...BUT WHEN THEY DO FIND YOU...
...ALL THERE'LL BE IS...

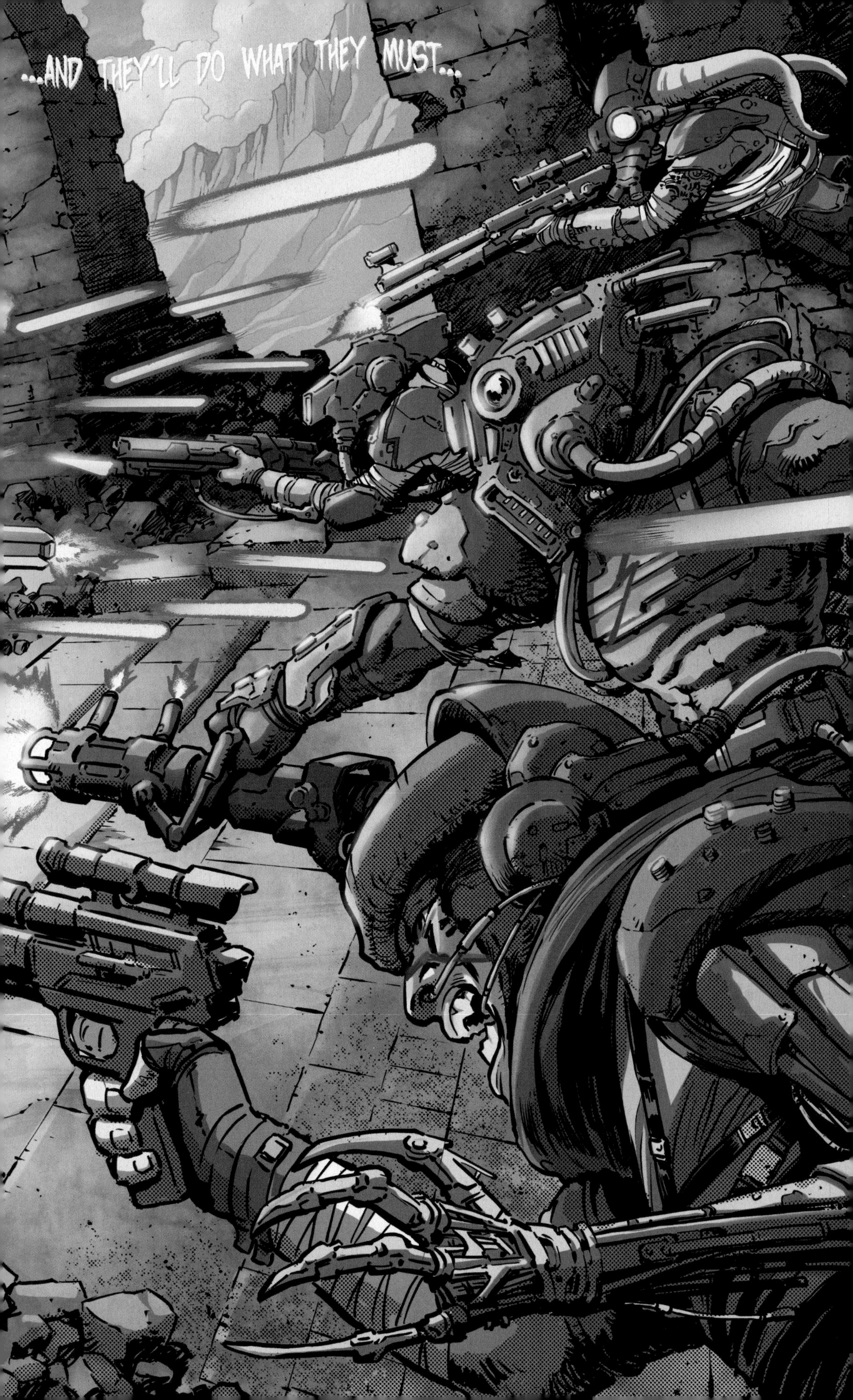
...AND THEY'LL DO WHAT THEY MUST...

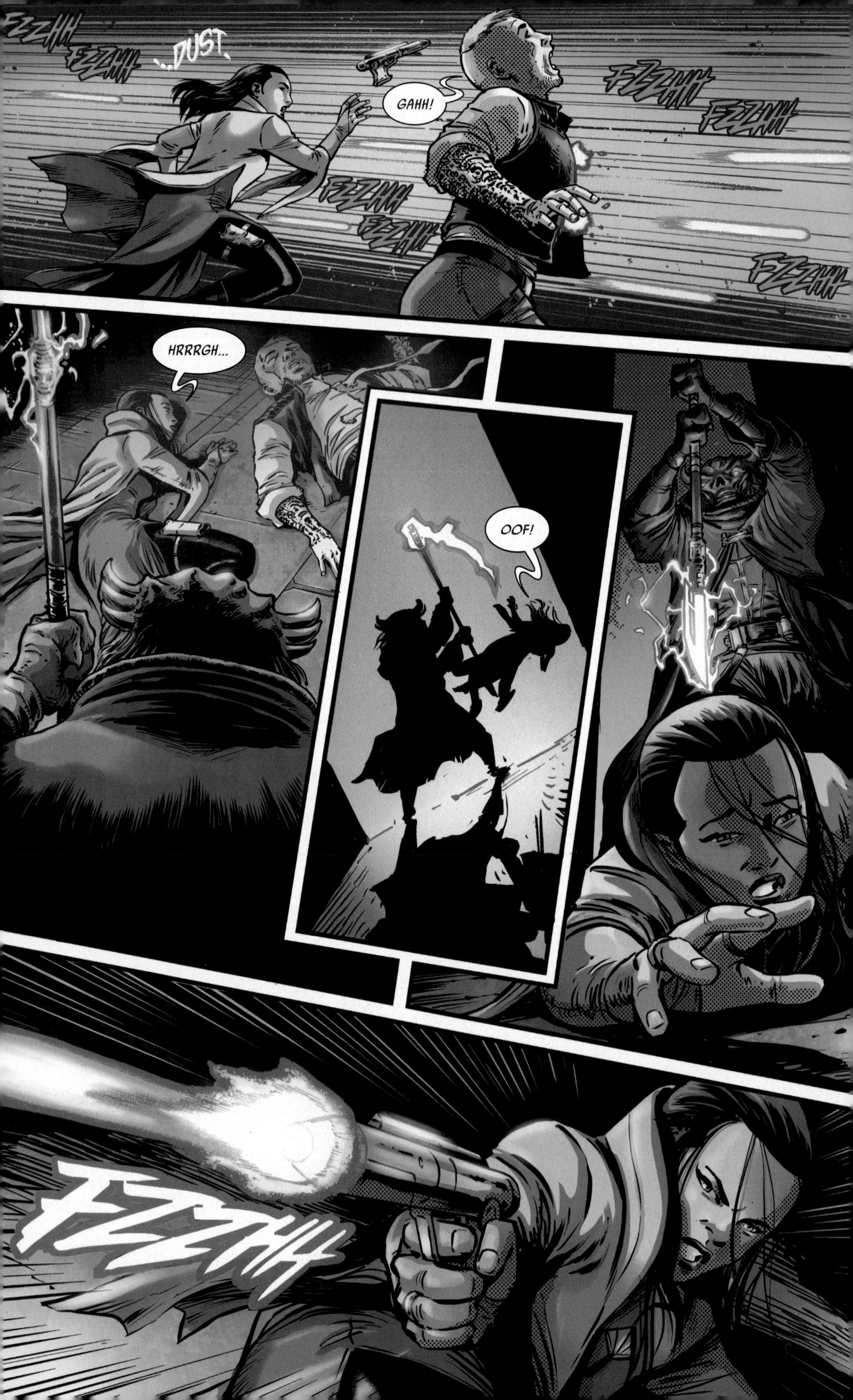
FZZHH
FZZHH
...DUST.
GAHH!
FZZHH
FZZHH
FZZHH
FZZHH
FZZHH
HRRRGH...
OOF!
FZZHH

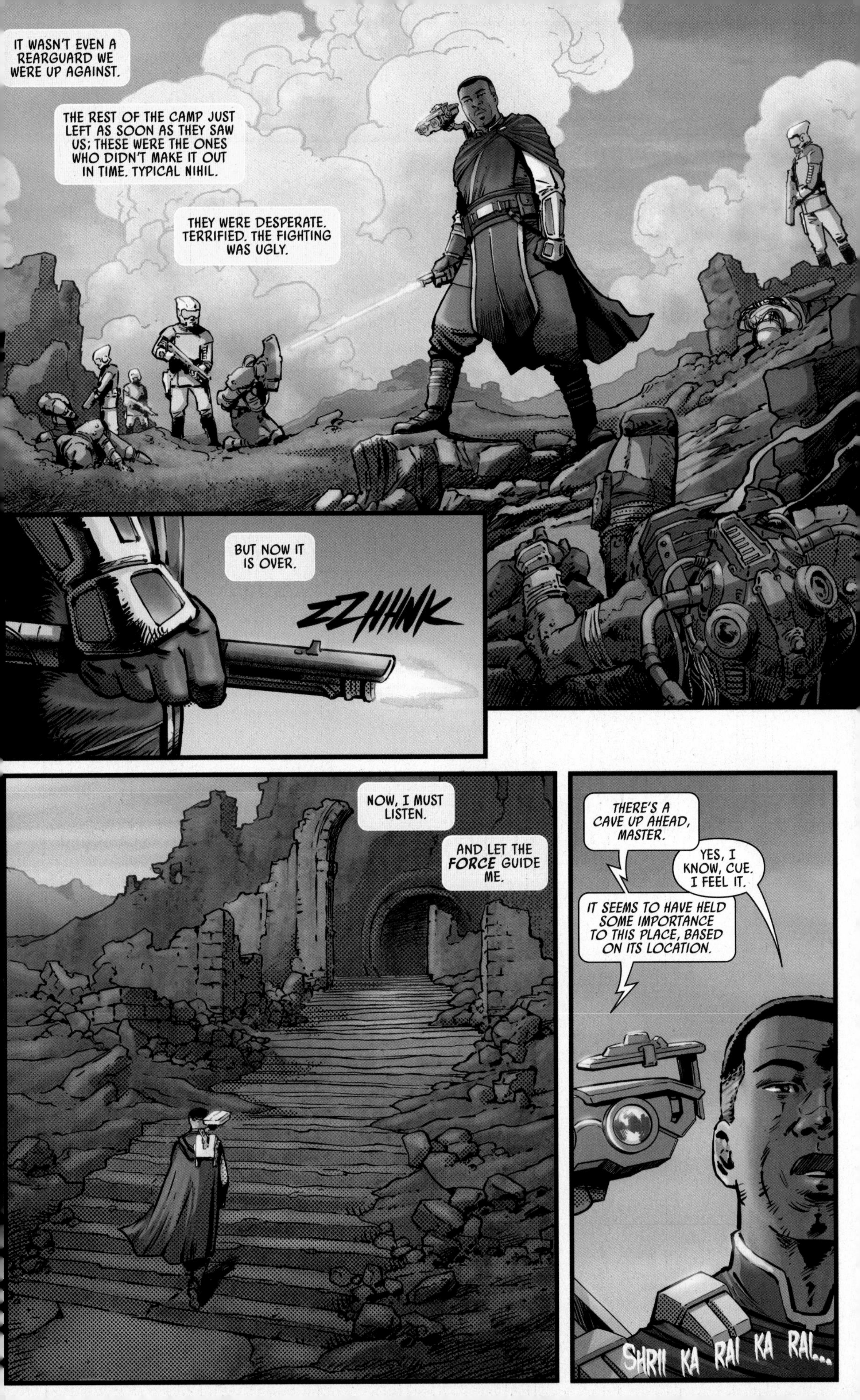
IT WASN'T EVEN A REARGUARD WE WERE UP AGAINST.
THE REST OF THE CAMP JUST LEFT AS SOON AS THEY SAW US; THESE WERE THE ONES WHO DIDN'T MAKE IT OUT IN TIME. TYPICAL NIHIL.
THEY WERE DESPERATE. TERRIFIED. THE FIGHTING WAS UGLY.
BUT NOW IT IS OVER.
ZZHHNK
NOW, I MUST LISTEN.
AND LET THE FORCE GUIDE ME.
THERE'S A CAVE UP AHEAD, MASTER.
YES, I KNOW, CUE. I FEEL IT.
IT SEEMS TO HAVE HELD SOME IMPORTANCE TO THIS PLACE, BASED ON ITS LOCATION.
SHRII KA RAI KA RAI...

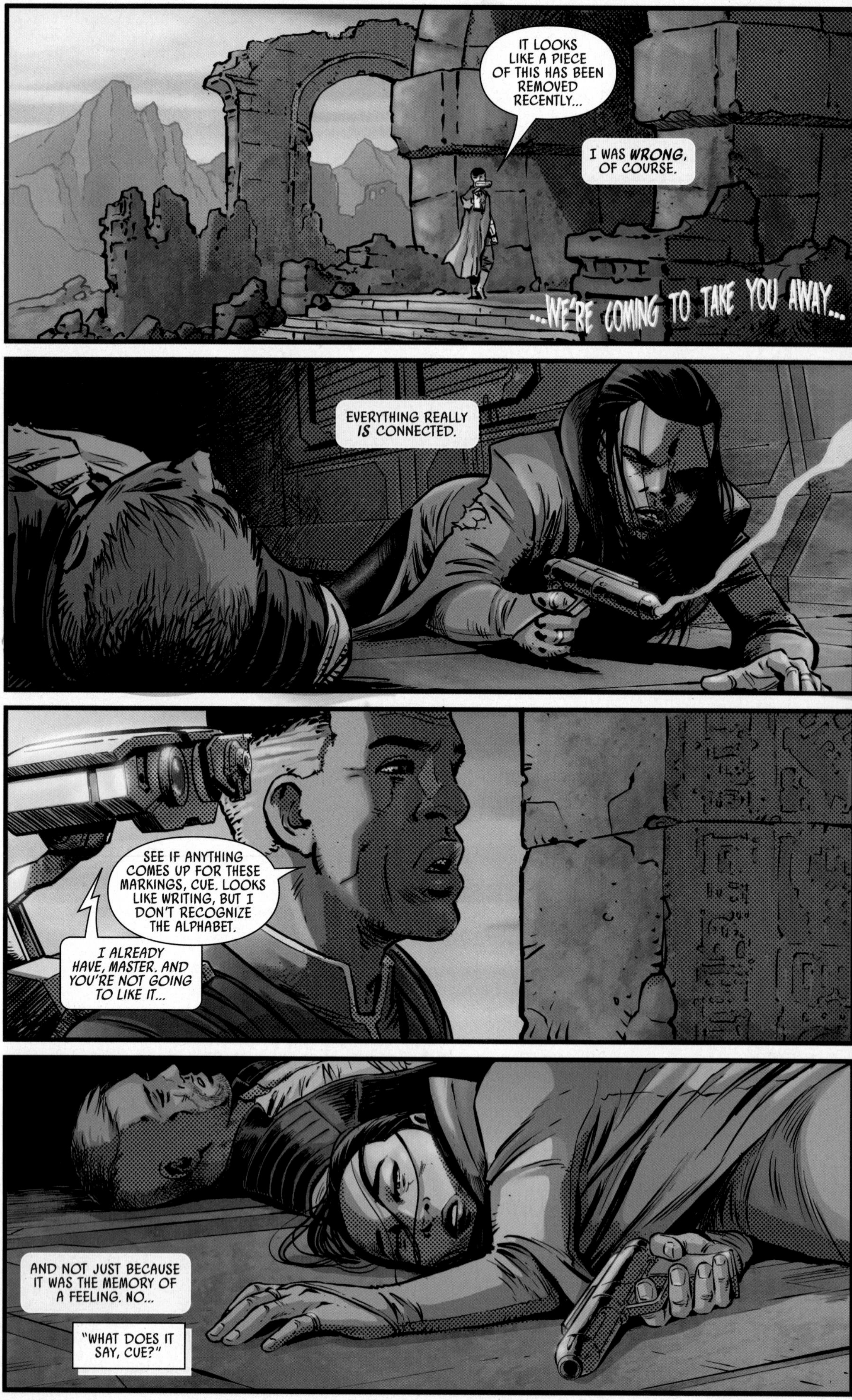
IT LOOKS LIKE A PIECE OF THIS HAS BEEN REMOVED RECENTLY...
I WAS WRONG, OF COURSE.
...WE'RE COMING TO TAKE YOU AWAY...
EVERYTHING REALLY IS CONNECTED.
SEE IF ANYTHING COMES UP FOR THESE MARKINGS, CUE. LOOKS LIKE WRITING, BUT I DON'T RECOGNIZE THE ALPHABET.
I ALREADY HAVE, MASTER. AND YOU'RE NOT GOING TO LIKE IT...
AND NOT JUST BECAUSE IT WAS THE MEMORY OF A FEELING. NO...
"WHAT DOES IT SAY, CUE?"

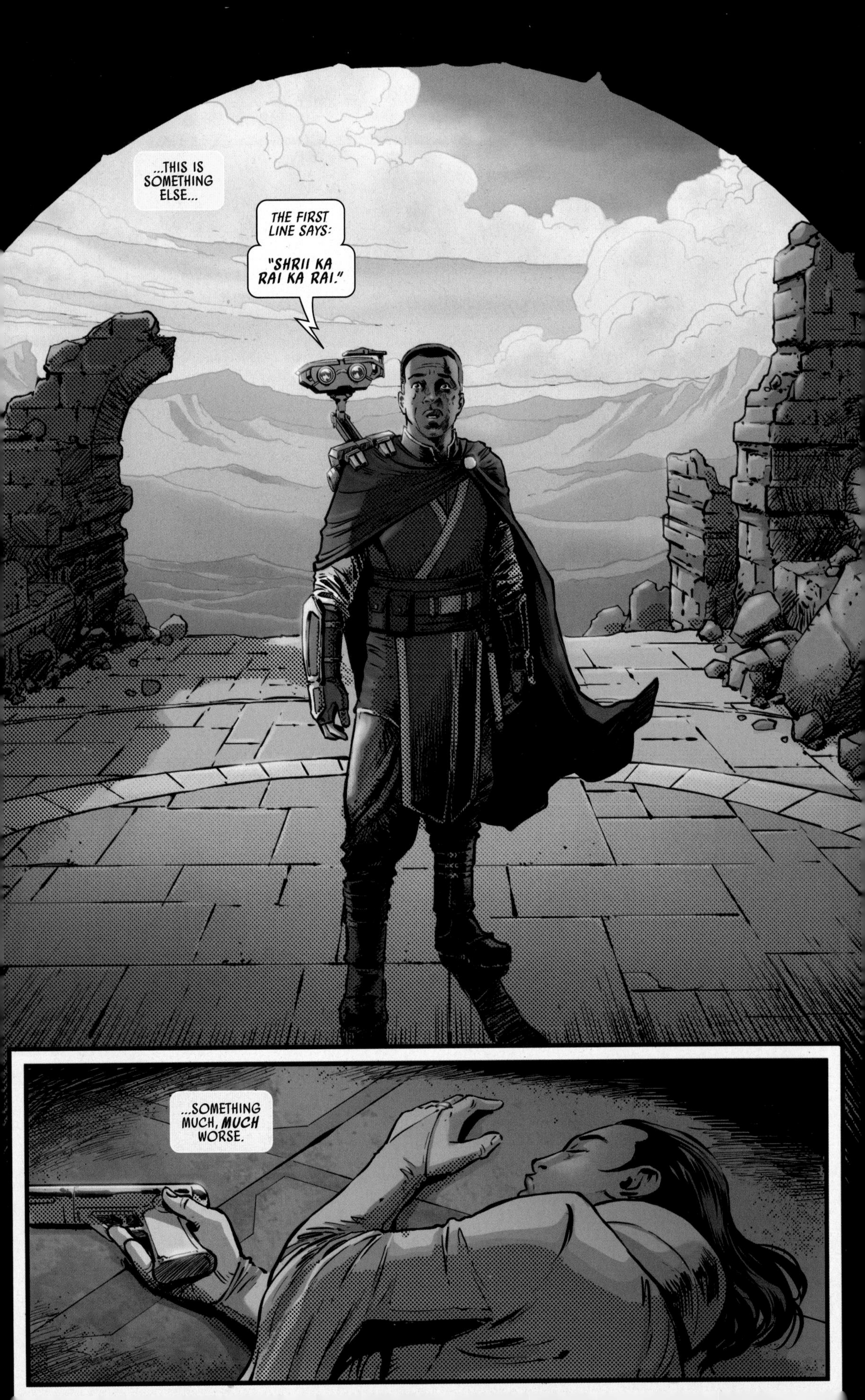
...THIS IS SOMETHING ELSE...
THE FIRST LINE SAYS:
"SHRII KA RAI KA RAI."
...SOMETHING MUCH, *MUCH* WORSE.

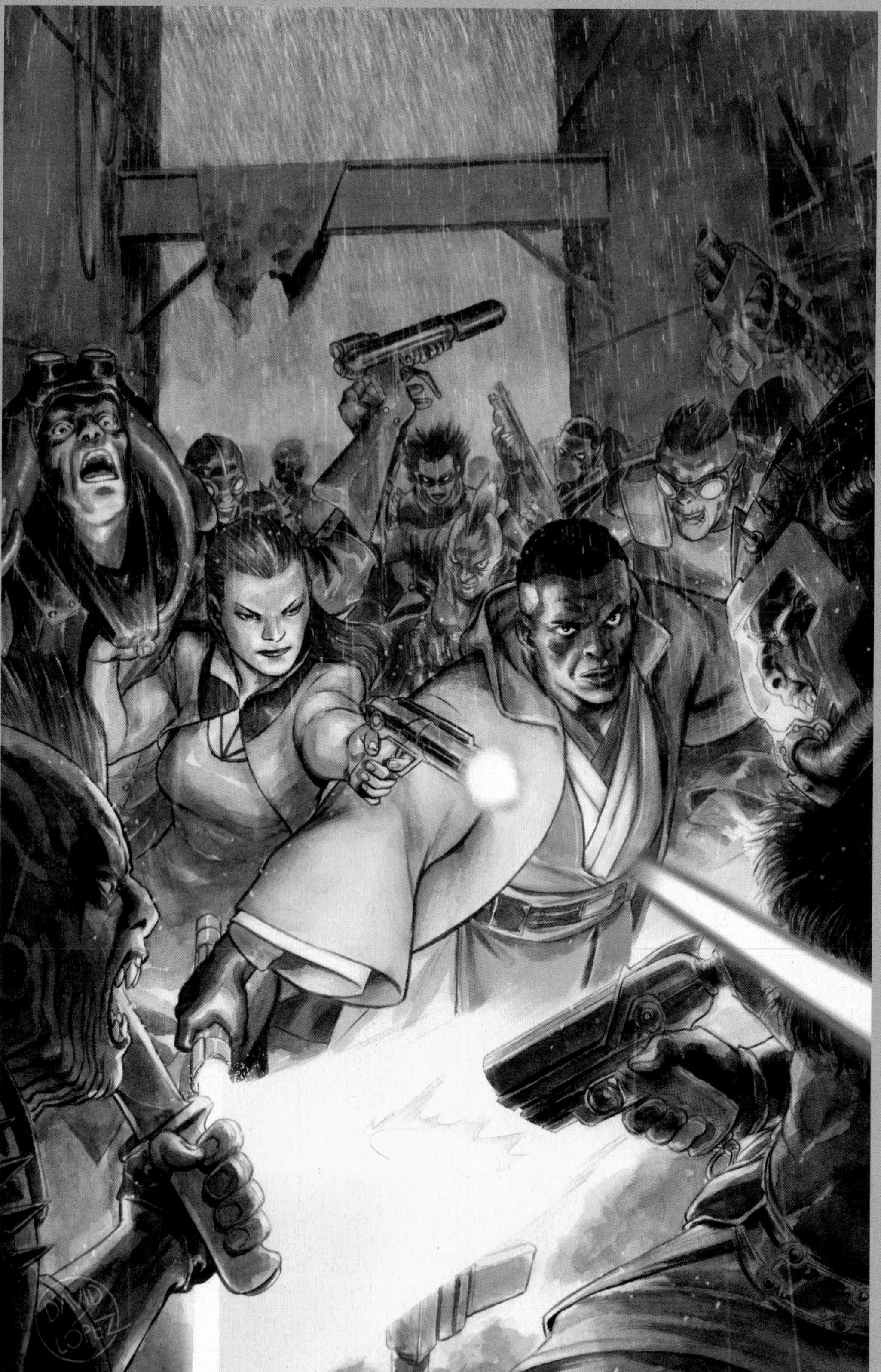
DAVID LOPEZ

2 | WAY DOWN DEEP IN THE DARK

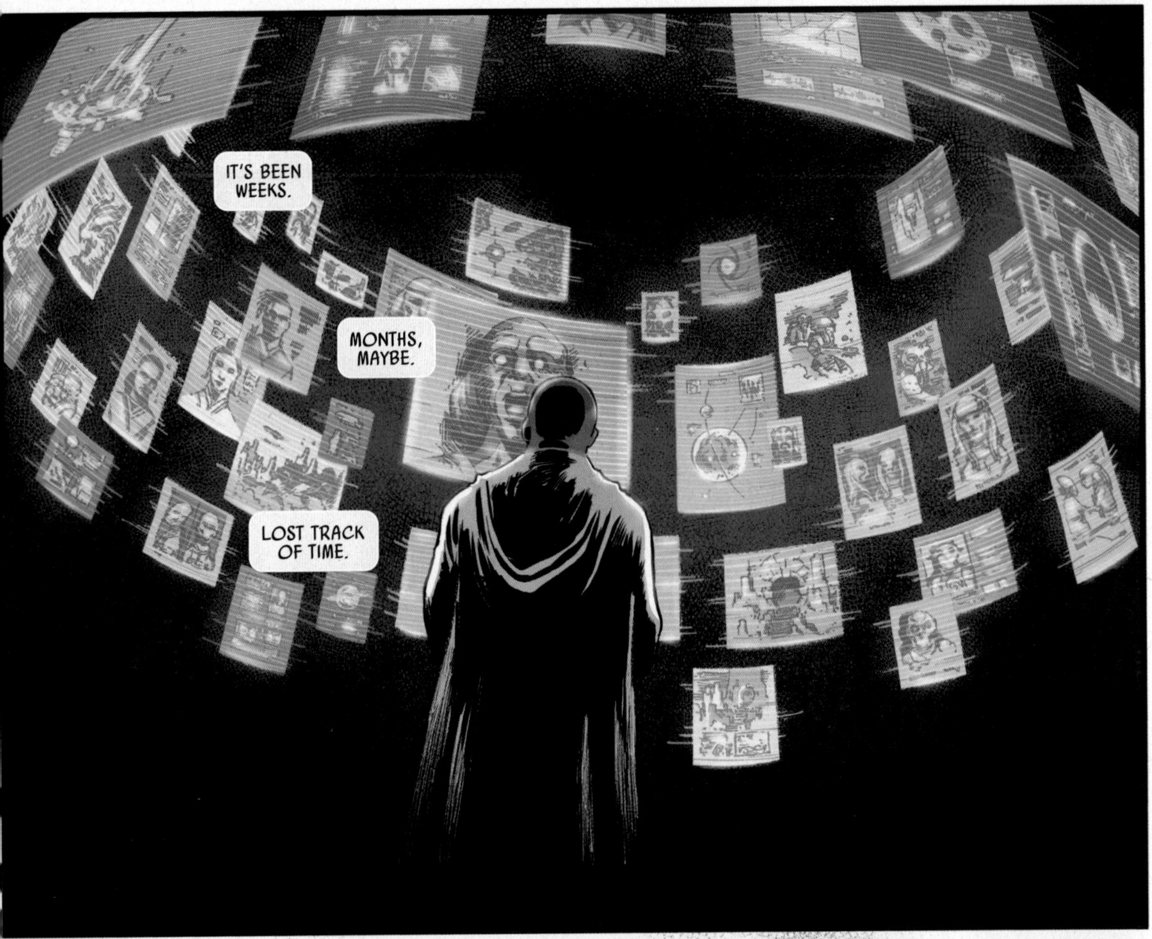
IT'S BEEN WEEKS.
MONTHS, MAYBE.
LOST TRACK OF TIME.

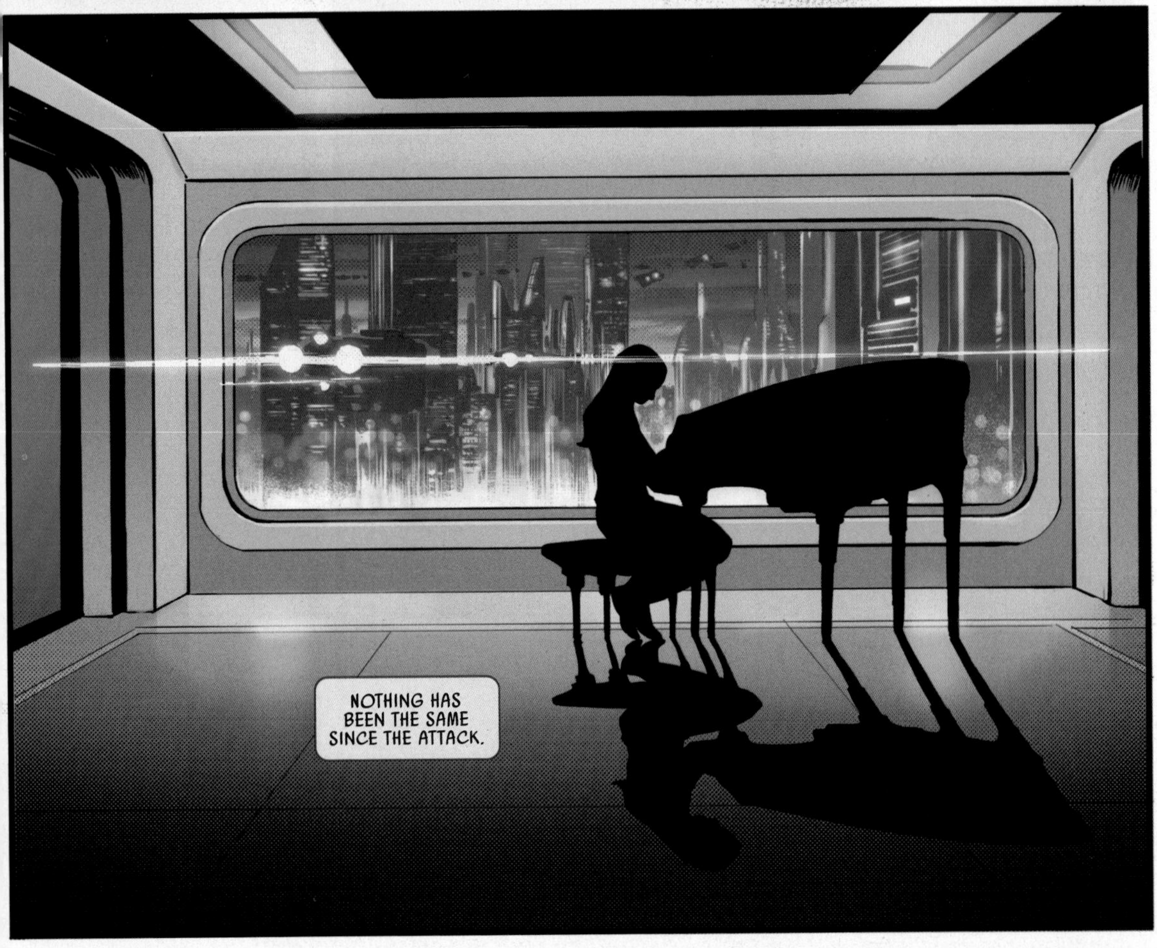
NOTHING HAS BEEN THE SAME SINCE THE ATTACK.

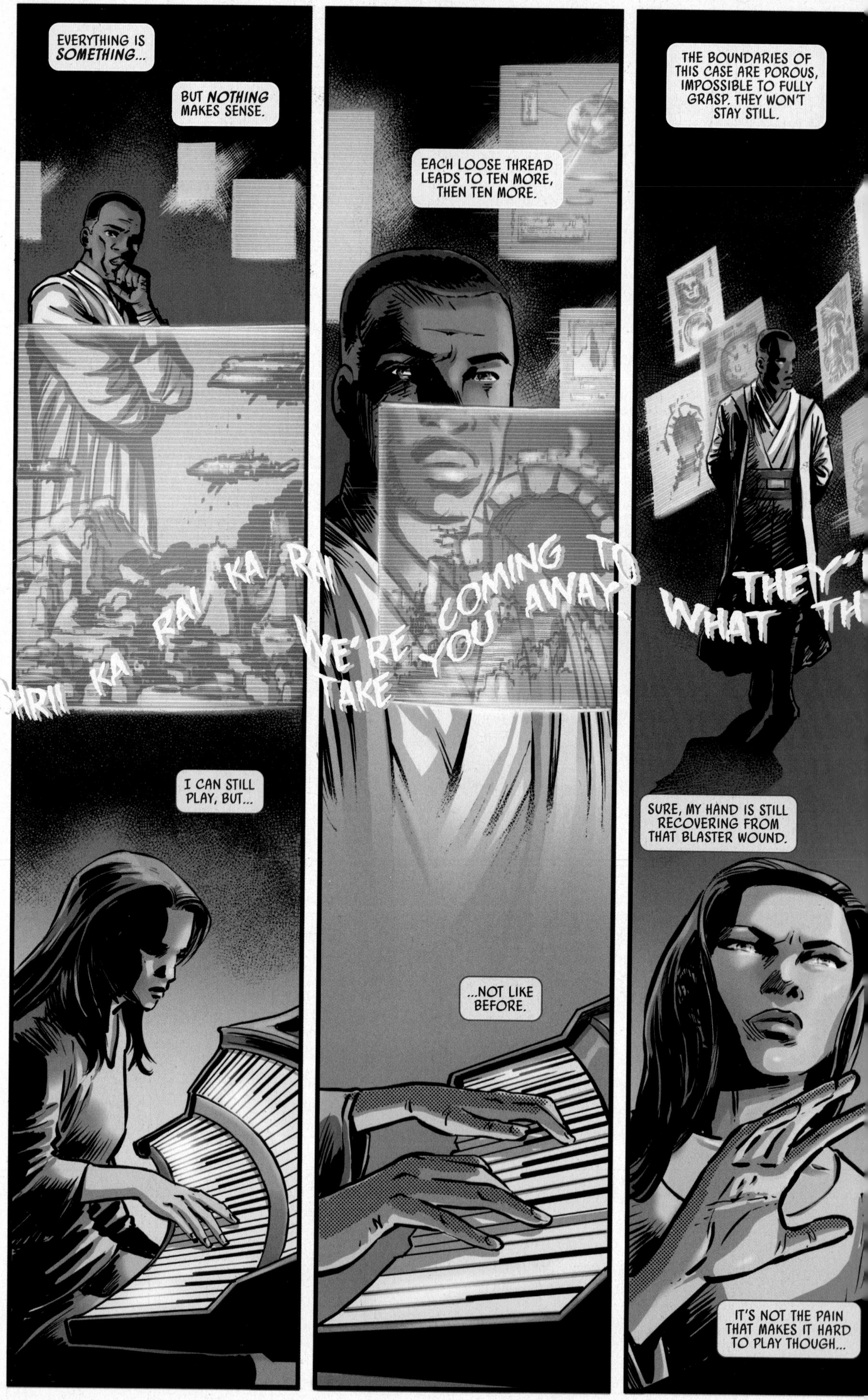
EVERYTHING IS SOMETHING...
BUT NOTHING MAKES SENSE.
EACH LOOSE THREAD LEADS TO TEN MORE, THEN TEN MORE.
THE BOUNDARIES OF THIS CASE ARE POROUS, IMPOSSIBLE TO FULLY GRASP. THEY WON'T STAY STILL.
SHRII KA RAI KA RAI
WE'RE COMING TO TAKE YOU AWAY!
I CAN STILL PLAY, BUT...
...NOT LIKE BEFORE.
SURE, MY HAND IS STILL RECOVERING FROM THAT BLASTER WOUND.
IT'S NOT THE PAIN THAT MAKES IT HARD TO PLAY THOUGH...

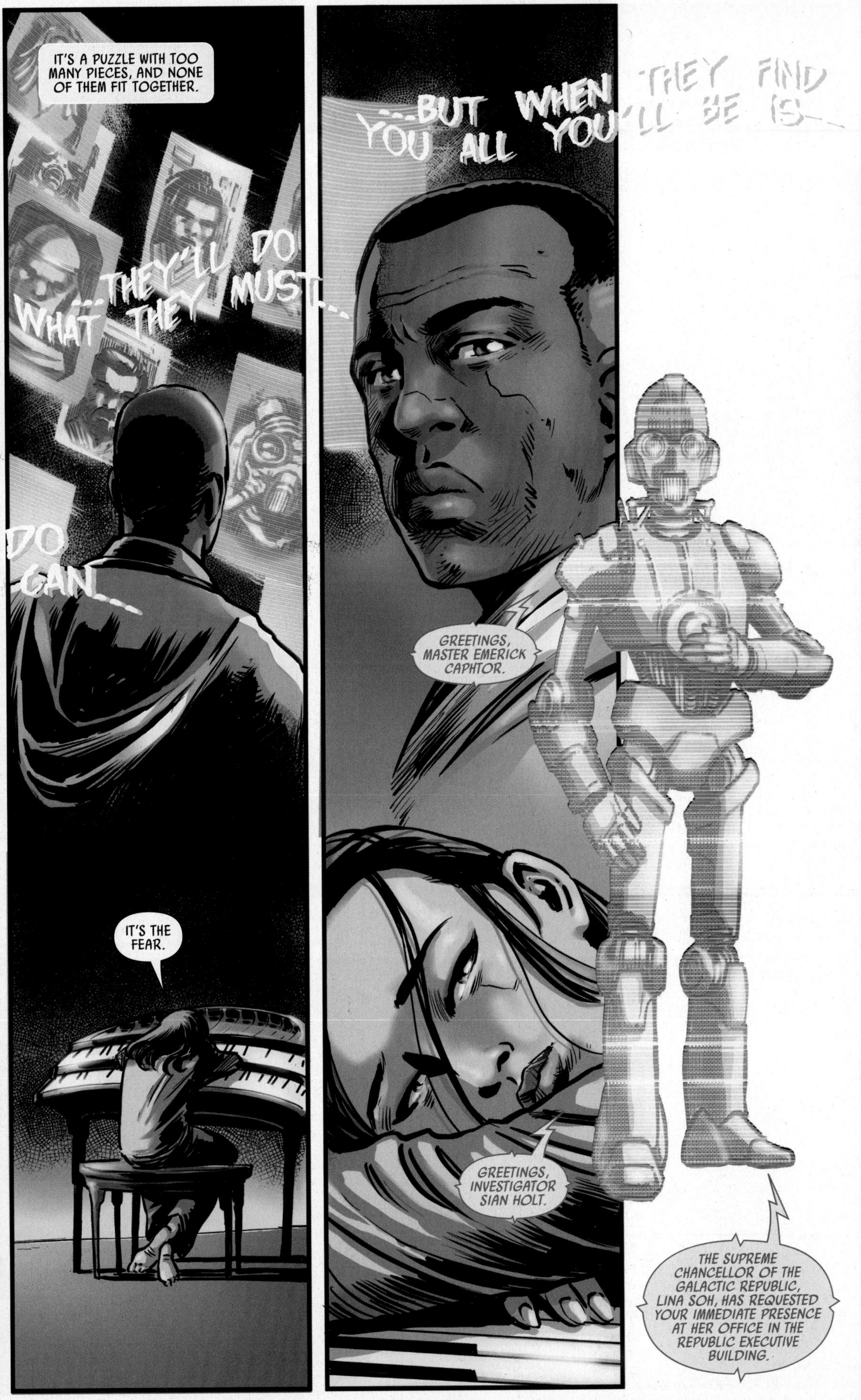
IT'S A PUZZLE WITH TOO MANY PIECES, AND NONE OF THEM FIT TOGETHER.
...THEY'LL DO WHAT THEY MUST...
DO CAN...
IT'S THE FEAR.
...BUT WHEN THEY FIND YOU ALL YOU'LL BE IS--
GREETINGS, MASTER EMERICK CAPHTOR.
GREETINGS, INVESTIGATOR SIAN HOLT.
THE SUPREME CHANCELLOR OF THE GALACTIC REPUBLIC, LINA SOH, HAS REQUESTED YOUR IMMEDIATE PRESENCE AT HER OFFICE IN THE REPUBLIC EXECUTIVE BUILDING.

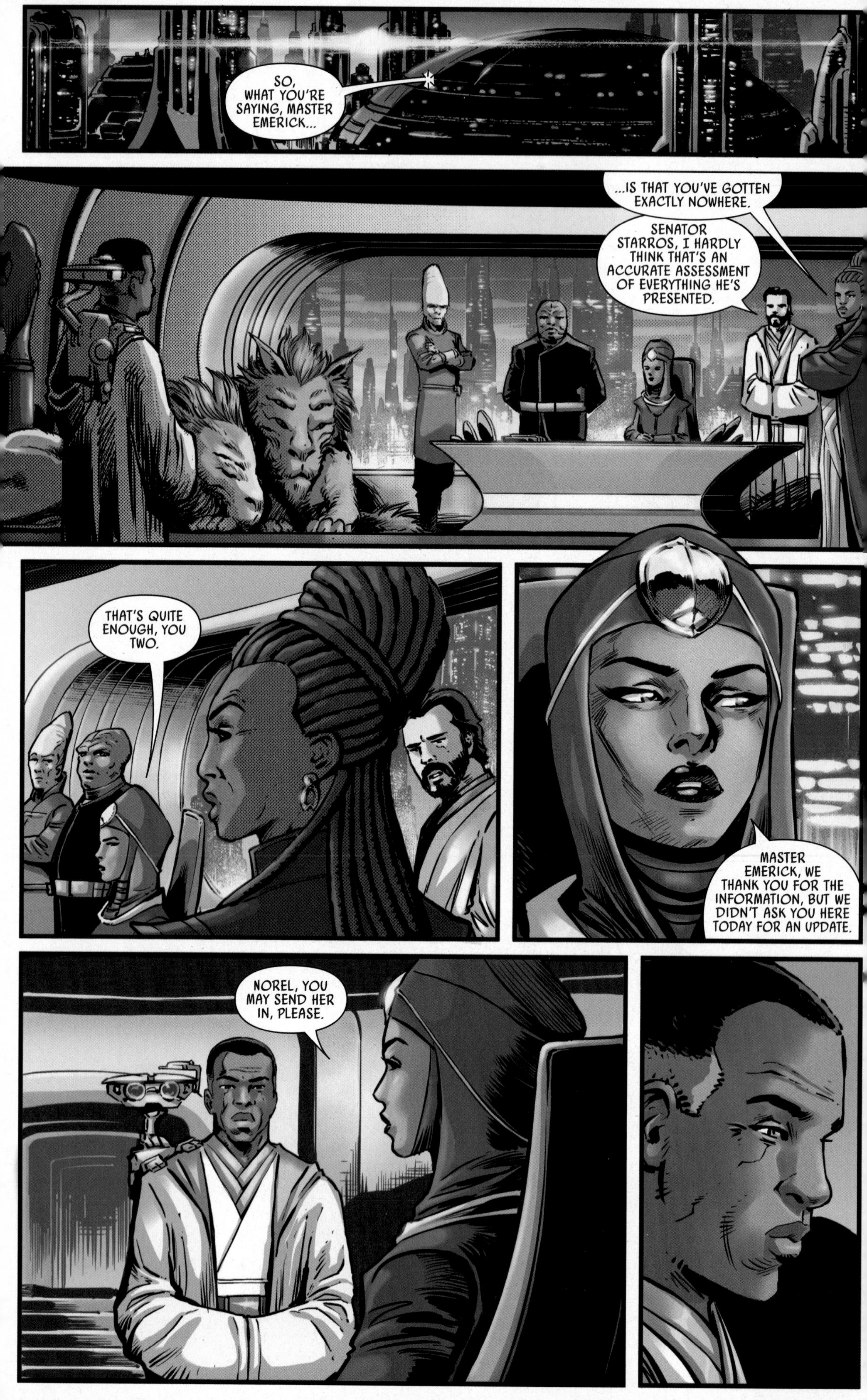
SO, WHAT YOU'RE SAYING, MASTER EMERICK...
...IS THAT YOU'VE GOTTEN EXACTLY NOWHERE.
SENATOR STARROS, I HARDLY THINK THAT'S AN ACCURATE ASSESSMENT OF EVERYTHING HE'S PRESENTED.
THAT'S QUITE ENOUGH, YOU TWO.
MASTER EMERICK, WE THANK YOU FOR THE INFORMATION, BUT WE DIDN'T ASK YOU HERE TODAY FOR AN UPDATE.
NOREL, YOU MAY SEND HER IN, PLEASE.

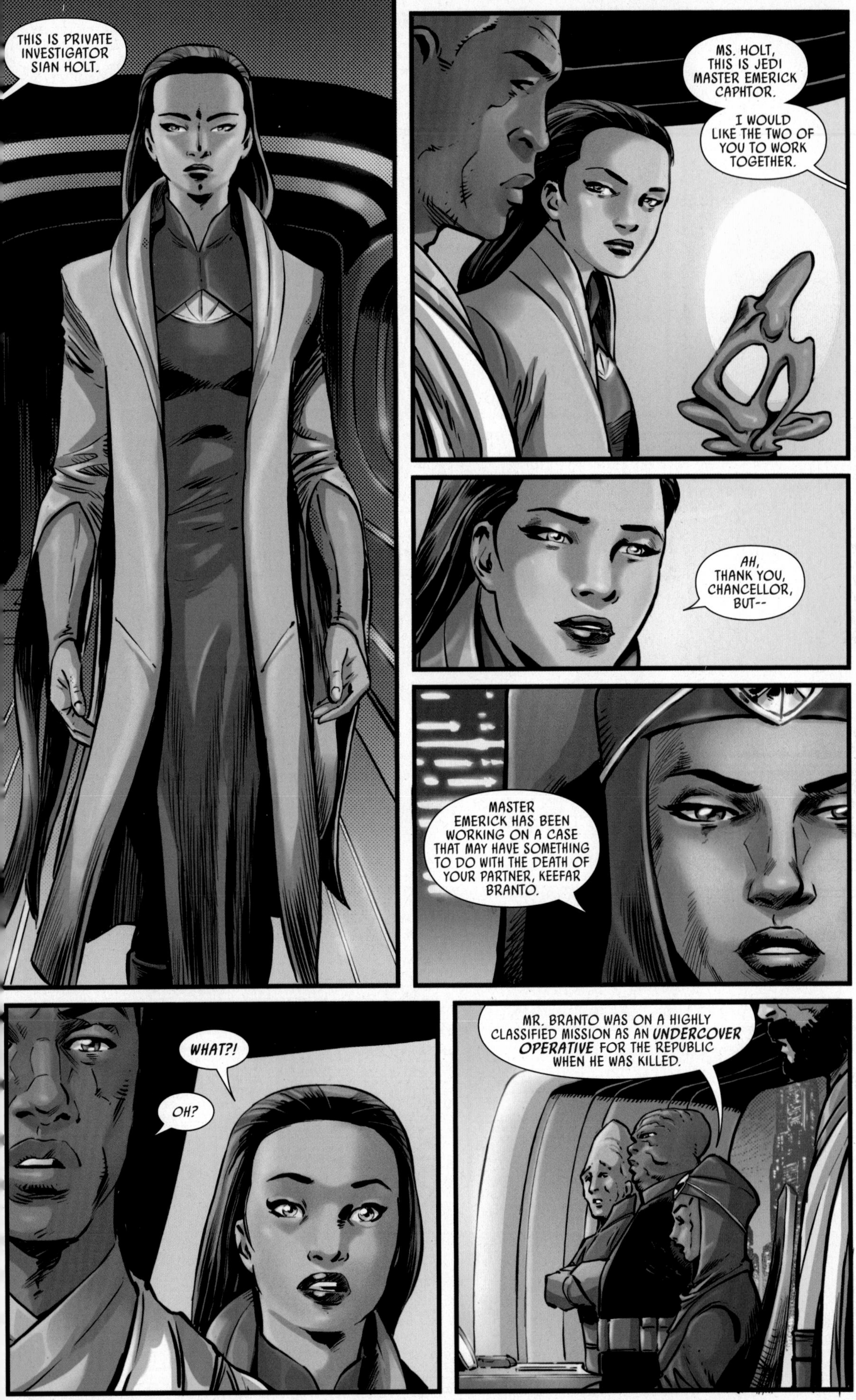
THIS IS PRIVATE INVESTIGATOR SIAN HOLT.
MS. HOLT, THIS IS JEDI MASTER EMERICK CAPHTOR.
I WOULD LIKE THE TWO OF YOU TO WORK TOGETHER.
AH, THANK YOU, CHANCELLOR, BUT--
MASTER EMERICK HAS BEEN WORKING ON A CASE THAT MAY HAVE SOMETHING TO DO WITH THE DEATH OF YOUR PARTNER, KEEFAR BRANTO.
WHAT?!
OH?
MR. BRANTO WAS ON A HIGHLY CLASSIFIED MISSION AS AN *UNDERCOVER OPERATIVE* FOR THE REPUBLIC WHEN HE WAS KILLED.

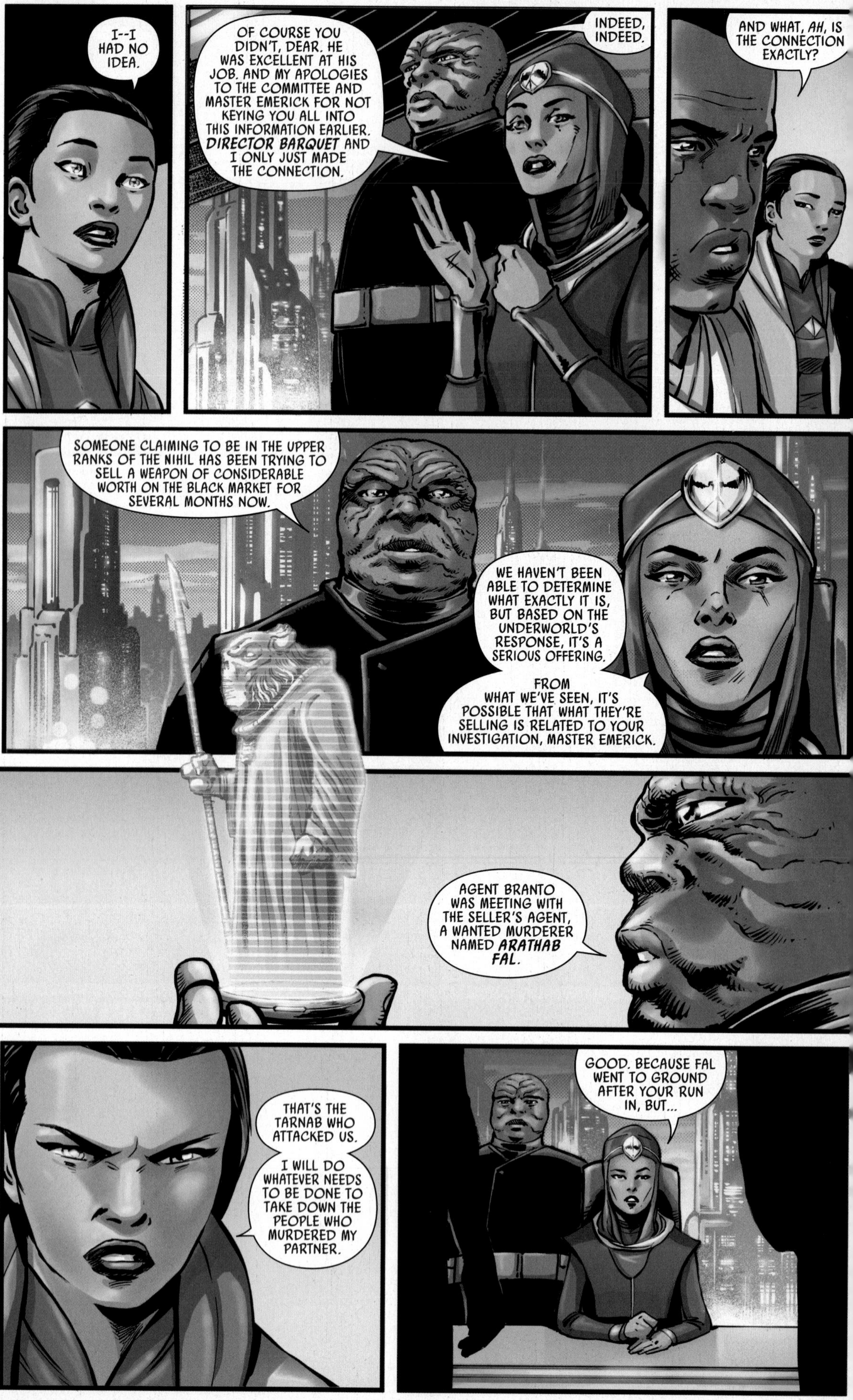
I--I HAD NO IDEA.
OF COURSE YOU DIDN'T, DEAR. HE WAS EXCELLENT AT HIS JOB. AND MY APOLOGIES TO THE COMMITTEE AND MASTER EMERICK FOR NOT KEYING YOU ALL INTO THIS INFORMATION EARLIER. DIRECTOR BARQUET AND I ONLY JUST MADE THE CONNECTION.
INDEED, INDEED.
AND WHAT, AH, IS THE CONNECTION EXACTLY?
SOMEONE CLAIMING TO BE IN THE UPPER RANKS OF THE NIHIL HAS BEEN TRYING TO SELL A WEAPON OF CONSIDERABLE WORTH ON THE BLACK MARKET FOR SEVERAL MONTHS NOW.
WE HAVEN'T BEEN ABLE TO DETERMINE WHAT EXACTLY IT IS, BUT BASED ON THE UNDERWORLD'S RESPONSE, IT'S A SERIOUS OFFERING.
FROM WHAT WE'VE SEEN, IT'S POSSIBLE THAT WHAT THEY'RE SELLING IS RELATED TO YOUR INVESTIGATION, MASTER EMERICK.
AGENT BRANTO WAS MEETING WITH THE SELLER'S AGENT, A WANTED MURDERER NAMED ARATHAB FAL.
THAT'S THE TARNAB WHO ATTACKED US.
I WILL DO WHATEVER NEEDS TO BE DONE TO TAKE DOWN THE PEOPLE WHO MURDERED MY PARTNER.
GOOD. BECAUSE FAL WENT TO GROUND AFTER YOUR RUN IN, BUT...

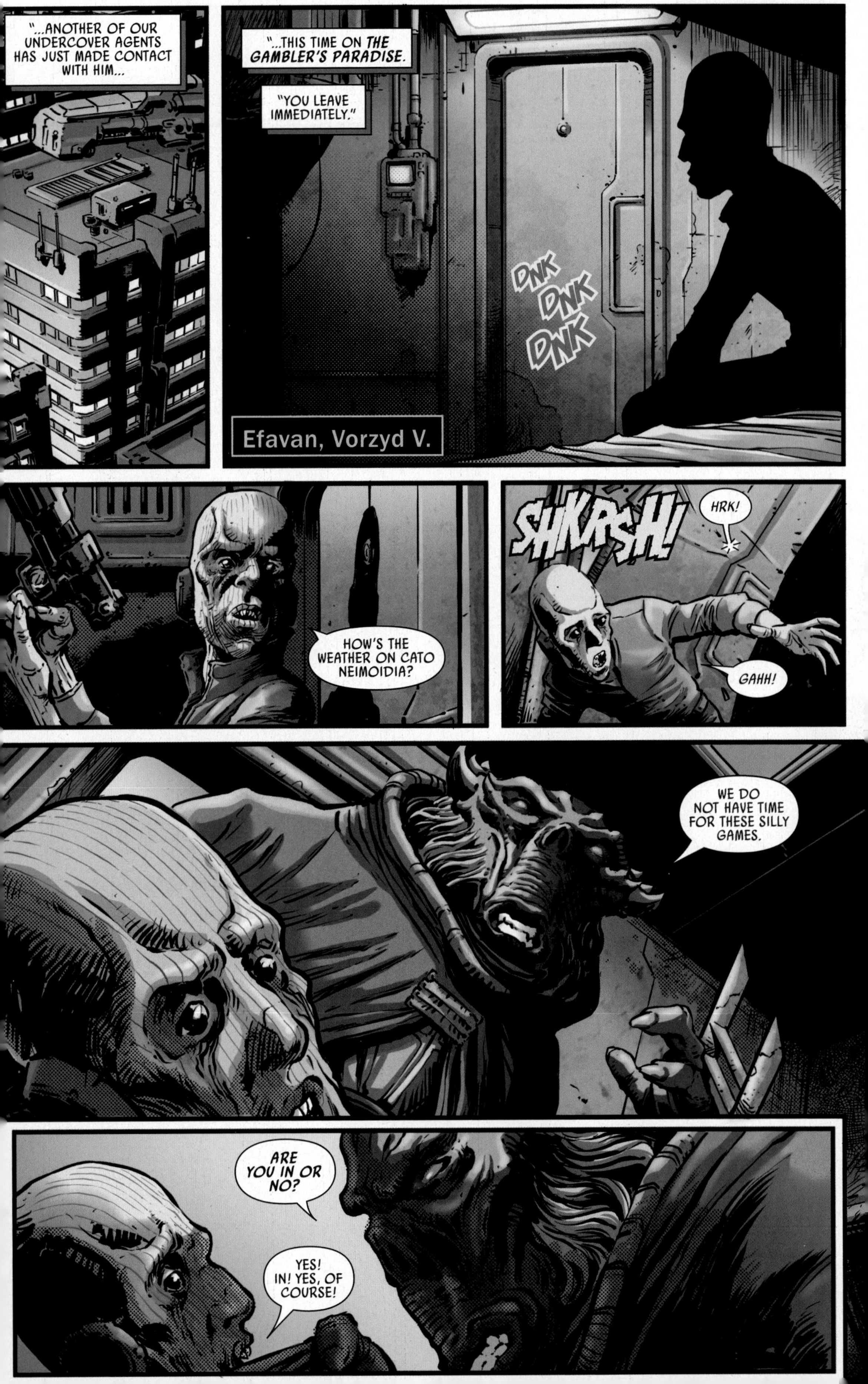
"...ANOTHER OF OUR UNDERCOVER AGENTS HAS JUST MADE CONTACT WITH HIM...
"...THIS TIME ON *THE GAMBLER'S PARADISE*.
"YOU LEAVE IMMEDIATELY."
Efavan, Vorzyd V.
DNK DNK DNK
HOW'S THE WEATHER ON CATO NEIMOIDIA?
SHKRSH!
HRK!
GAHH!
WE DO NOT HAVE TIME FOR THESE SILLY GAMES.
ARE YOU IN OR NO?
YES! IN! YES, OF COURSE!

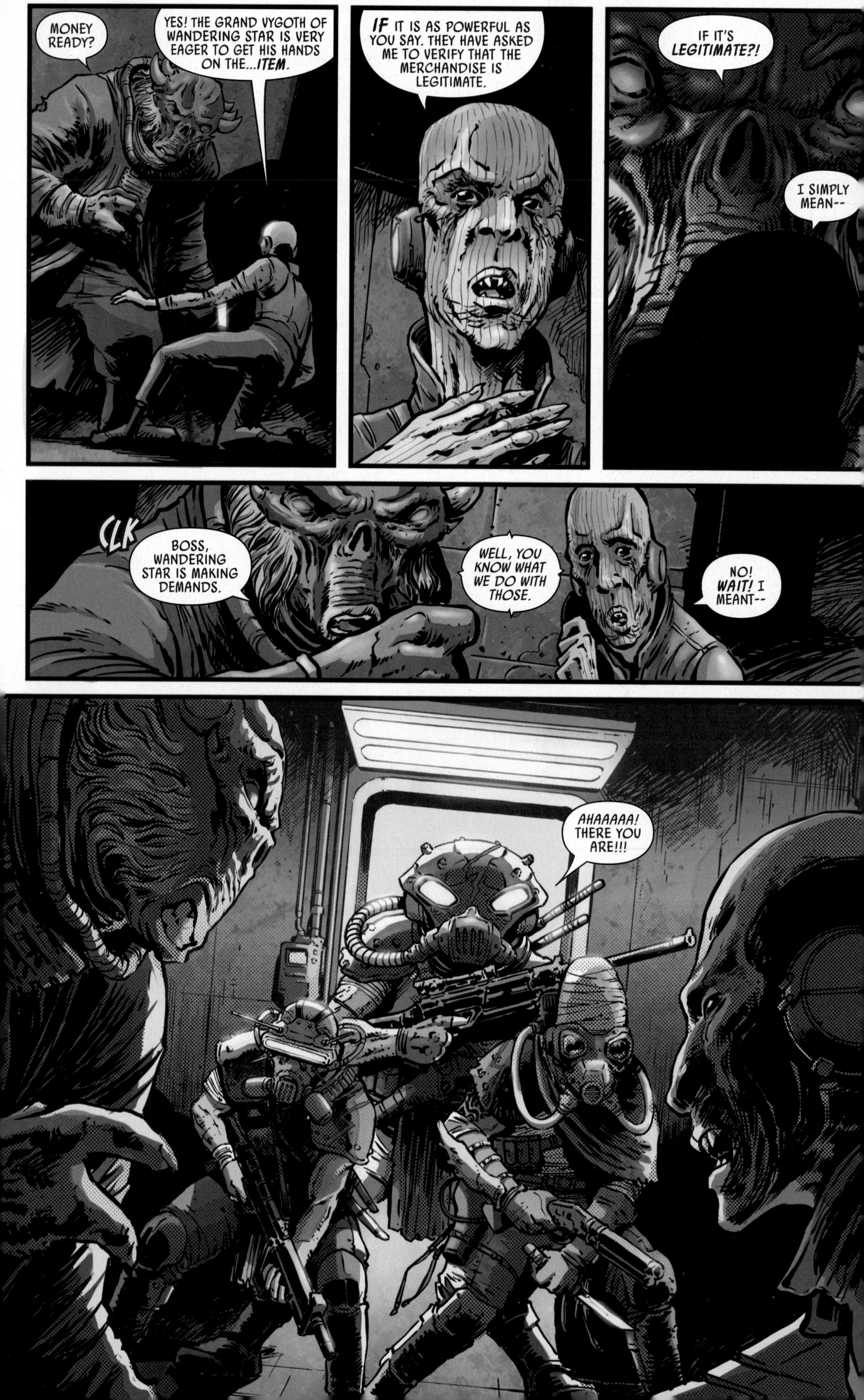
MONEY READY?
YES! THE GRAND VYGOTH OF WANDERING STAR IS VERY EAGER TO GET HIS HANDS ON THE...ITEM.
IF IT IS AS POWERFUL AS YOU SAY. THEY HAVE ASKED ME TO VERIFY THAT THE MERCHANDISE IS LEGITIMATE.
IF IT'S LEGITIMATE?!
I SIMPLY MEAN--
CLK
BOSS, WANDERING STAR IS MAKING DEMANDS.
WELL, YOU KNOW WHAT WE DO WITH THOSE.
NO! WAIT! I MEANT--
AHAAAAA! THERE YOU ARE!!!

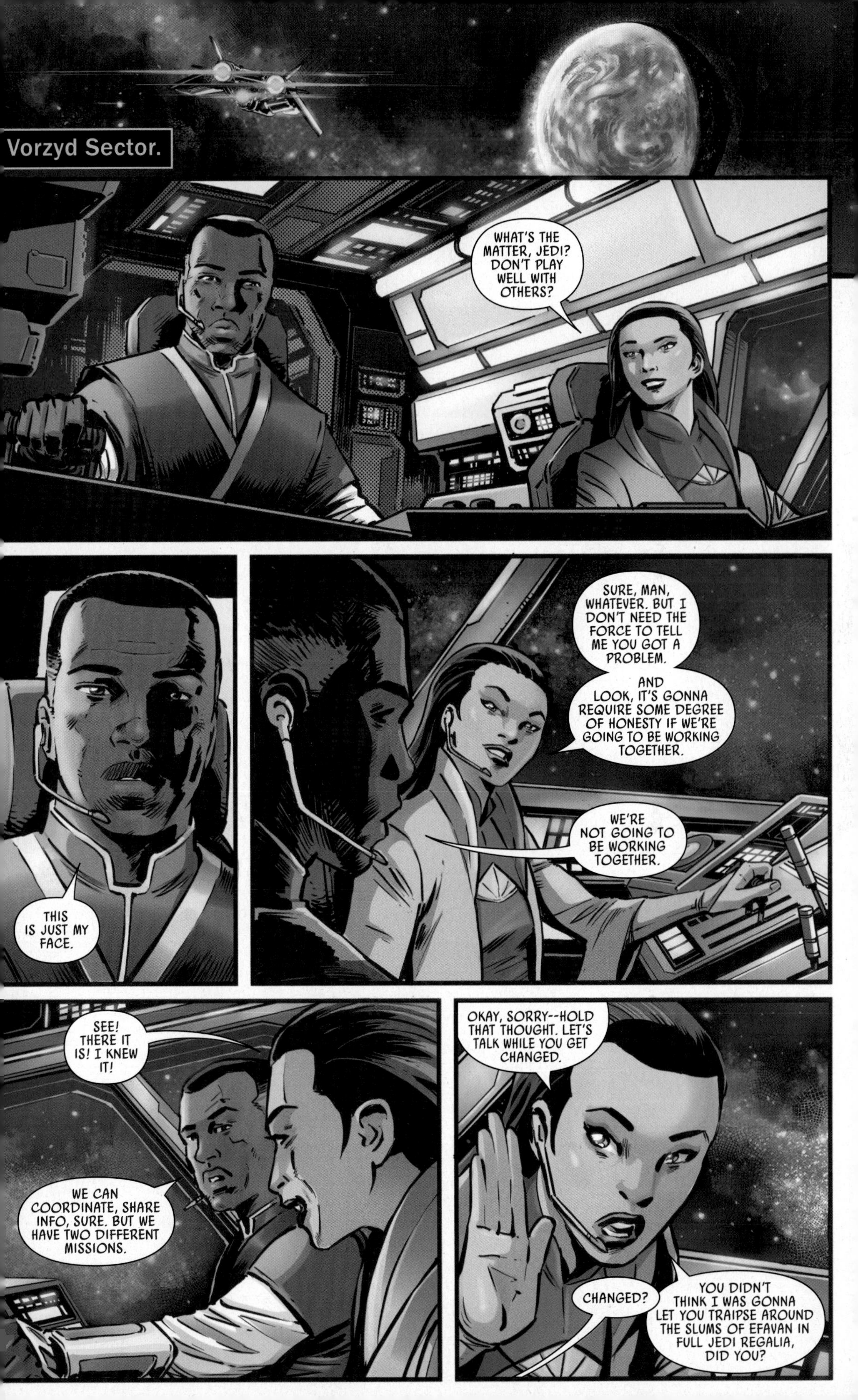
Vorzyd Sector.
WHAT'S THE MATTER, JEDI? DON'T PLAY WELL WITH OTHERS?
THIS IS JUST MY FACE.
SURE, MAN, WHATEVER. BUT I DON'T NEED THE FORCE TO TELL ME YOU GOT A PROBLEM.
AND LOOK, IT'S GONNA REQUIRE SOME DEGREE OF HONESTY IF WE'RE GOING TO BE WORKING TOGETHER.
WE'RE NOT GOING TO BE WORKING TOGETHER.
SEE! THERE IT IS! I KNEW IT!
WE CAN COORDINATE, SHARE INFO, SURE. BUT WE HAVE TWO DIFFERENT MISSIONS.
OKAY, SORRY--HOLD THAT THOUGHT. LET'S TALK WHILE YOU GET CHANGED.
CHANGED?
YOU DIDN'T THINK I WAS GONNA LET YOU TRAIPSE AROUND THE SLUMS OF EFAVAN IN FULL JEDI REGALIA, DID YOU?

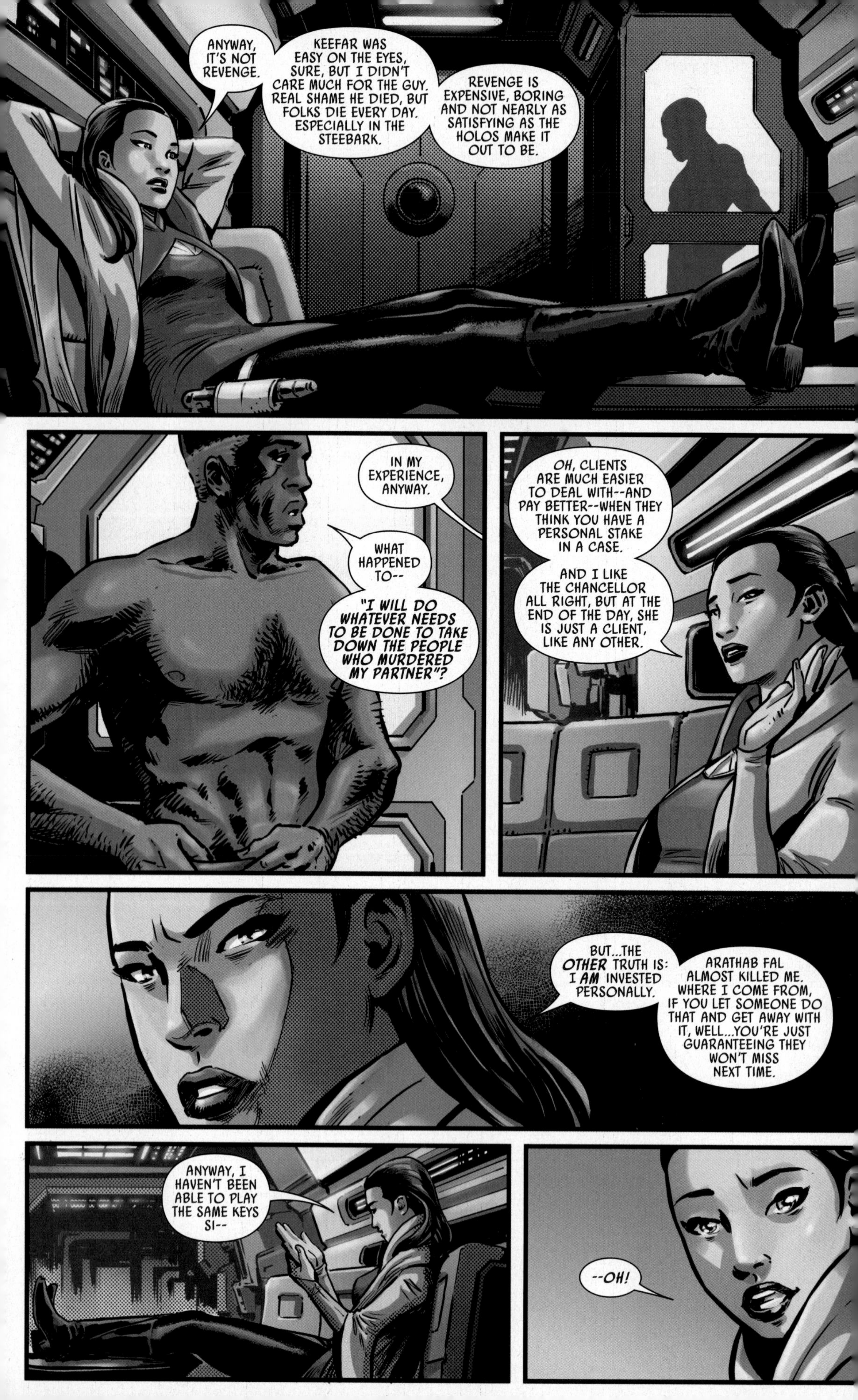
ANYWAY, IT'S NOT REVENGE.
KEEFAR WAS EASY ON THE EYES, SURE, BUT I DIDN'T CARE MUCH FOR THE GUY. REAL SHAME HE DIED, BUT FOLKS DIE EVERY DAY. ESPECIALLY IN THE STEEBARK.
REVENGE IS EXPENSIVE, BORING AND NOT NEARLY AS SATISFYING AS THE HOLOS MAKE IT OUT TO BE.
IN MY EXPERIENCE, ANYWAY.
WHAT HAPPENED TO--
"I WILL DO WHATEVER NEEDS TO BE DONE TO TAKE DOWN THE PEOPLE WHO MURDERED MY PARTNER"?
OH, CLIENTS ARE MUCH EASIER TO DEAL WITH--AND PAY BETTER--WHEN THEY THINK YOU HAVE A PERSONAL STAKE IN A CASE.
AND I LIKE THE CHANCELLOR ALL RIGHT, BUT AT THE END OF THE DAY, SHE IS JUST A CLIENT, LIKE ANY OTHER.
BUT...THE OTHER TRUTH IS: I AM INVESTED PERSONALLY.
ARATHAB FAL ALMOST KILLED ME. WHERE I COME FROM, IF YOU LET SOMEONE DO THAT AND GET AWAY WITH IT, WELL...YOU'RE JUST GUARANTEEING THEY WON'T MISS NEXT TIME.
ANYWAY, I HAVEN'T BEEN ABLE TO PLAY THE SAME KEYS SI--
--OH!

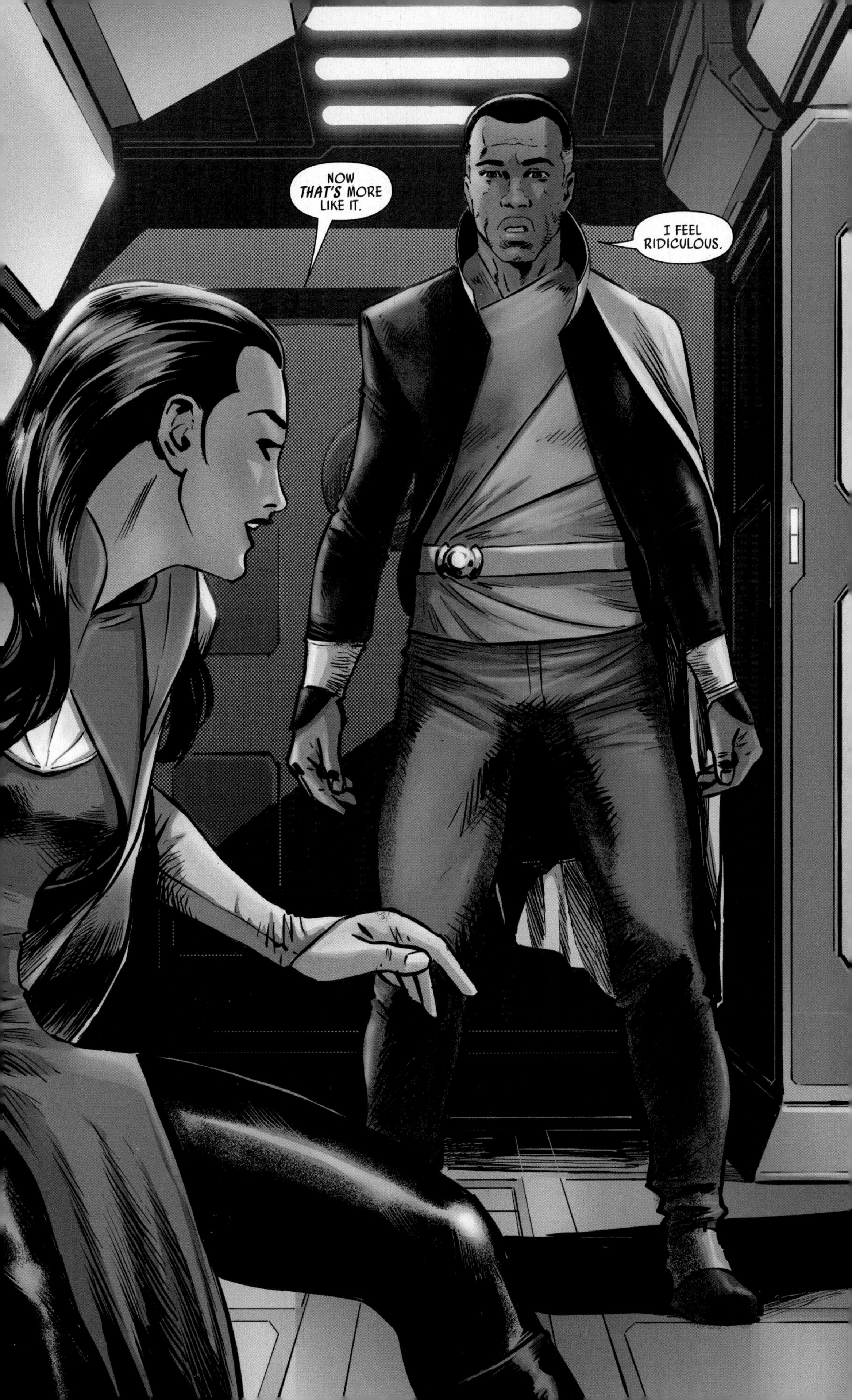
NOW THAT'S MORE LIKE IT.
I FEEL RIDICULOUS.

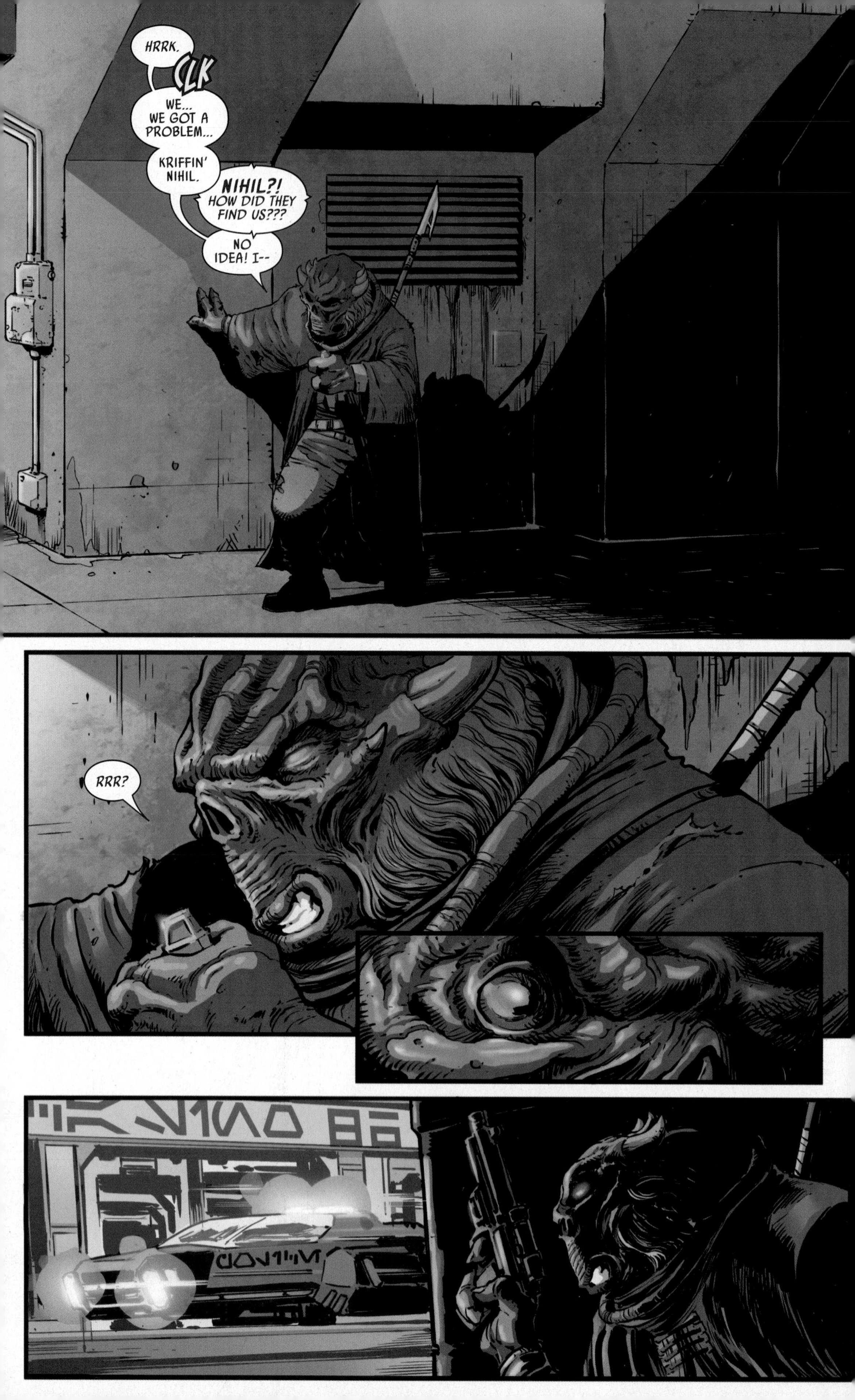
HRRK.
CLK
WE... WE GOT A PROBLEM...
KRIFFIN' NIHIL.
NIHIL?! HOW DID THEY FIND US???
NO IDEA! I--
RRR?

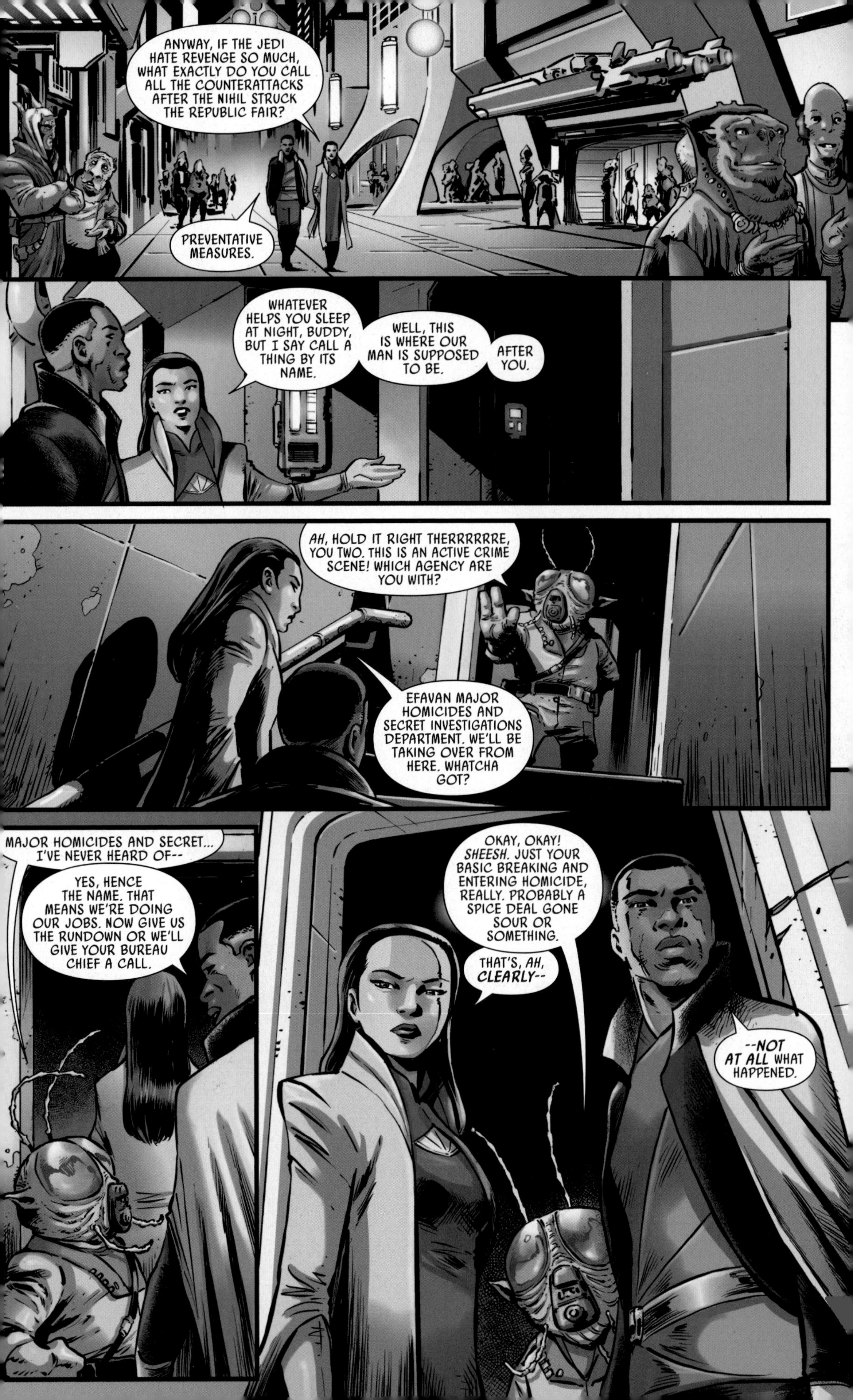

ANYWAY, IF THE JEDI HATE REVENGE SO MUCH, WHAT EXACTLY DO YOU CALL ALL THE COUNTERATTACKS AFTER THE NIHIL STRUCK THE REPUBLIC FAIR?
PREVENTATIVE MEASURES.
WHATEVER HELPS YOU SLEEP AT NIGHT, BUDDY, BUT I SAY CALL A THING BY ITS NAME.
WELL, THIS IS WHERE OUR MAN IS SUPPOSED TO BE.
AFTER YOU.
AH, HOLD IT RIGHT THERRRRRRE, YOU TWO. THIS IS AN ACTIVE CRIME SCENE! WHICH AGENCY ARE YOU WITH?
EFAVAN MAJOR HOMICIDES AND SECRET INVESTIGATIONS DEPARTMENT. WE'LL BE TAKING OVER FROM HERE. WHATCHA GOT?
MAJOR HOMICIDES AND SECRET... I'VE NEVER HEARD OF--
YES, HENCE THE NAME. THAT MEANS WE'RE DOING OUR JOBS. NOW GIVE US THE RUNDOWN OR WE'LL GIVE YOUR BUREAU CHIEF A CALL.
OKAY, OKAY! *SHEESH.* JUST YOUR BASIC BREAKING AND ENTERING HOMICIDE, REALLY. PROBABLY A SPICE DEAL GONE SOUR OR SOMETHING.
THAT'S, AH, ***CLEARLY***--
--***NOT AT ALL*** WHAT HAPPENED.

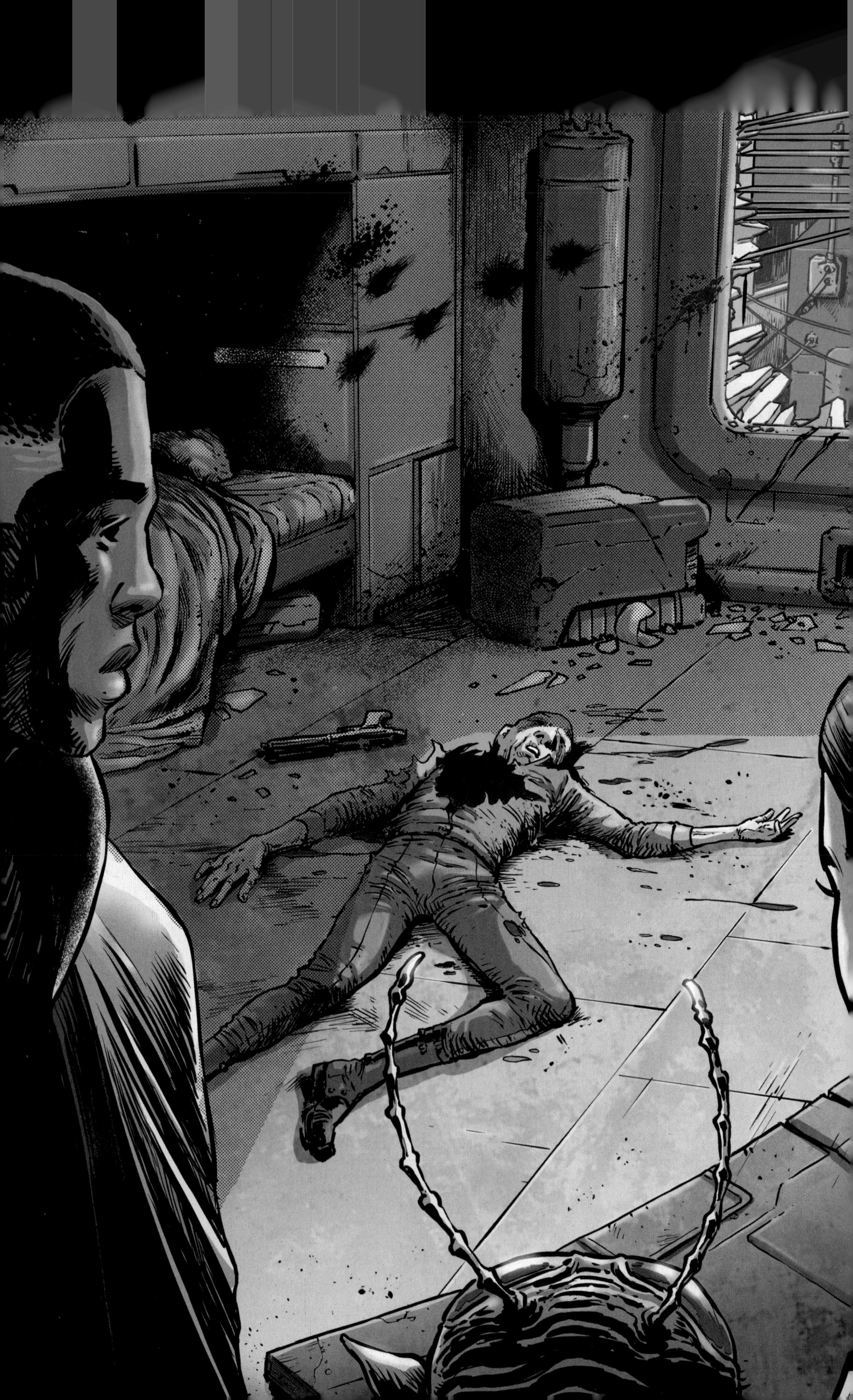

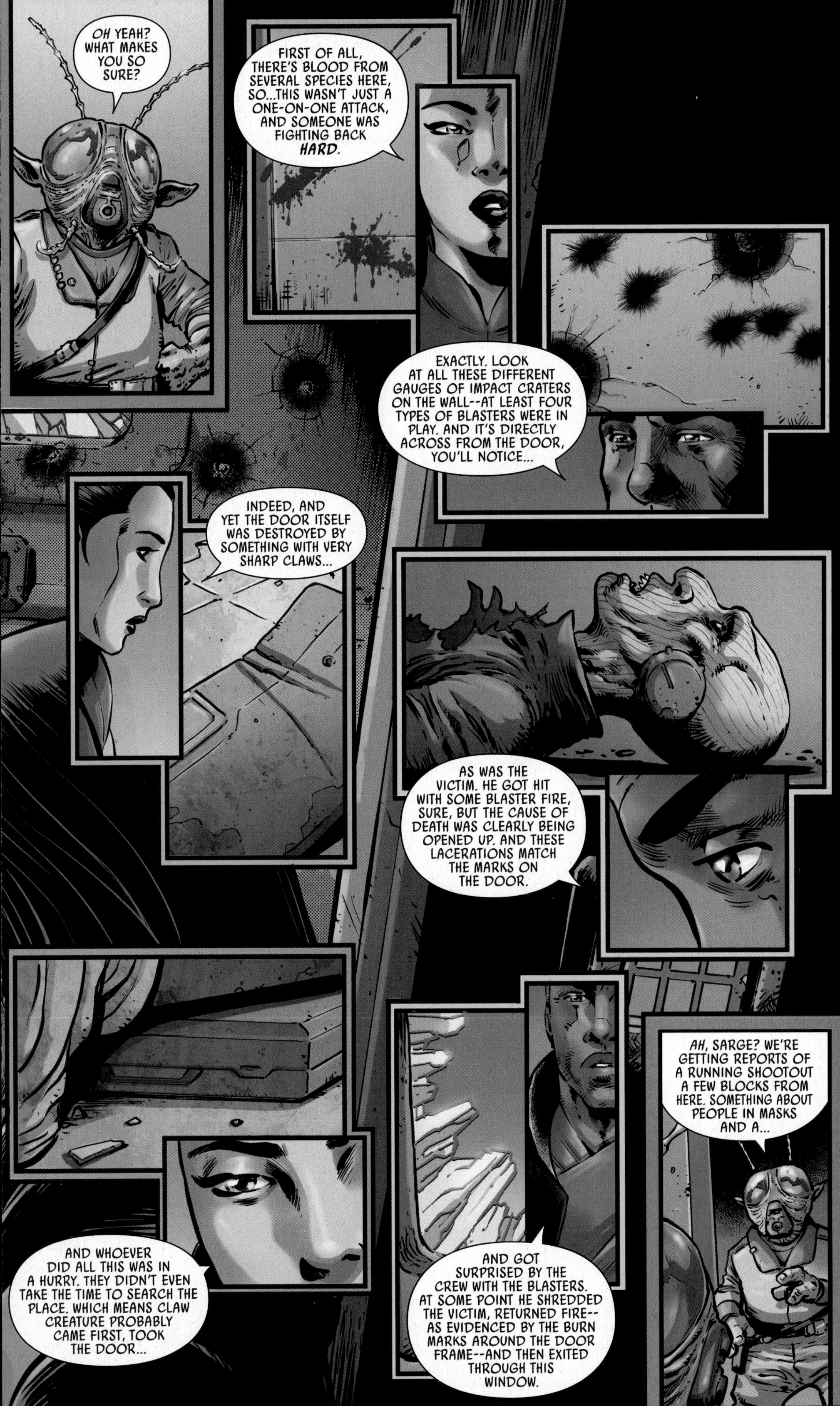
OH YEAH? WHAT MAKES YOU SO SURE?
FIRST OF ALL, THERE'S BLOOD FROM SEVERAL SPECIES HERE, SO...THIS WASN'T JUST A ONE-ON-ONE ATTACK, AND SOMEONE WAS FIGHTING BACK HARD.
EXACTLY. LOOK AT ALL THESE DIFFERENT GAUGES OF IMPACT CRATERS ON THE WALL--AT LEAST FOUR TYPES OF BLASTERS WERE IN PLAY. AND IT'S DIRECTLY ACROSS FROM THE DOOR, YOU'LL NOTICE...
INDEED, AND YET THE DOOR ITSELF WAS DESTROYED BY SOMETHING WITH VERY SHARP CLAWS...
AS WAS THE VICTIM. HE GOT HIT WITH SOME BLASTER FIRE, SURE, BUT THE CAUSE OF DEATH WAS CLEARLY BEING OPENED UP. AND THESE LACERATIONS MATCH THE MARKS ON THE DOOR.
AND WHOEVER DID ALL THIS WAS IN A HURRY. THEY DIDN'T EVEN TAKE THE TIME TO SEARCH THE PLACE. WHICH MEANS CLAW CREATURE PROBABLY CAME FIRST, TOOK THE DOOR...
AND GOT SURPRISED BY THE CREW WITH THE BLASTERS. AT SOME POINT HE SHREDDED THE VICTIM, RETURNED FIRE--AS EVIDENCED BY THE BURN MARKS AROUND THE DOOR FRAME--AND THEN EXITED THROUGH THIS WINDOW.
AH, SARGE? WE'RE GETTING REPORTS OF A RUNNING SHOOTOUT A FEW BLOCKS FROM HERE. SOMETHING ABOUT PEOPLE IN MASKS AND A...

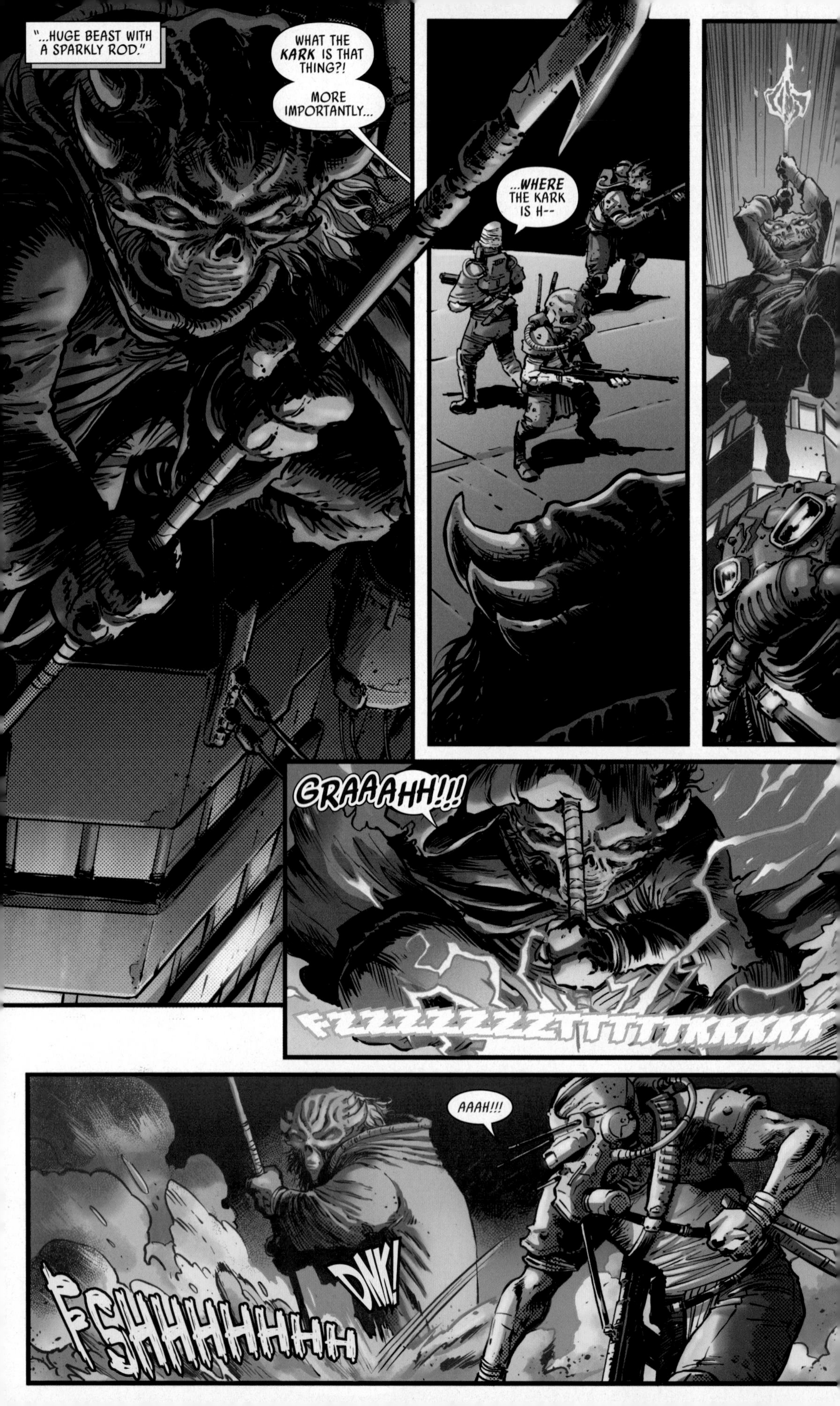
"...HUGE BEAST WITH A SPARKLY ROD."
WHAT THE KARK IS THAT THING?!
MORE IMPORTANTLY...
...WHERE THE KARK IS H--
GRAAAHH!!!
FZZZZZZZZZTTTTTTKKKKK
AAAH!!!
DNK!
FSHHHHHHHH

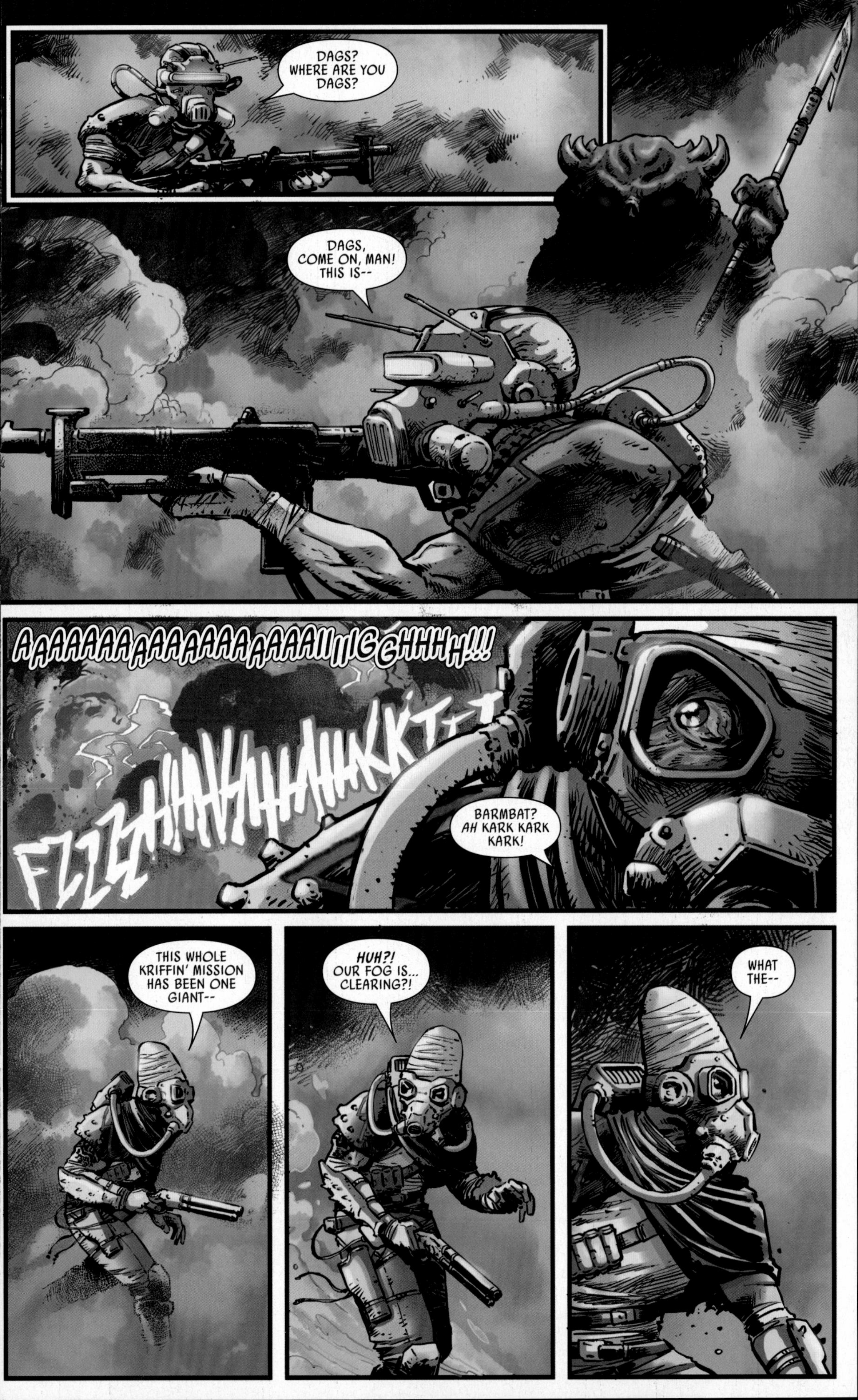
DAGS? WHERE ARE YOU DAGS?
DAGS, COME ON, MAN! THIS IS--
AAAAAAAAAAAAAAAAAIIIIGGHHHH!!!
FZZZZHHHSHHHHHKT-T-T
BARMBAT? AH KARK KARK KARK!
THIS WHOLE KRIFFIN' MISSION HAS BEEN ONE GIANT--
HUH?! OUR FOG IS... CLEARING?!
WHAT THE--

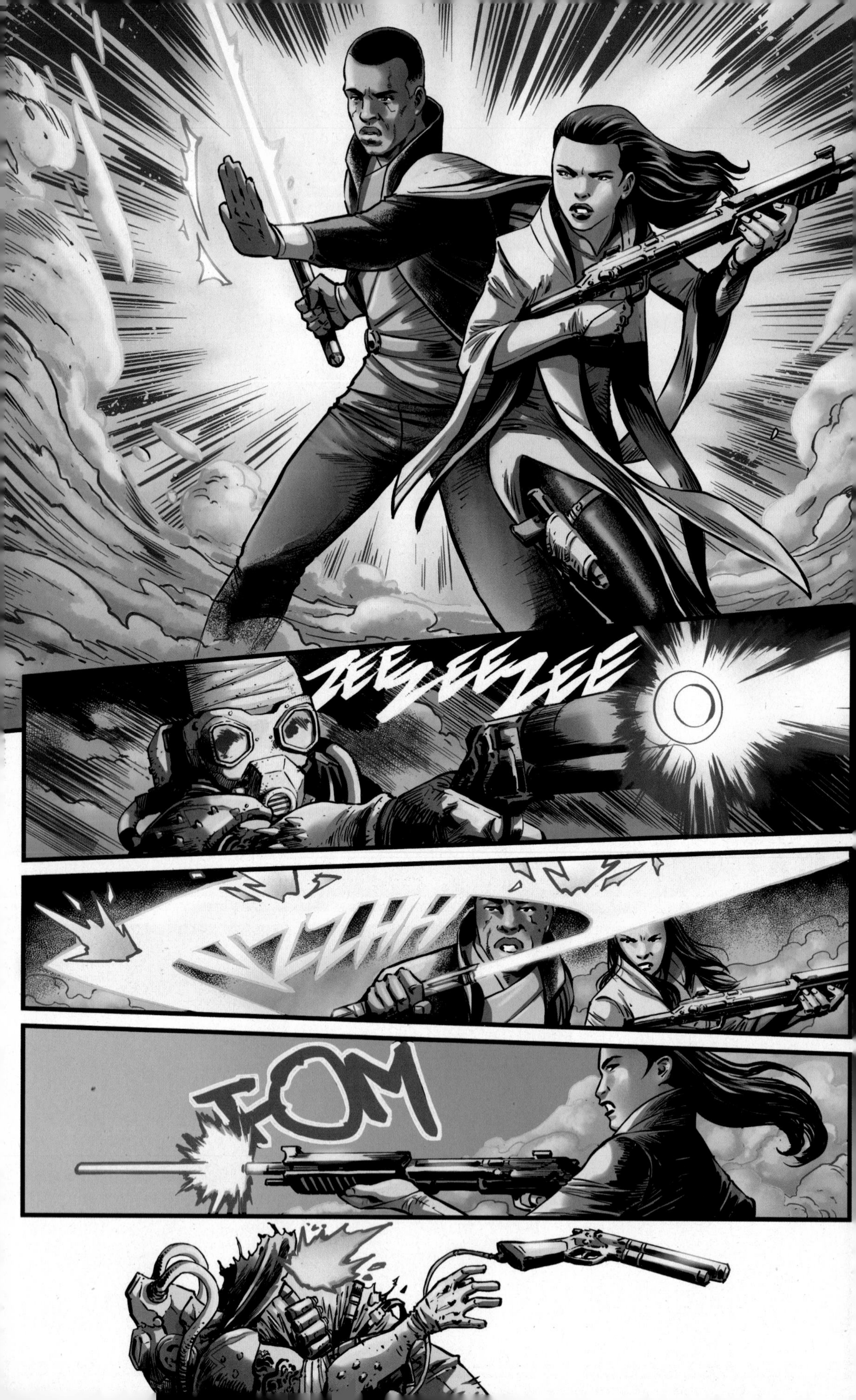
ZEE ZEE ZEE
VZZHH
TCHOM

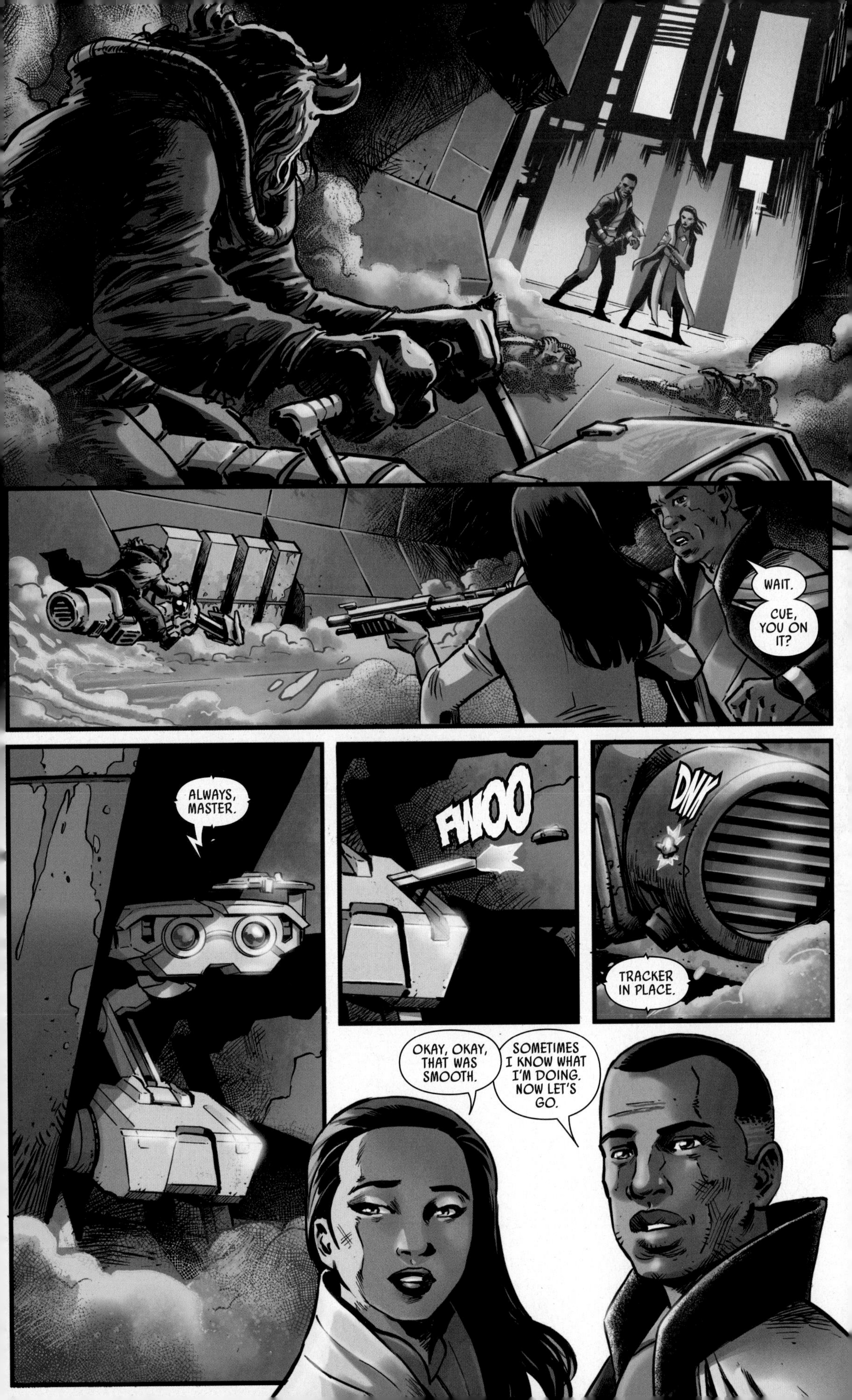
WAIT.
CUE, YOU ON IT?
ALWAYS, MASTER.
FWOO
DNK
TRACKER IN PLACE.
OKAY, OKAY, THAT WAS SMOOTH.
SOMETIMES I KNOW WHAT I'M DOING. NOW LET'S GO.

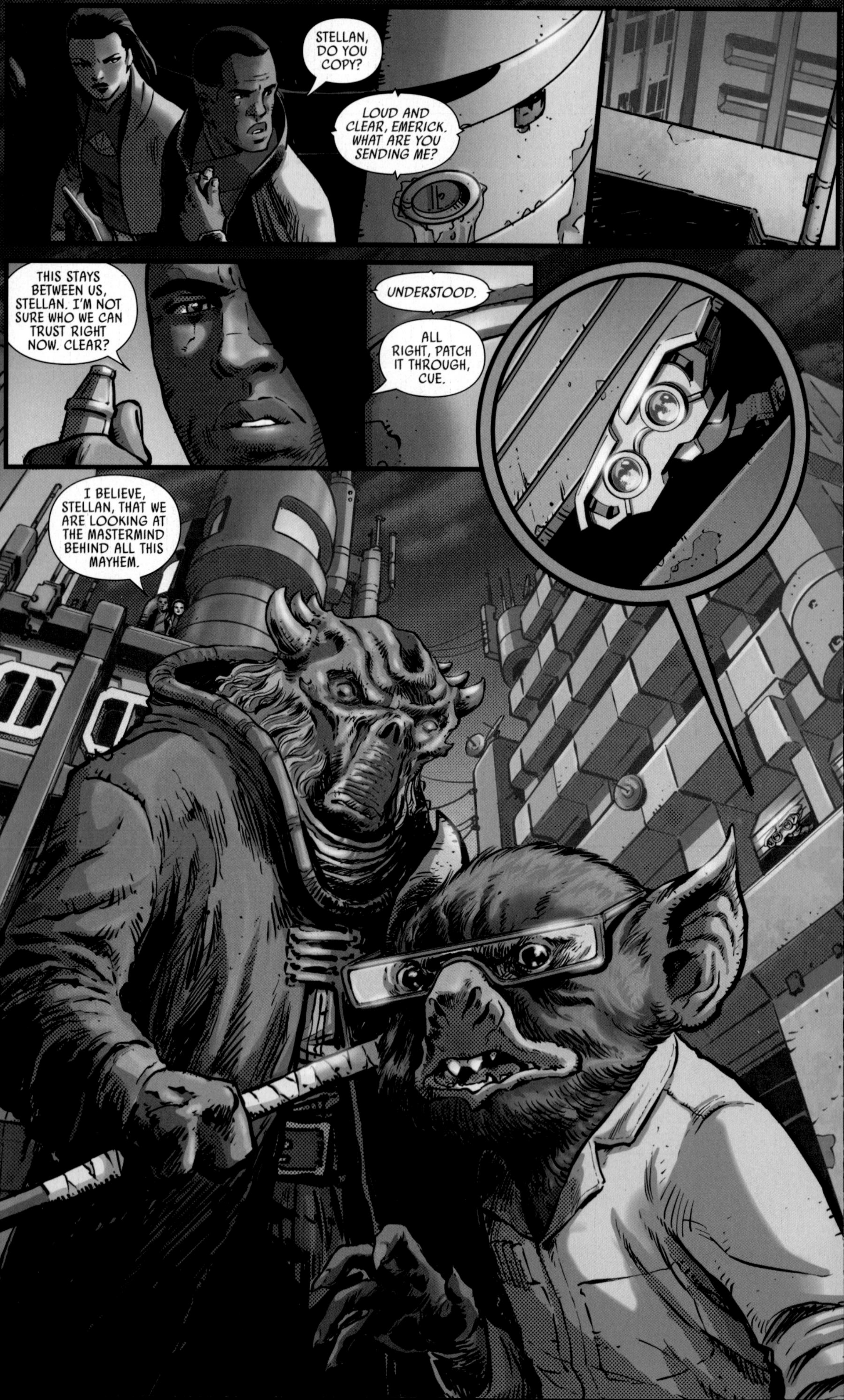
STELLAN, DO YOU COPY?
LOUD AND CLEAR, EMERICK. WHAT ARE YOU SENDING ME?
THIS STAYS BETWEEN US, STELLAN. I'M NOT SURE WHO WE CAN TRUST RIGHT NOW. CLEAR?
UNDERSTOOD.
ALL RIGHT, PATCH IT THROUGH, CUE.
I BELIEVE, STELLAN, THAT WE ARE LOOKING AT THE MASTERMIND BEHIND ALL THIS MAYHEM.

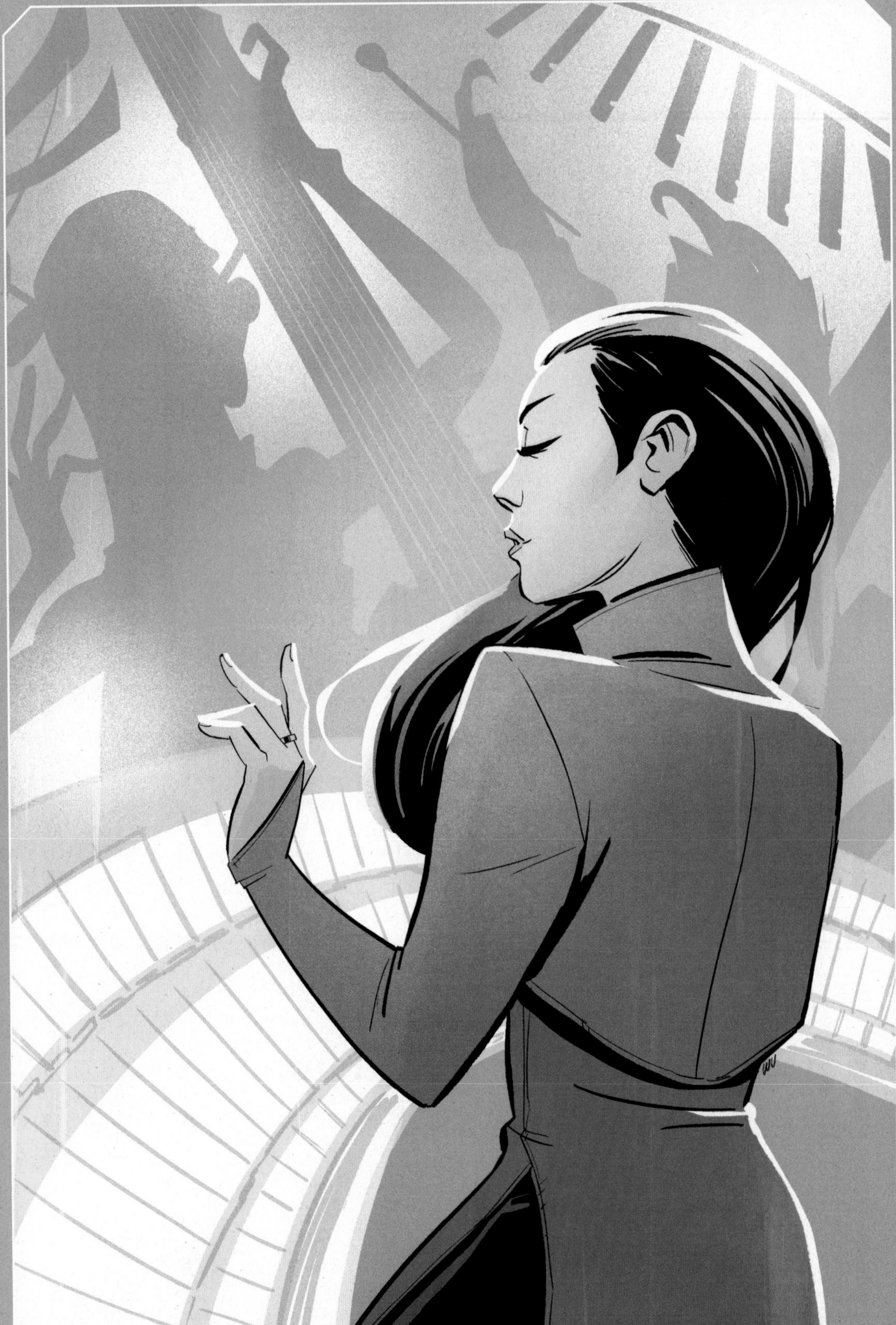
WU

#3 Variant by
ANNIE WU

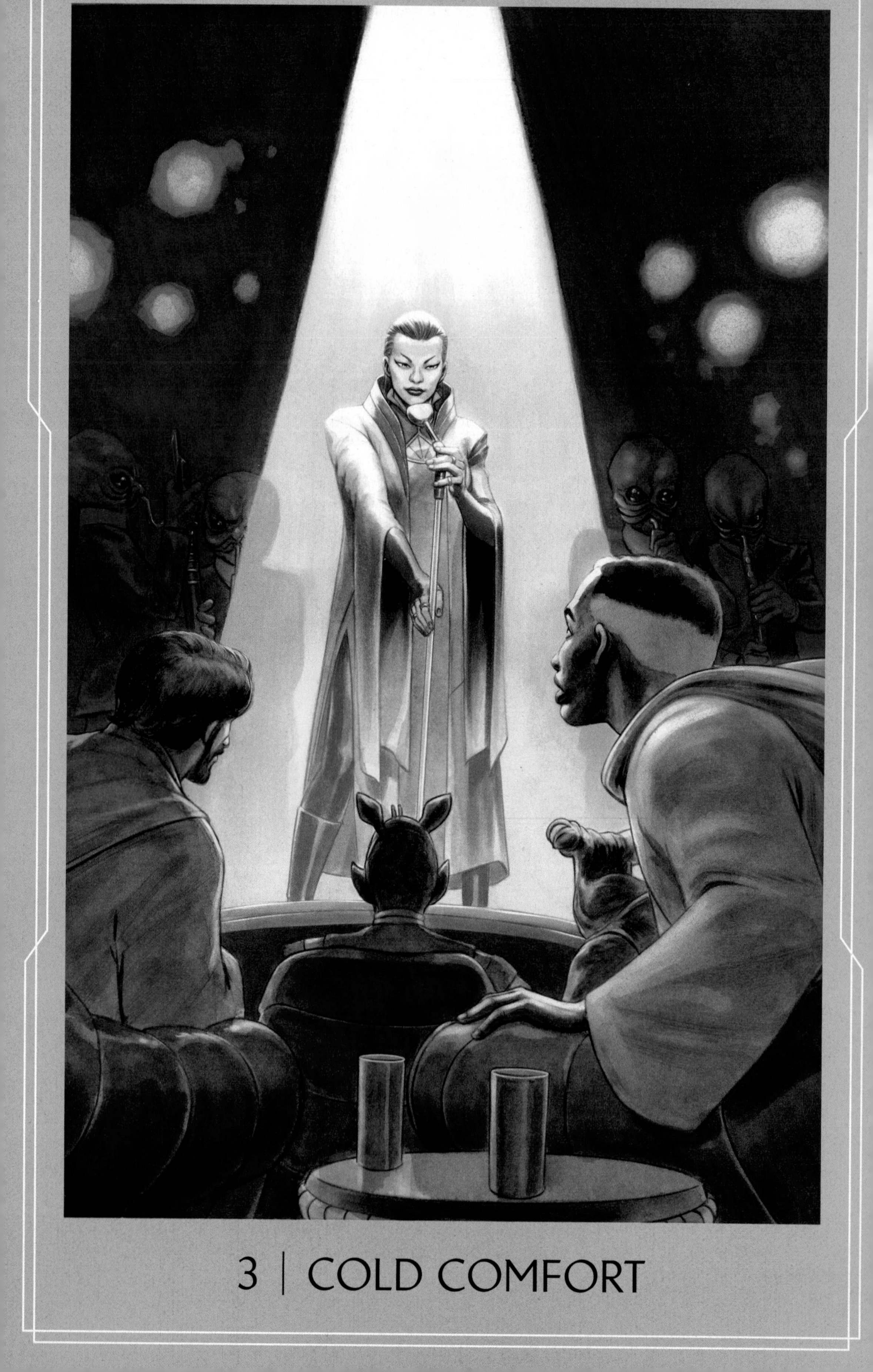

3 | COLD COMFORT

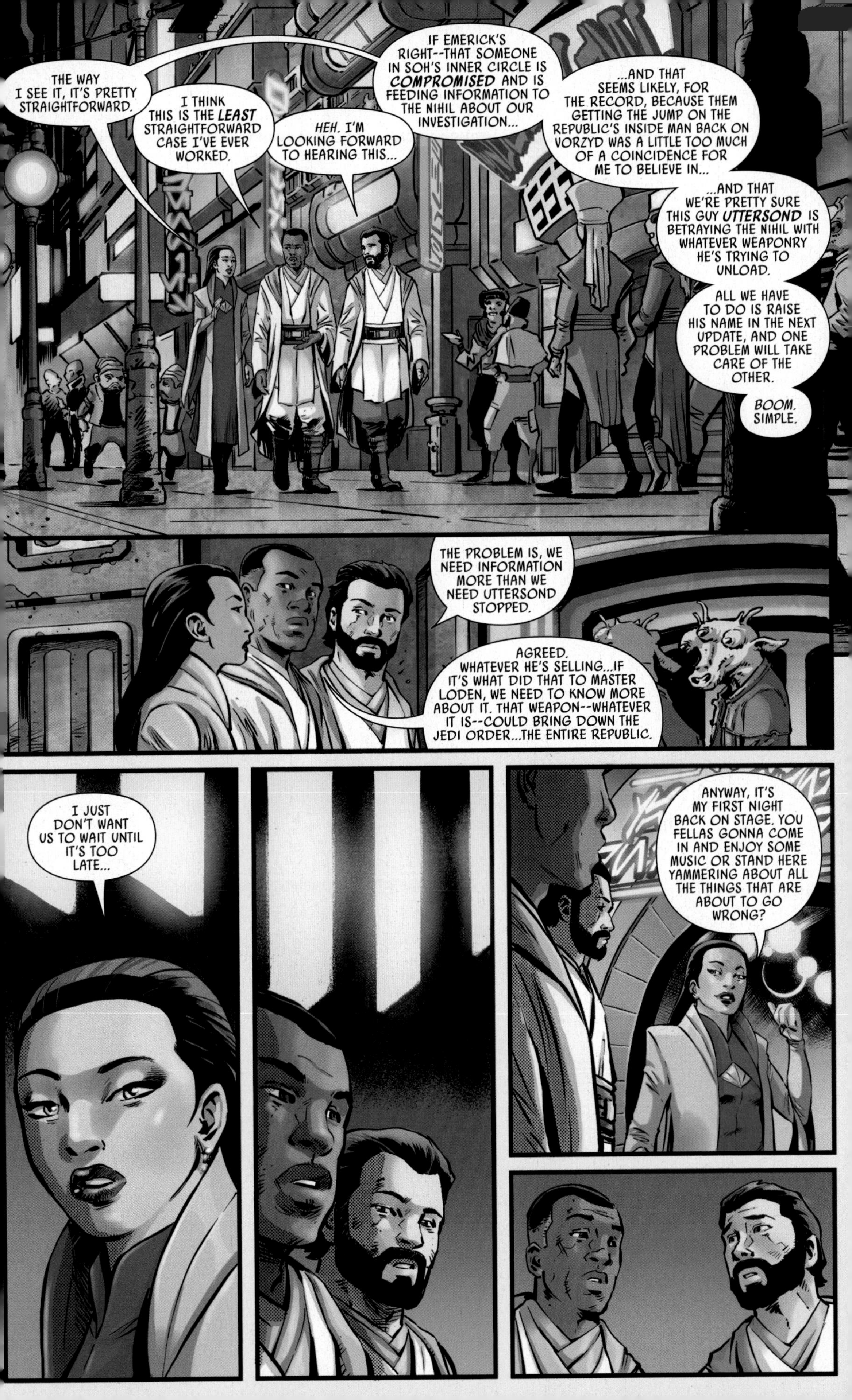
THE WAY I SEE IT, IT'S PRETTY STRAIGHTFORWARD.
I THINK THIS IS THE *LEAST* STRAIGHTFORWARD CASE I'VE EVER WORKED.
HEH. I'M LOOKING FORWARD TO HEARING THIS...
IF EMERICK'S RIGHT--THAT SOMEONE IN SOH'S INNER CIRCLE IS ***COMPROMISED*** AND IS FEEDING INFORMATION TO THE NIHIL ABOUT OUR INVESTIGATION...
...AND THAT SEEMS LIKELY, FOR THE RECORD, BECAUSE THEM GETTING THE JUMP ON THE REPUBLIC'S INSIDE MAN BACK ON VORZYD WAS A LITTLE TOO MUCH OF A COINCIDENCE FOR ME TO BELIEVE IN...
...AND THAT WE'RE PRETTY SURE THIS GUY ***UTTERSOND*** IS BETRAYING THE NIHIL WITH WHATEVER WEAPONRY HE'S TRYING TO UNLOAD.
ALL WE HAVE TO DO IS RAISE HIS NAME IN THE NEXT UPDATE, AND ONE PROBLEM WILL TAKE CARE OF THE OTHER.
BOOM. SIMPLE.
THE PROBLEM IS, WE NEED INFORMATION MORE THAN WE NEED UTTERSOND STOPPED.
AGREED. WHATEVER HE'S SELLING...IF IT'S WHAT DID THAT TO MASTER LODEN, WE NEED TO KNOW MORE ABOUT IT. THAT WEAPON--WHATEVER IT IS--COULD BRING DOWN THE JEDI ORDER...THE ENTIRE REPUBLIC.
I JUST DON'T WANT US TO WAIT UNTIL IT'S TOO LATE...
ANYWAY, IT'S MY FIRST NIGHT BACK ON STAGE. YOU FELLAS GONNA COME IN AND ENJOY SOME MUSIC OR STAND HERE YAMMERING ABOUT ALL THE THINGS THAT ARE ABOUT TO GO WRONG?

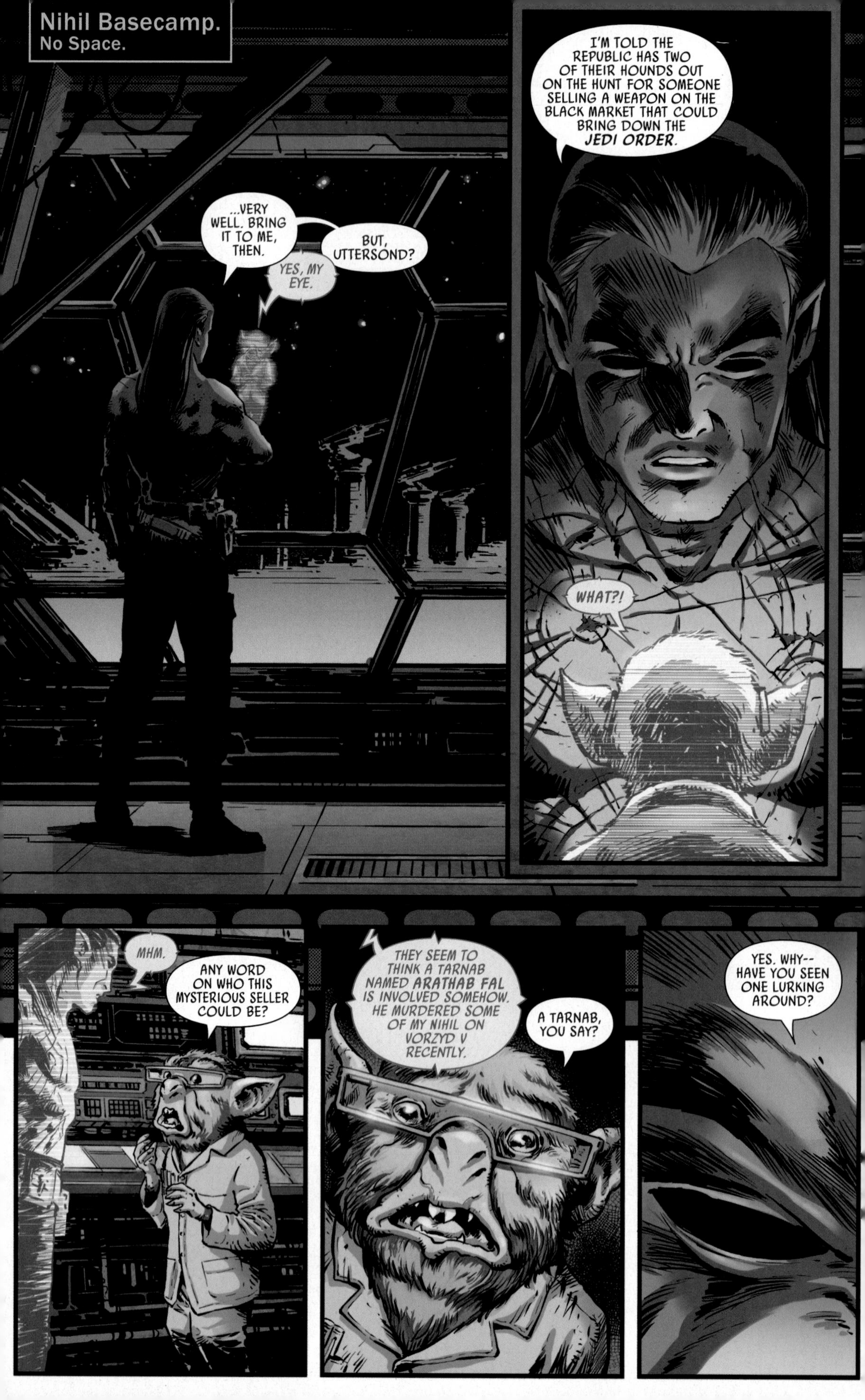
Nihil Basecamp.
No Space.
I'M TOLD THE REPUBLIC HAS TWO OF THEIR HOUNDS OUT ON THE HUNT FOR SOMEONE SELLING A WEAPON ON THE BLACK MARKET THAT COULD BRING DOWN THE JEDI ORDER.
WHAT?!
...VERY WELL. BRING IT TO ME, THEN.
YES, MY EYE.
BUT, UTTERSOND?
MHM.
ANY WORD ON WHO THIS MYSTERIOUS SELLER COULD BE?
THEY SEEM TO THINK A TARNAB NAMED ARATHAB FAL IS INVOLVED SOMEHOW. HE MURDERED SOME OF MY NIHIL ON VORZYD V RECENTLY.
A TARNAB, YOU SAY?
YES. WHY--HAVE YOU SEEN ONE LURKING AROUND?

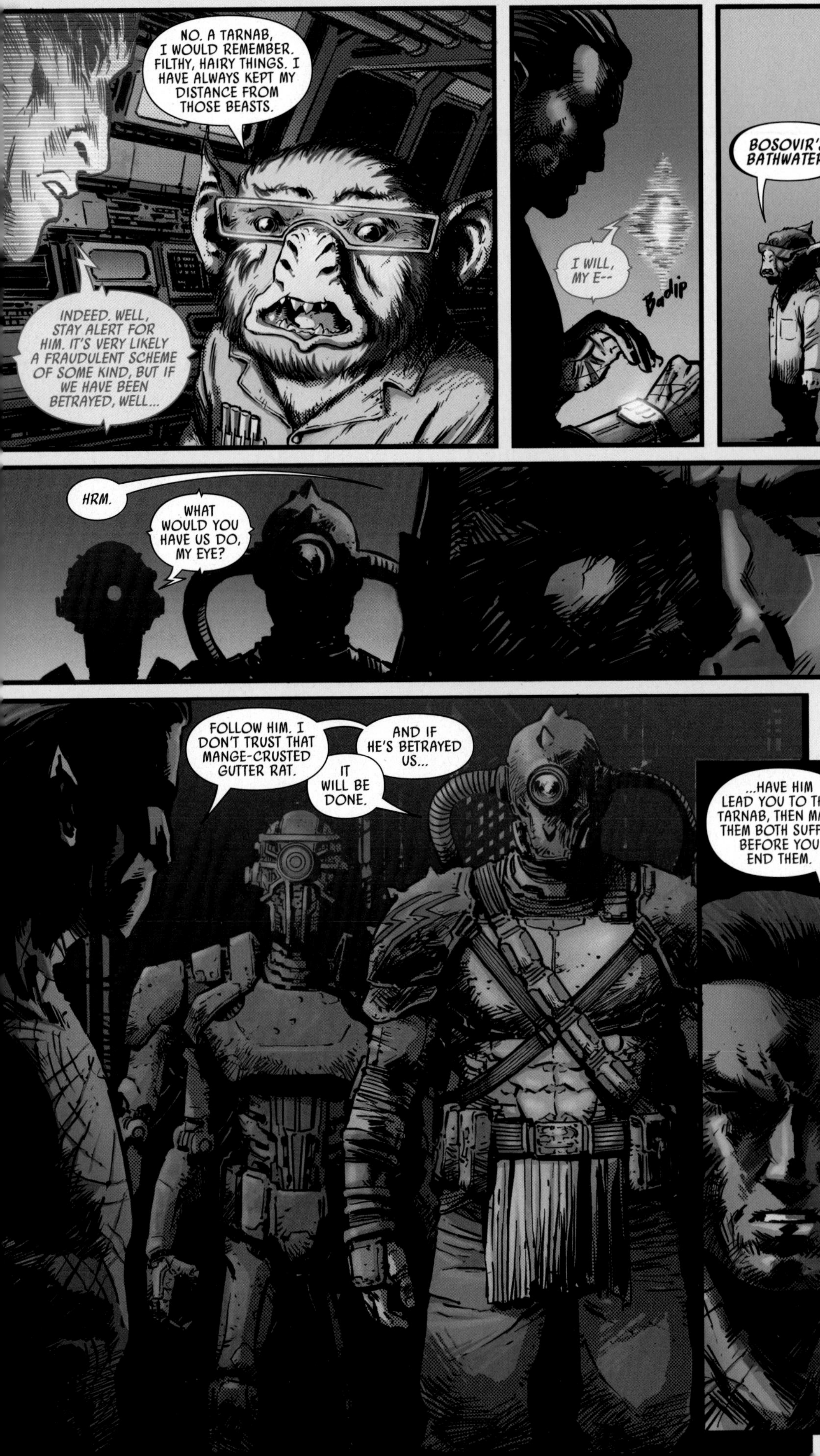
NO. A TARNAB, I WOULD REMEMBER. FILTHY, HAIRY THINGS. I HAVE ALWAYS KEPT MY DISTANCE FROM THOSE BEASTS.
INDEED. WELL, STAY ALERT FOR HIM. IT'S VERY LIKELY A FRAUDULENT SCHEME OF SOME KIND, BUT IF WE HAVE BEEN BETRAYED, WELL...
I WILL, MY E--
Badip
BOSOVIR'S BATHWATER!
HRM.
WHAT WOULD YOU HAVE US DO, MY EYE?
FOLLOW HIM. I DON'T TRUST THAT MANGE-CRUSTED GUTTER RAT.
AND IF HE'S BETRAYED US...
IT WILL BE DONE.
...HAVE HIM LEAD YOU TO THIS TARNAB, THEN MAKE THEM BOTH SUFFER BEFORE YOU END THEM.

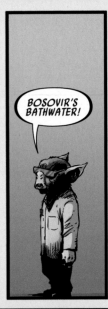

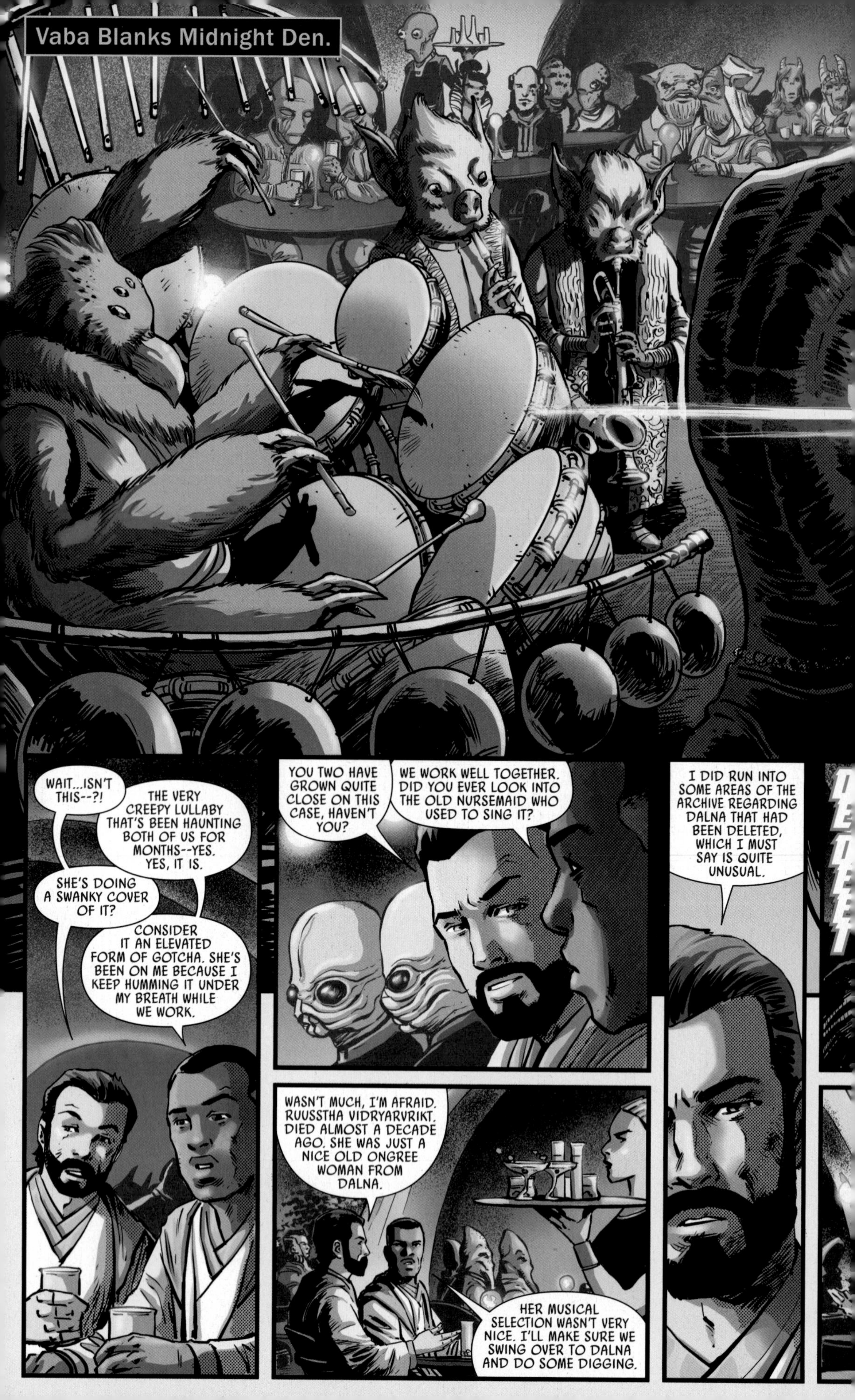
Vaba Blanks Midnight Den.
WAIT...ISN'T THIS--?!
THE VERY CREEPY LULLABY THAT'S BEEN HAUNTING BOTH OF US FOR MONTHS--YES. YES, IT IS.
SHE'S DOING A SWANKY COVER OF IT?
CONSIDER IT AN ELEVATED FORM OF GOTCHA. SHE'S BEEN ON ME BECAUSE I KEEP HUMMING IT UNDER MY BREATH WHILE WE WORK.
YOU TWO HAVE GROWN QUITE CLOSE ON THIS CASE, HAVEN'T YOU?
WE WORK WELL TOGETHER. DID YOU EVER LOOK INTO THE OLD NURSEMAID WHO USED TO SING IT?
WASN'T MUCH, I'M AFRAID. RUUSSTHA VIDRYARVRIKT. DIED ALMOST A DECADE AGO. SHE WAS JUST A NICE OLD ONGREE WOMAN FROM DALNA.
HER MUSICAL SELECTION WASN'T VERY NICE. I'LL MAKE SURE WE SWING OVER TO DALNA AND DO SOME DIGGING.
I DID RUN INTO SOME AREAS OF THE ARCHIVE REGARDING DALNA THAT HAD BEEN DELETED, WHICH I MUST SAY IS QUITE UNUSUAL.

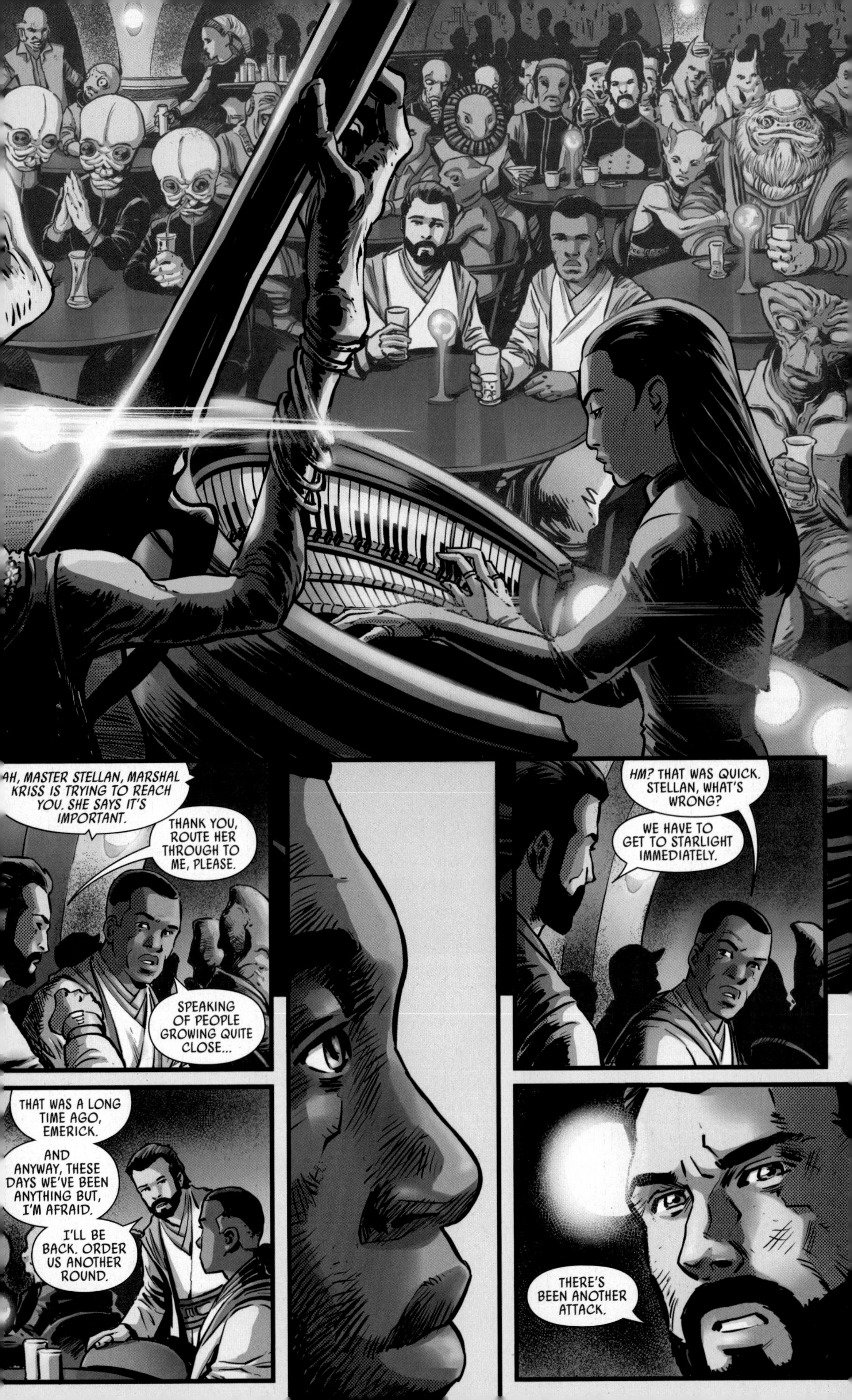
AH, MASTER STELLAN, MARSHAL KRISS IS TRYING TO REACH YOU. SHE SAYS IT'S IMPORTANT.
THANK YOU, ROUTE HER THROUGH TO ME, PLEASE.
SPEAKING OF PEOPLE GROWING QUITE CLOSE...
HM? THAT WAS QUICK. STELLAN, WHAT'S WRONG?
WE HAVE TO GET TO STARLIGHT IMMEDIATELY.
THAT WAS A LONG TIME AGO, EMERICK.
AND ANYWAY, THESE DAYS WE'VE BEEN ANYTHING BUT, I'M AFRAID.
I'LL BE BACK. ORDER US ANOTHER ROUND.
THERE'S BEEN ANOTHER ATTACK.

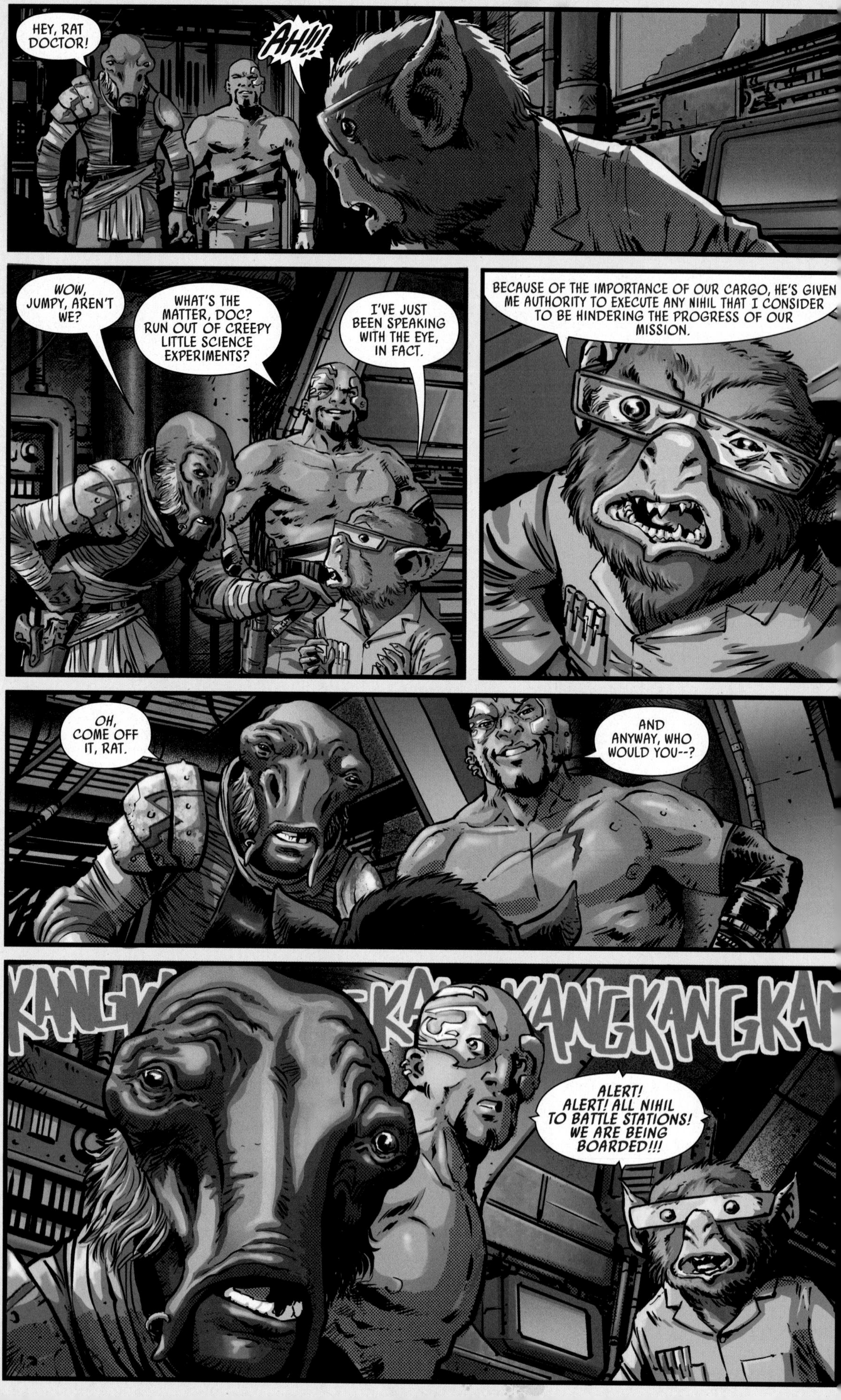
HEY, RAT DOCTOR!
AH!!!
WOW, JUMPY, AREN'T WE?
WHAT'S THE MATTER, DOC? RUN OUT OF CREEPY LITTLE SCIENCE EXPERIMENTS?
I'VE JUST BEEN SPEAKING WITH THE EYE, IN FACT.
BECAUSE OF THE IMPORTANCE OF OUR CARGO, HE'S GIVEN ME AUTHORITY TO EXECUTE ANY NIHIL THAT I CONSIDER TO BE HINDERING THE PROGRESS OF OUR MISSION.
OH, COME OFF IT, RAT.
AND ANYWAY, WHO WOULD YOU--?
KANG KANG KANG
ALERT! ALERT! ALL NIHIL TO BATTLE STATIONS! WE ARE BEING BOARDED!!!

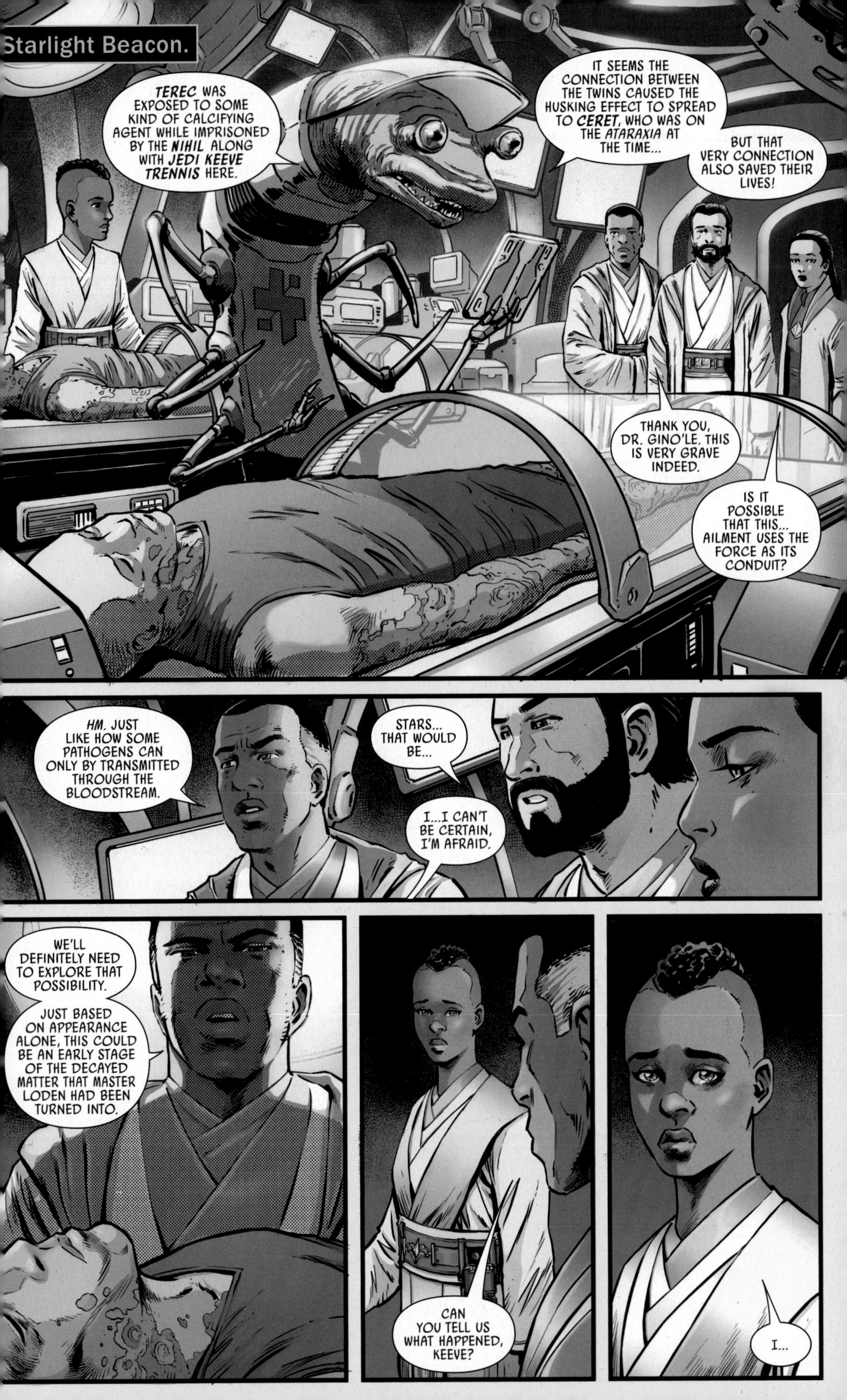
Starlight Beacon.
TEREC WAS EXPOSED TO SOME KIND OF CALCIFYING AGENT WHILE IMPRISONED BY THE NIHIL ALONG WITH JEDI KEEVE TRENNIS HERE.
IT SEEMS THE CONNECTION BETWEEN THE TWINS CAUSED THE HUSKING EFFECT TO SPREAD TO CERET, WHO WAS ON THE ATARAXIA AT THE TIME...
BUT THAT VERY CONNECTION ALSO SAVED THEIR LIVES!
THANK YOU, DR. GINO'LE. THIS IS VERY GRAVE INDEED.
IS IT POSSIBLE THAT THIS... AILMENT USES THE FORCE AS ITS CONDUIT?
HM. JUST LIKE HOW SOME PATHOGENS CAN ONLY BY TRANSMITTED THROUGH THE BLOODSTREAM.
STARS... THAT WOULD BE...
I...I CAN'T BE CERTAIN, I'M AFRAID.
WE'LL DEFINITELY NEED TO EXPLORE THAT POSSIBILITY.
JUST BASED ON APPEARANCE ALONE, THIS COULD BE AN EARLY STAGE OF THE DECAYED MATTER THAT MASTER LODEN HAD BEEN TURNED INTO.
CAN YOU TELL US WHAT HAPPENED, KEEVE?
I...

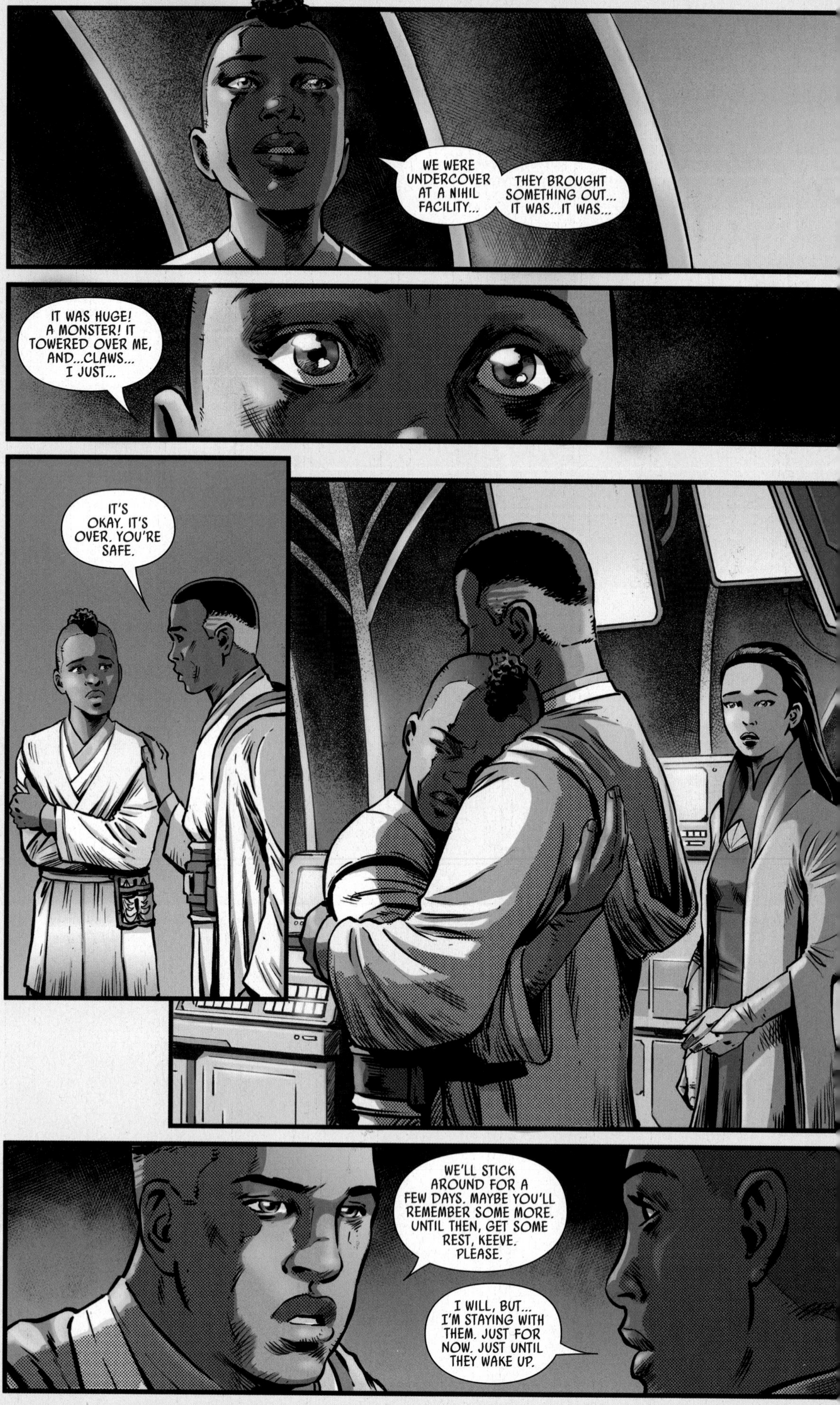
WE WERE UNDERCOVER AT A NIHIL FACILITY...
THEY BROUGHT SOMETHING OUT... IT WAS...IT WAS...
IT WAS HUGE! A MONSTER! IT TOWERED OVER ME, AND...CLAWS... I JUST...
IT'S OKAY. IT'S OVER. YOU'RE SAFE.
WE'LL STICK AROUND FOR A FEW DAYS. MAYBE YOU'LL REMEMBER SOME MORE. UNTIL THEN, GET SOME REST, KEEVE. PLEASE.
I WILL, BUT... I'M STAYING WITH THEM. JUST FOR NOW. JUST UNTIL THEY WAKE UP.

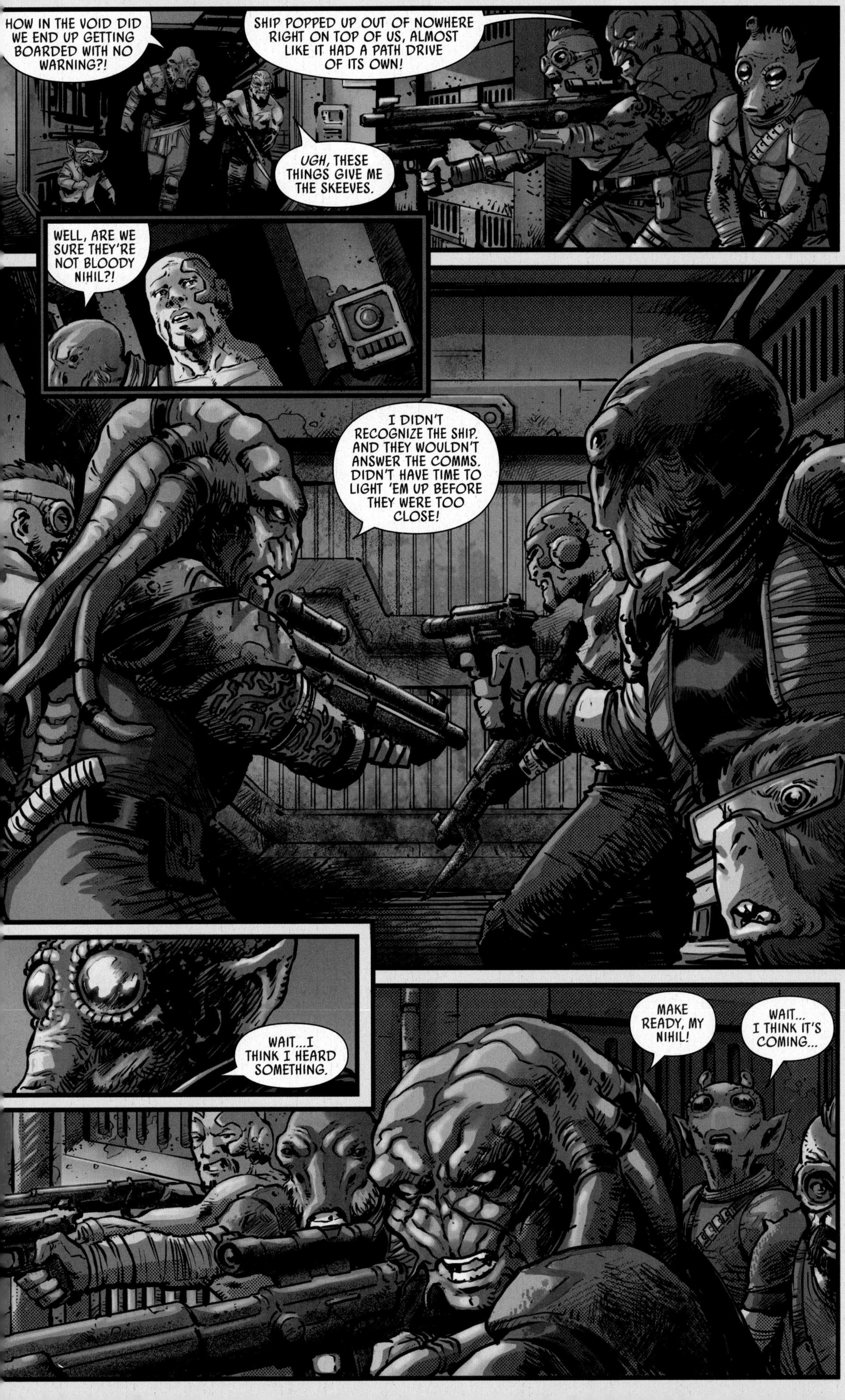
HOW IN THE VOID DID WE END UP GETTING BOARDED WITH NO WARNING?!
SHIP POPPED UP OUT OF NOWHERE RIGHT ON TOP OF US, ALMOST LIKE IT HAD A PATH DRIVE OF ITS OWN!
UGH, THESE THINGS GIVE ME THE SKEEVES.
WELL, ARE WE SURE THEY'RE NOT BLOODY NIHIL?!
I DIDN'T RECOGNIZE THE SHIP. AND THEY WOULDN'T ANSWER THE COMMS. DIDN'T HAVE TIME TO LIGHT 'EM UP BEFORE THEY WERE TOO CLOSE!
WAIT...I THINK I HEARD SOMETHING.
MAKE READY, MY NIHIL!
WAIT... I THINK IT'S COMING...

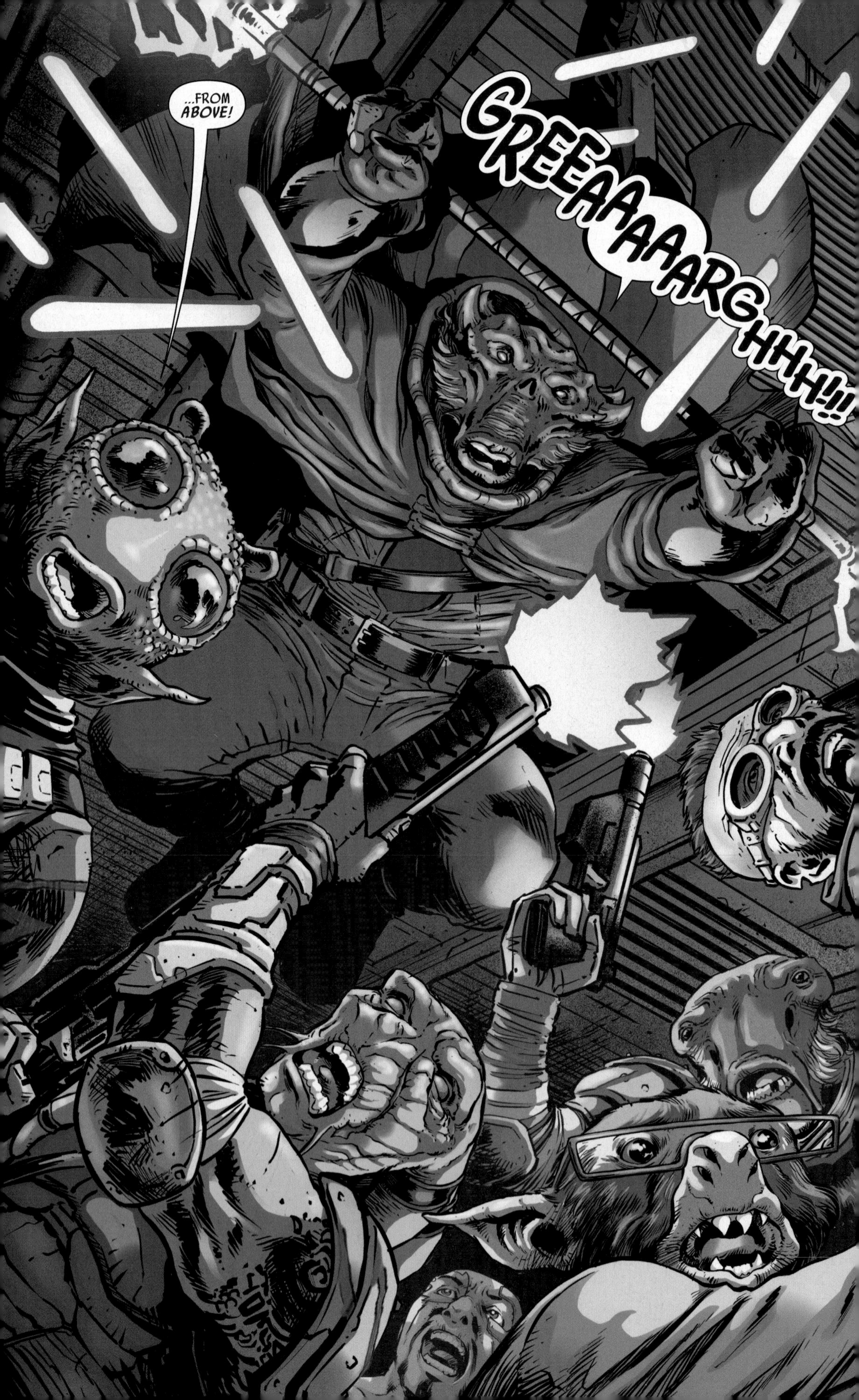
...FROM ABOVE!
GREEAAAAARGHHH!!!

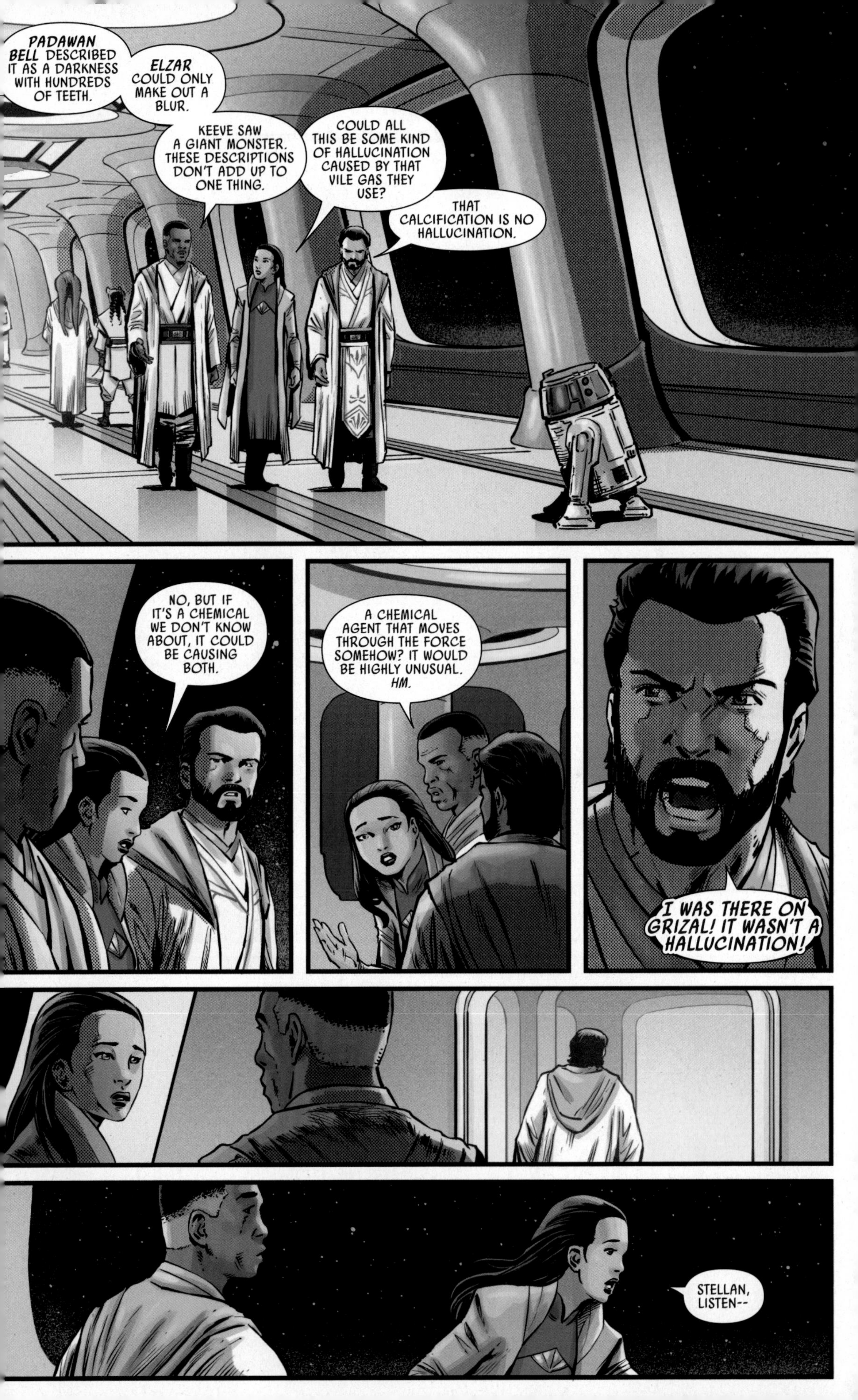
PADAWAN BELL DESCRIBED IT AS A DARKNESS WITH HUNDREDS OF TEETH.
ELZAR COULD ONLY MAKE OUT A BLUR.
KEEVE SAW A GIANT MONSTER. THESE DESCRIPTIONS DON'T ADD UP TO ONE THING.
COULD ALL THIS BE SOME KIND OF HALLUCINATION CAUSED BY THAT VILE GAS THEY USE?
THAT CALCIFICATION IS NO HALLUCINATION.
NO, BUT IF IT'S A CHEMICAL WE DON'T KNOW ABOUT, IT COULD BE CAUSING BOTH.
A CHEMICAL AGENT THAT MOVES THROUGH THE FORCE SOMEHOW? IT WOULD BE HIGHLY UNUSUAL. HM.
I WAS THERE ON GRIZAL! IT WASN'T A HALLUCINATION!
STELLAN, LISTEN--

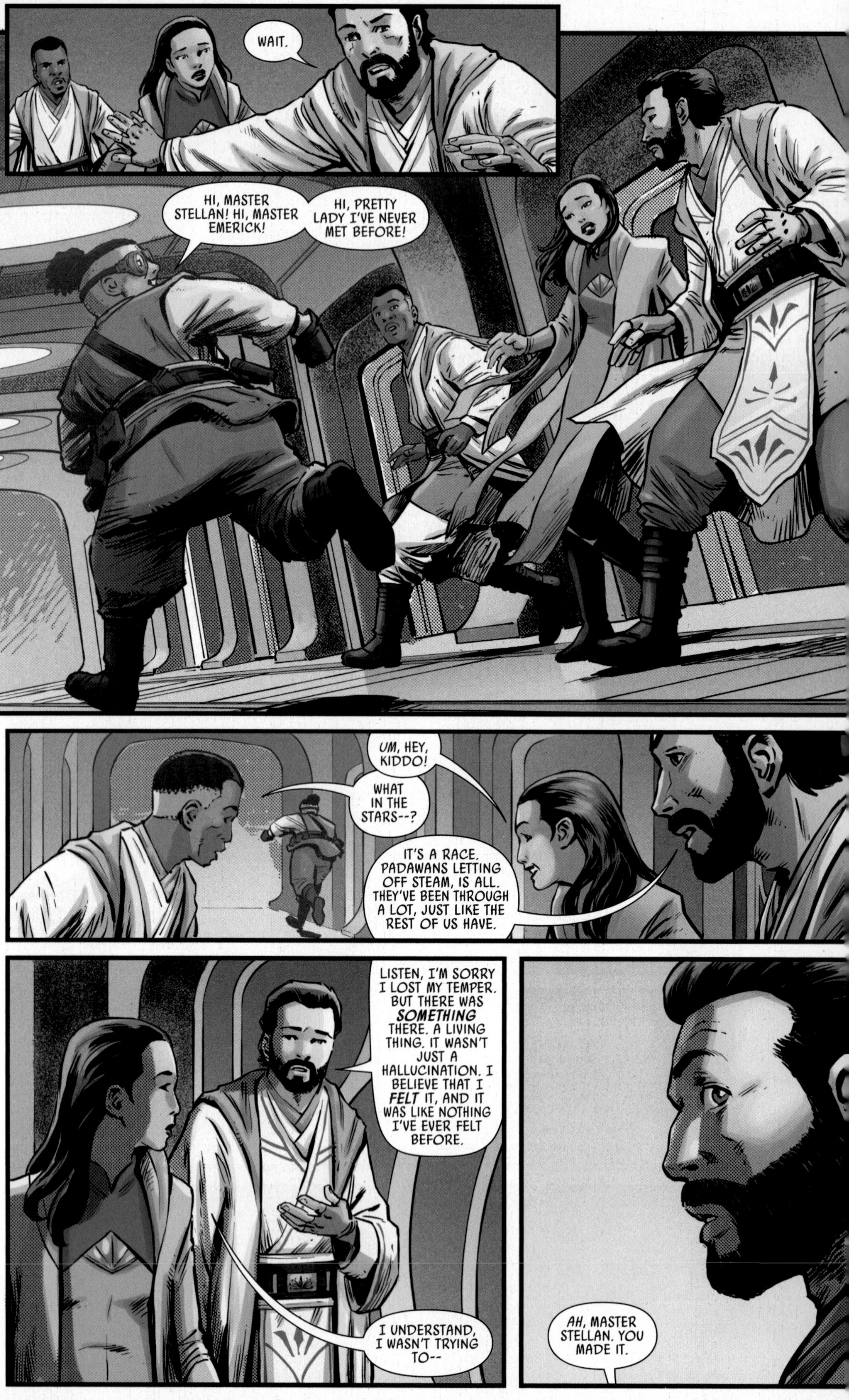
WAIT.
HI, MASTER STELLAN! HI, MASTER EMERICK!
HI, PRETTY LADY I'VE NEVER MET BEFORE!
UM, HEY, KIDDO!
WHAT IN THE STARS--?
IT'S A RACE. PADAWANS LETTING OFF STEAM, IS ALL. THEY'VE BEEN THROUGH A LOT, JUST LIKE THE REST OF US HAVE.
LISTEN, I'M SORRY I LOST MY TEMPER. BUT THERE WAS SOMETHING THERE. A LIVING THING. IT WASN'T JUST A HALLUCINATION. I BELIEVE THAT I FELT IT, AND IT WAS LIKE NOTHING I'VE EVER FELT BEFORE.
I UNDERSTAND, I WASN'T TRYING TO--
AH, MASTER STELLAN. YOU MADE IT.

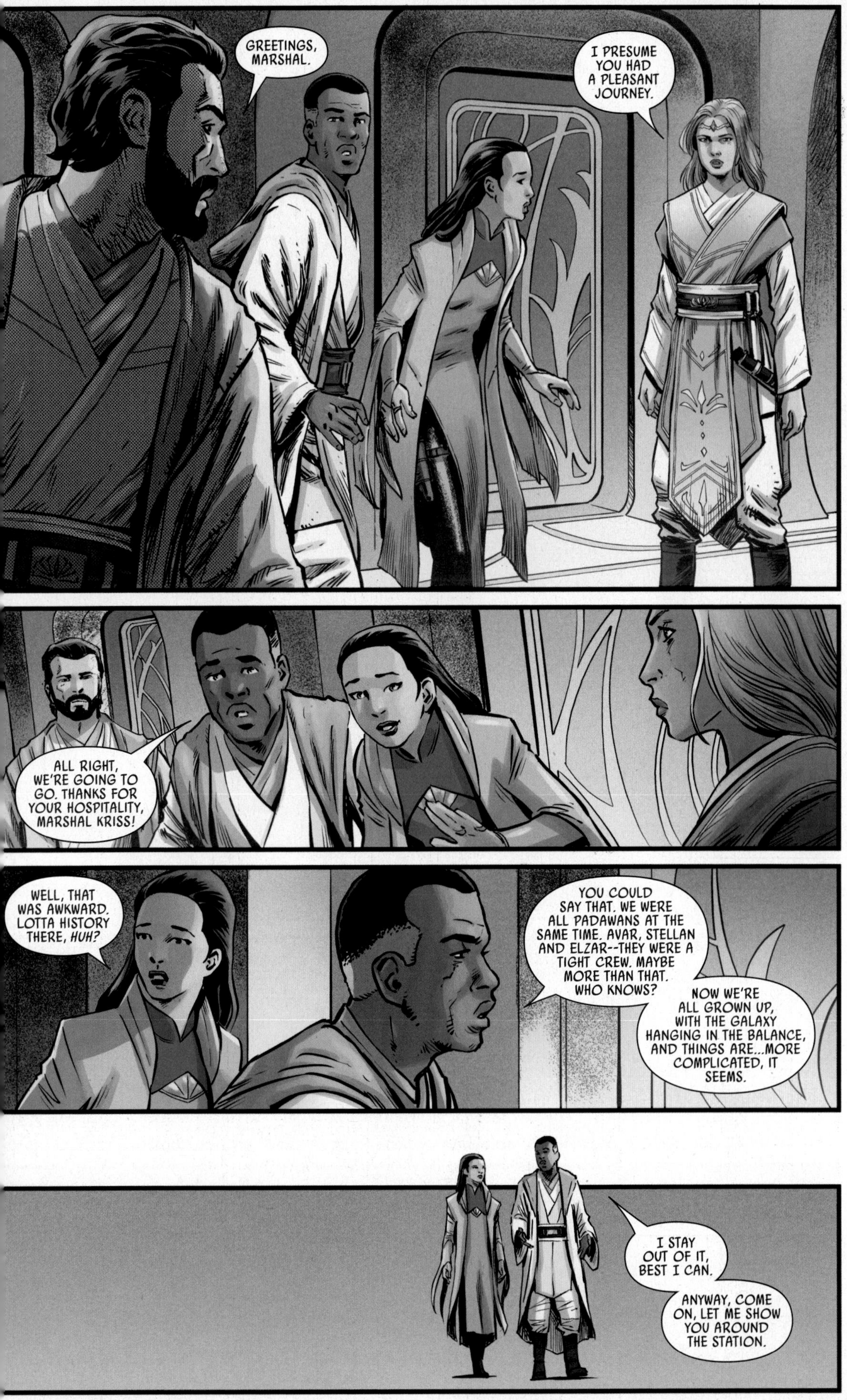
GREETINGS, MARSHAL.
I PRESUME YOU HAD A PLEASANT JOURNEY.
ALL RIGHT, WE'RE GOING TO GO. THANKS FOR YOUR HOSPITALITY, MARSHAL KRISS!
WELL, THAT WAS AWKWARD. LOTTA HISTORY THERE, *HUH?*
YOU COULD SAY THAT. WE WERE ALL PADAWANS AT THE SAME TIME. AVAR, STELLAN AND ELZAR--THEY WERE A TIGHT CREW. MAYBE MORE THAN THAT. WHO KNOWS?
NOW WE'RE ALL GROWN UP, WITH THE GALAXY HANGING IN THE BALANCE, AND THINGS ARE...MORE COMPLICATED, IT SEEMS.
I STAY OUT OF IT, BEST I CAN.
ANYWAY, COME ON, LET ME SHOW YOU AROUND THE STATION.

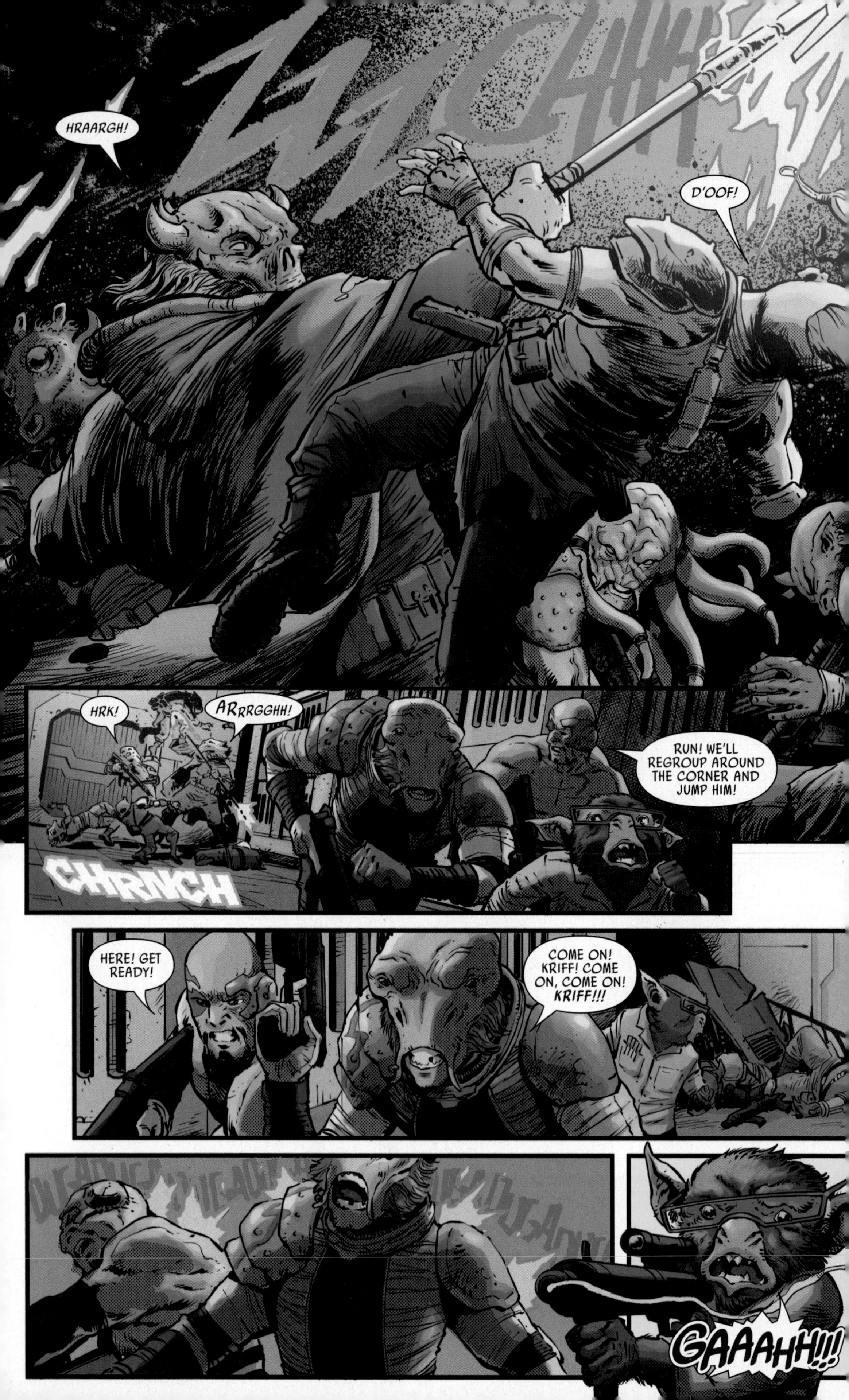
ZAZZCHHH
HRAARGH!
D'OOF!
HRK!
ARRRGGHH!
RUN! WE'LL REGROUP AROUND THE CORNER AND JUMP HIM!
CHRNCH
HERE! GET READY!
COME ON! KRIFF! COME ON, COME ON! KRIFF!!!
GAAAHH!!!

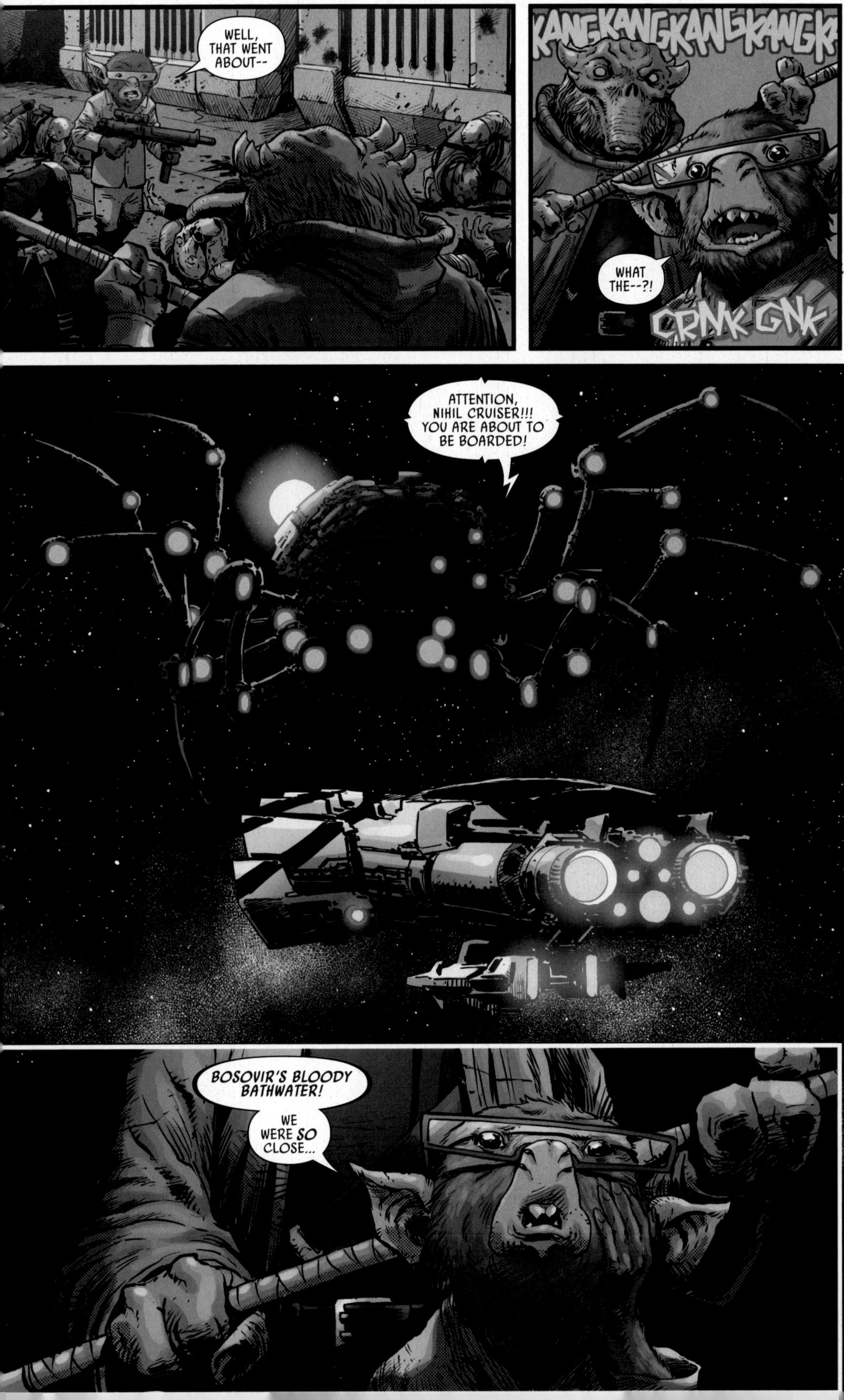
WELL, THAT WENT ABOUT--
KANGKANGKANGKANGK
WHAT THE--?!
CRNK GNK
ATTENTION, NIHIL CRUISER!!! YOU ARE ABOUT TO BE BOARDED!
BOSOVIR'S BLOODY BATHWATER!
WE WERE SO CLOSE...

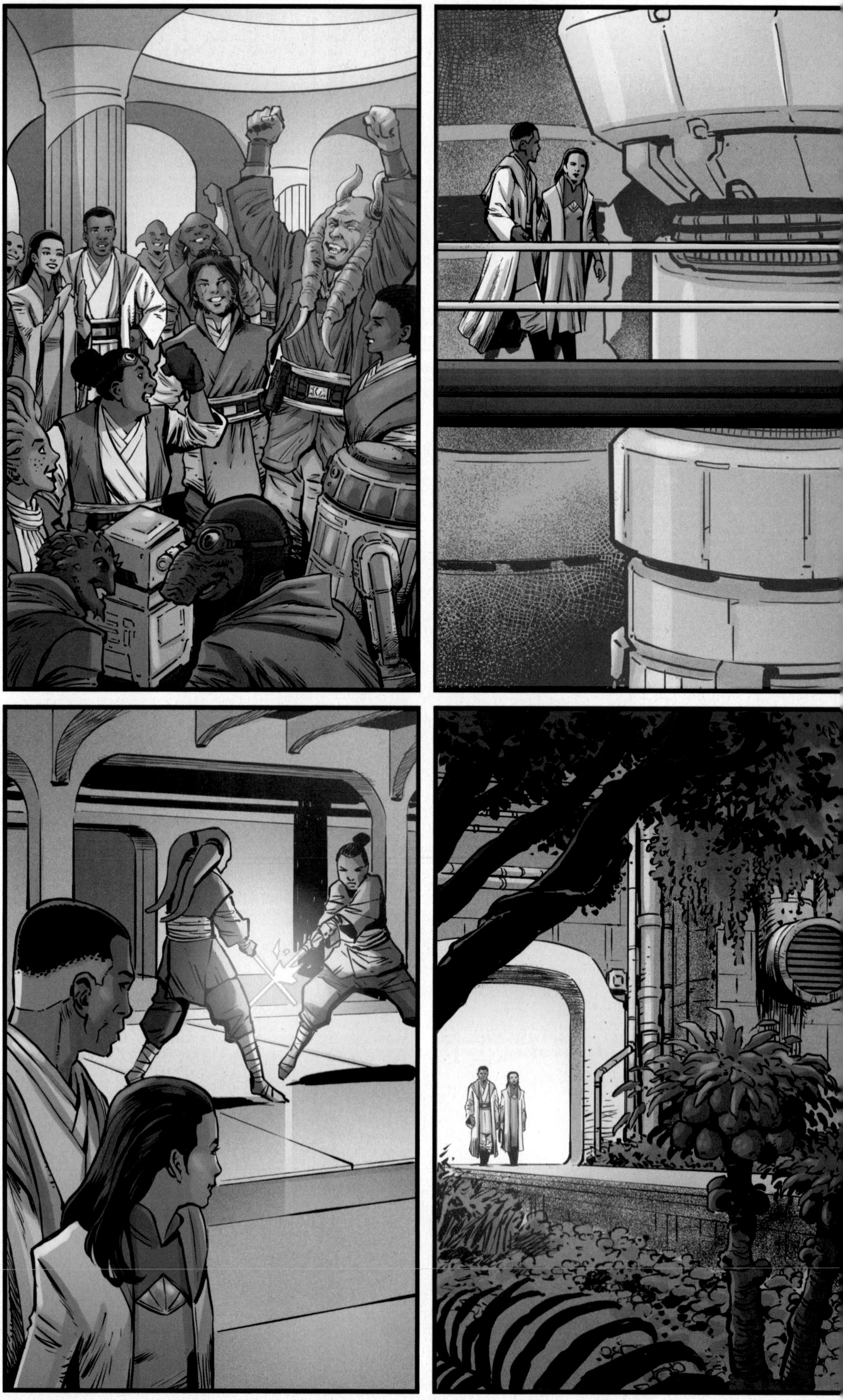

WHAT A VOID FORSAKEN MESS.

THESE NIHIL WERE KILLED BY DISMEMBERMENT...

IT'S A MASSACRE HERE, MY EYE. NO SURVIVORS FROM WHAT I CAN TELL.

AND THE SHIP THAT ATTACKED THEM?

...EVISCERATION... SOMETHING WITH CLAWS--THAT TARNAB MOST LIKELY... AH, ELECTROCUTION, JUDGING FROM THIS CHARRING, HM...

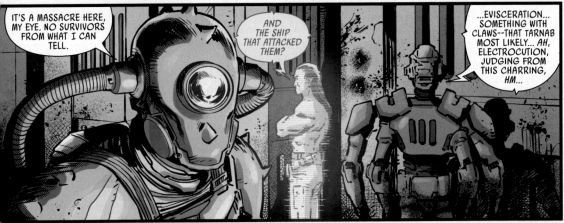

IT JUMPED AWAY JUST AS WE ARRIVED.

RRRRRRRR...

COULD BE WRONG, BUT JUST GOING FROM THE LOOK OF IT AND THE WAY IT HIT THAT LEAP TO HYPERSPACE...GOOD CHANCE IT'S GOT ONE OF OUR PATH ENGINES.

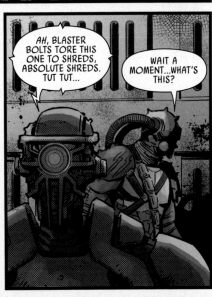

AH, BLASTER BOLTS TORE THIS ONE TO SHREDS, ABSOLUTE SHREDS. TUT TUT...

WAIT A MOMENT...WHAT'S THIS?

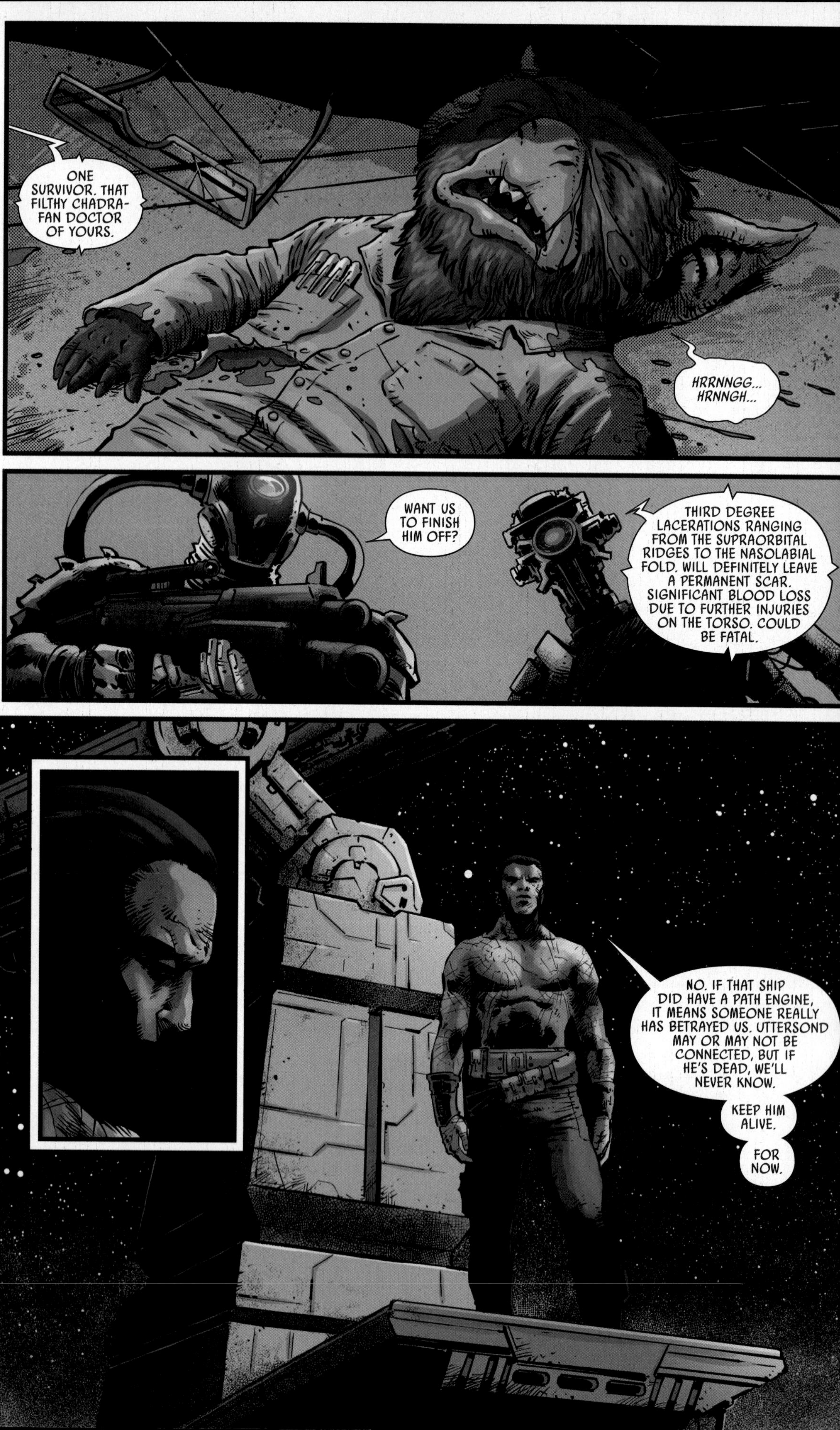
ONE SURVIVOR. THAT FILTHY CHADRA-FAN DOCTOR OF YOURS.
HRRNNGG... HRNNGH...
WANT US TO FINISH HIM OFF?
THIRD DEGREE LACERATIONS RANGING FROM THE SUPRAORBITAL RIDGES TO THE NASOLABIAL FOLD. WILL DEFINITELY LEAVE A PERMANENT SCAR. SIGNIFICANT BLOOD LOSS DUE TO FURTHER INJURIES ON THE TORSO. COULD BE FATAL.
NO. IF THAT SHIP DID HAVE A PATH ENGINE, IT MEANS SOMEONE REALLY HAS BETRAYED US. UTTERSOND MAY OR MAY NOT BE CONNECTED, BUT IF HE'S DEAD, WE'LL NEVER KNOW.
KEEP HIM ALIVE.
FOR NOW.

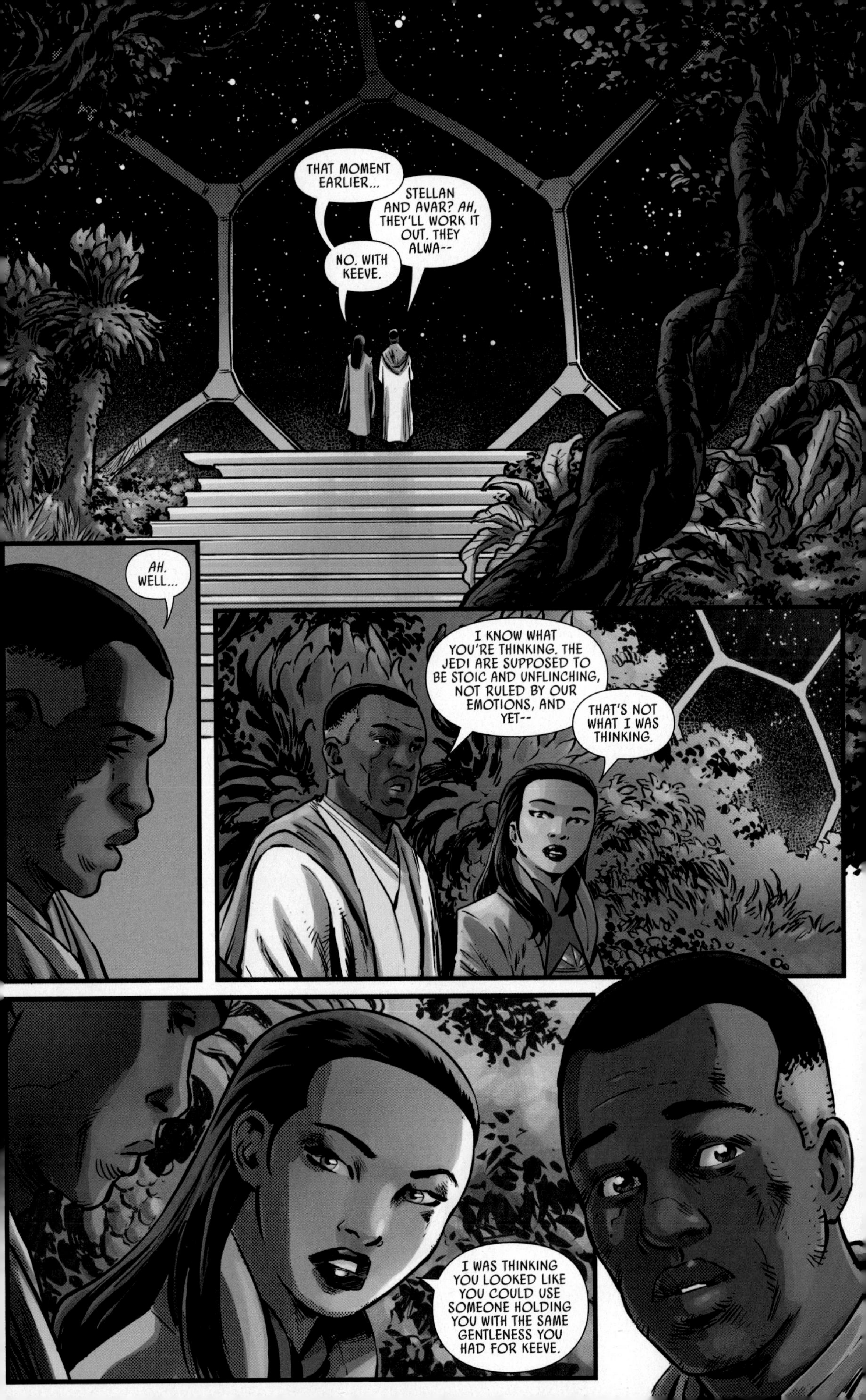
THAT MOMENT EARLIER...
STELLAN AND AVAR? AH, THEY'LL WORK IT OUT. THEY ALWA--
NO. WITH KEEVE.
AH. WELL...
I KNOW WHAT YOU'RE THINKING. THE JEDI ARE SUPPOSED TO BE STOIC AND UNFLINCHING, NOT RULED BY OUR EMOTIONS, AND YET--
THAT'S NOT WHAT I WAS THINKING.
I WAS THINKING YOU LOOKED LIKE YOU COULD USE SOMEONE HOLDING YOU WITH THE SAME GENTLENESS YOU HAD FOR KEEVE.

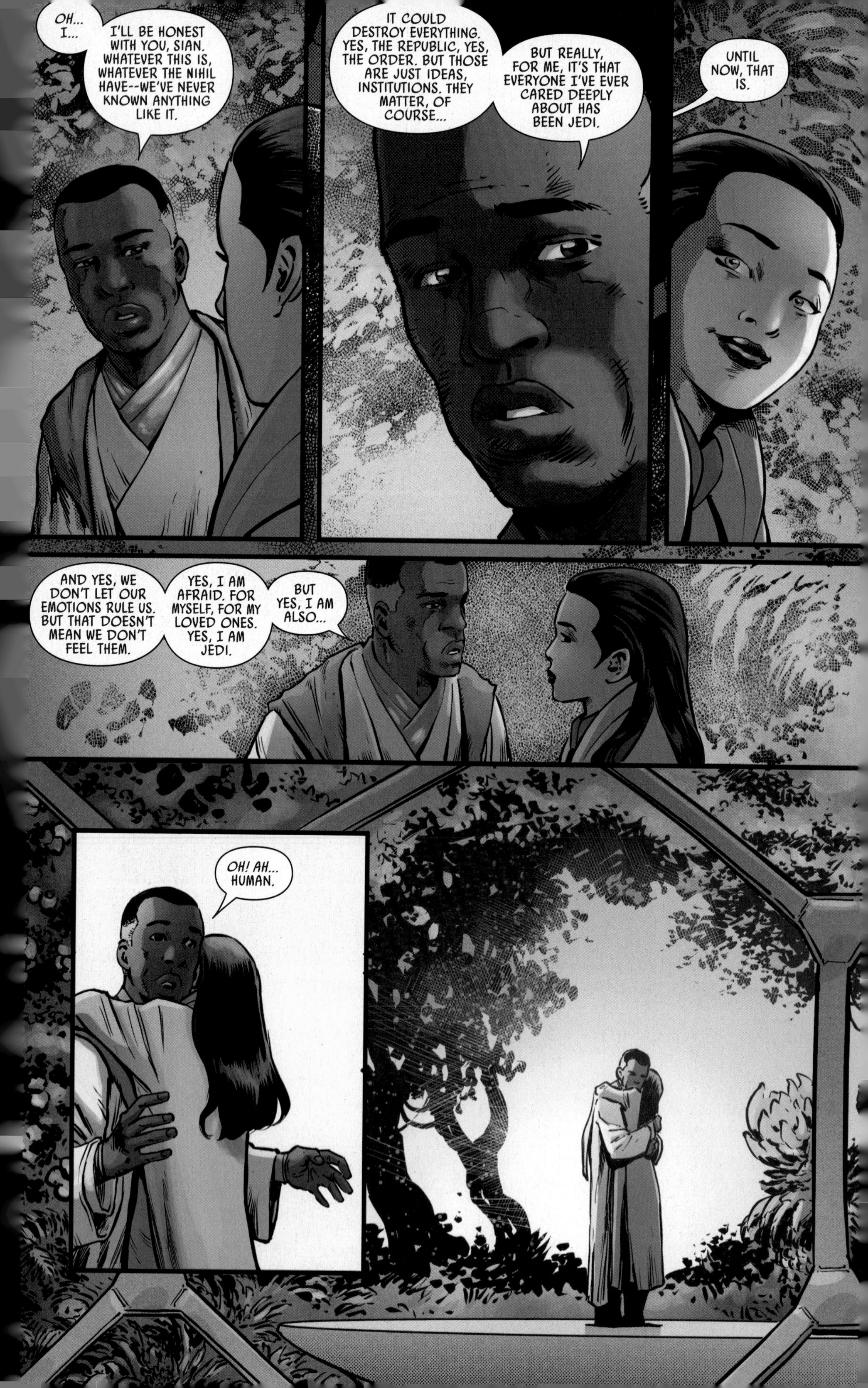
OH... I...
I'LL BE HONEST WITH YOU, SIAN. WHATEVER THIS IS, WHATEVER THE NIHIL HAVE--WE'VE NEVER KNOWN ANYTHING LIKE IT.
IT COULD DESTROY EVERYTHING. YES, THE REPUBLIC, YES, THE ORDER. BUT THOSE ARE JUST IDEAS, INSTITUTIONS. THEY MATTER, OF COURSE...
BUT REALLY, FOR ME, IT'S THAT EVERYONE I'VE EVER CARED DEEPLY ABOUT HAS BEEN JEDI.
UNTIL NOW, THAT IS.
AND YES, WE DON'T LET OUR EMOTIONS RULE US. BUT THAT DOESN'T MEAN WE DON'T FEEL THEM.
YES, I AM AFRAID. FOR MYSELF, FOR MY LOVED ONES. YES, I AM JEDI.
BUT YES, I AM ALSO...
OH! AH... HUMAN.

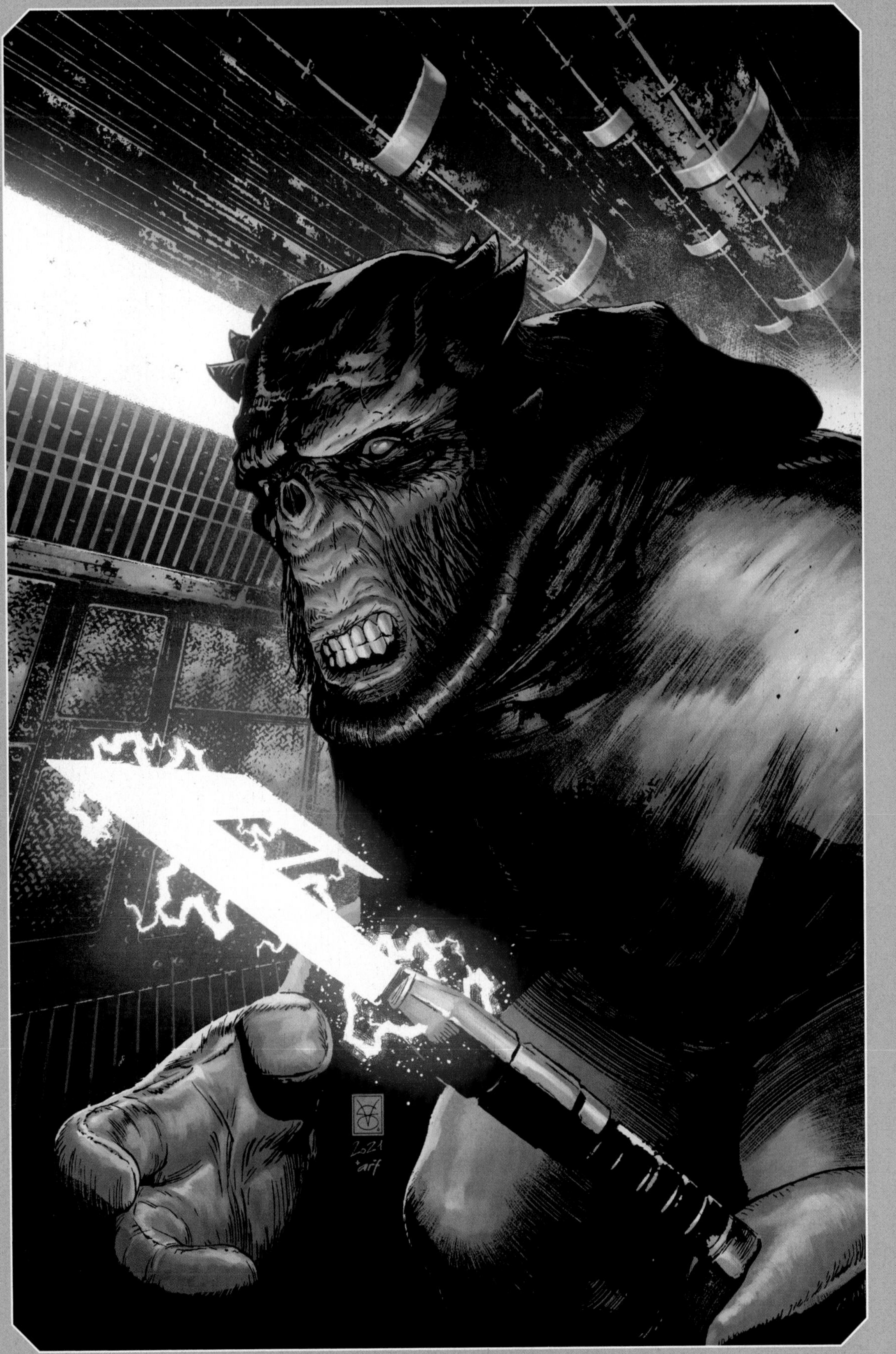

#4 Variant by
VALERIO GIANGIORDANO & ARIF PRIANTO

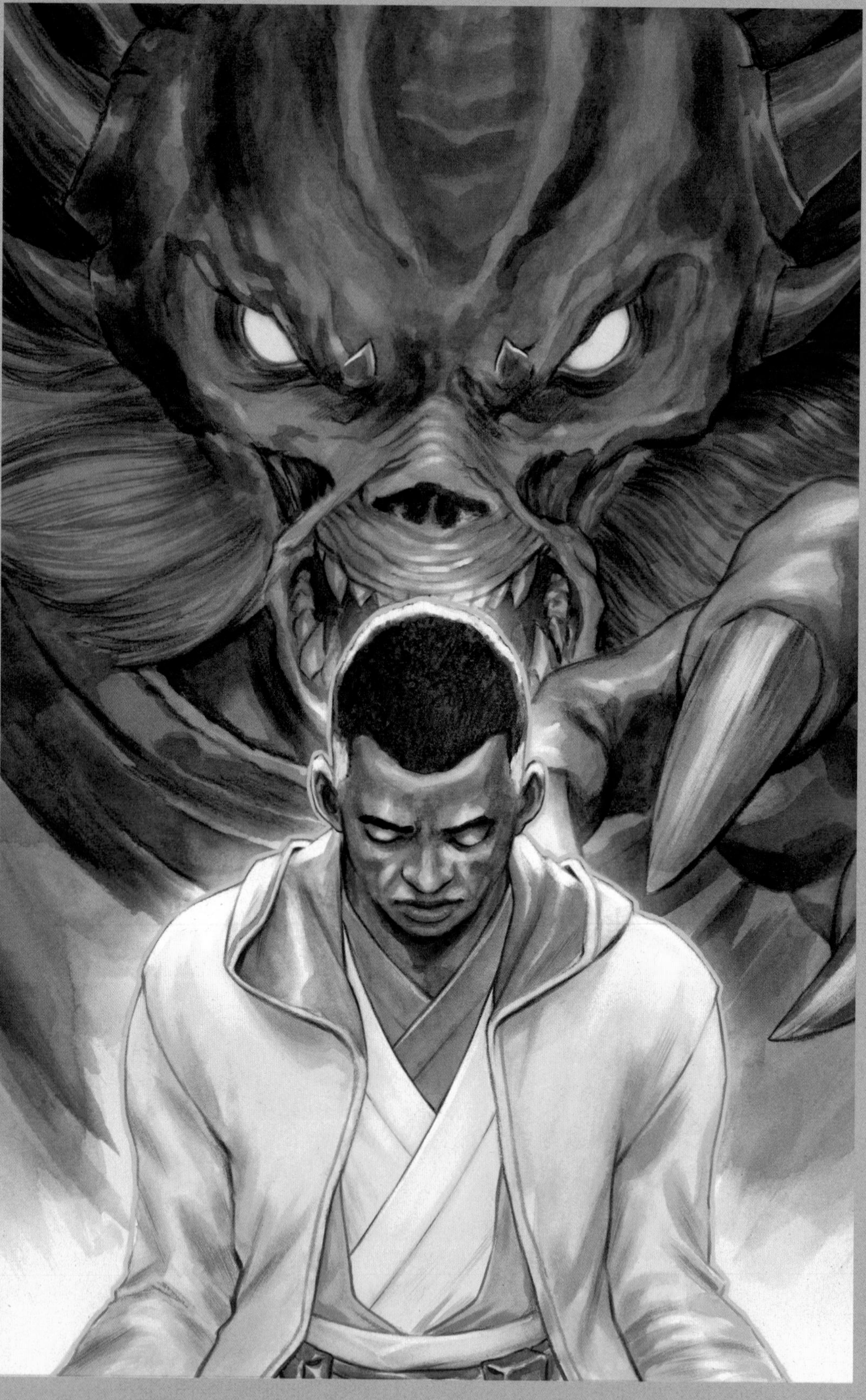

4 | WHATEVER IT TAKES

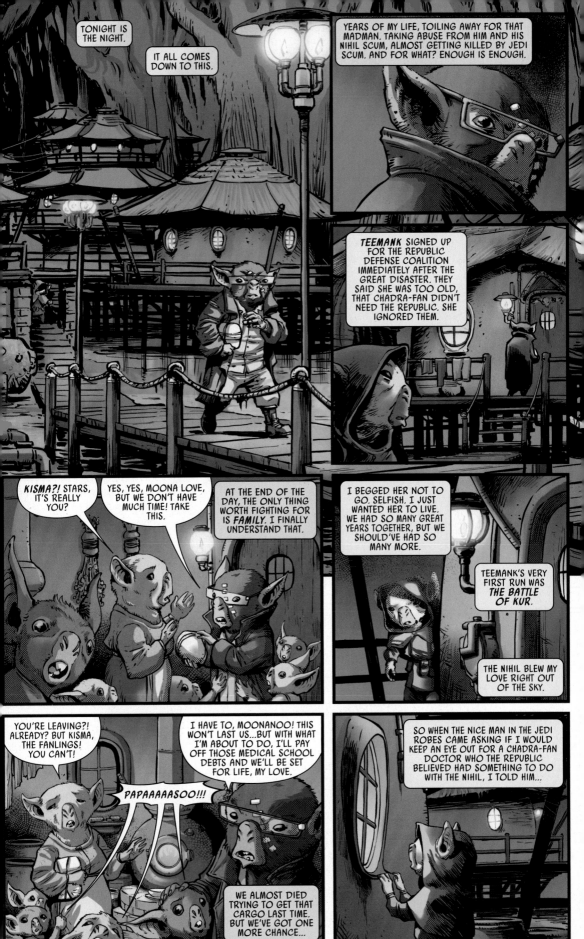

TONIGHT IS THE NIGHT.

IT ALL COMES DOWN TO THIS.

YEARS OF MY LIFE, TOILING AWAY FOR THAT MADMAN. TAKING ABUSE FROM HIM AND HIS NIHIL SCUM. ALMOST GETTING KILLED BY JEDI SCUM. AND FOR WHAT? ENOUGH IS ENOUGH.

TEEMANK SIGNED UP FOR THE REPUBLIC DEFENSE COALITION IMMEDIATELY AFTER THE GREAT DISASTER. THEY SAID SHE WAS TOO OLD, THAT CHADRA-FAN DIDN'T NEED THE REPUBLIC. SHE IGNORED THEM.

KISMA?! STARS, IT'S REALLY YOU?

YES, YES, MOONA LOVE, BUT WE DON'T HAVE MUCH TIME! TAKE THIS.

AT THE END OF THE DAY, THE ONLY THING WORTH FIGHTING FOR IS *FAMILY*. I FINALLY UNDERSTAND THAT.

I BEGGED HER NOT TO GO. SELFISH. I JUST WANTED HER TO LIVE. WE HAD SO MANY GREAT YEARS TOGETHER, BUT WE SHOULD'VE HAD SO MANY MORE.

TEEMANK'S VERY FIRST RUN WAS *THE BATTLE OF KUR*.

THE NIHIL BLEW MY LOVE RIGHT OUT OF THE SKY.

YOU'RE LEAVING?! ALREADY? BUT KISMA, THE FANLINGS! YOU CAN'T!

I HAVE TO, MOONANOO! THIS WON'T LAST US...BUT WITH WHAT I'M ABOUT TO DO, I'LL PAY OFF THOSE MEDICAL SCHOOL DEBTS AND WE'LL BE SET FOR LIFE, MY LOVE.

PAPAAAAASOO!!!

WE ALMOST DIED TRYING TO GET THAT CARGO LAST TIME. BUT WE'VE GOT ONE MORE CHANCE...

SO WHEN THE NICE MAN IN THE JEDI ROBES CAME ASKING IF I WOULD KEEP AN EYE OUT FOR A CHADRA-FAN DOCTOR WHO THE REPUBLIC BELIEVED HAD SOMETHING TO DO WITH THE NIHIL, I TOLD HIM...

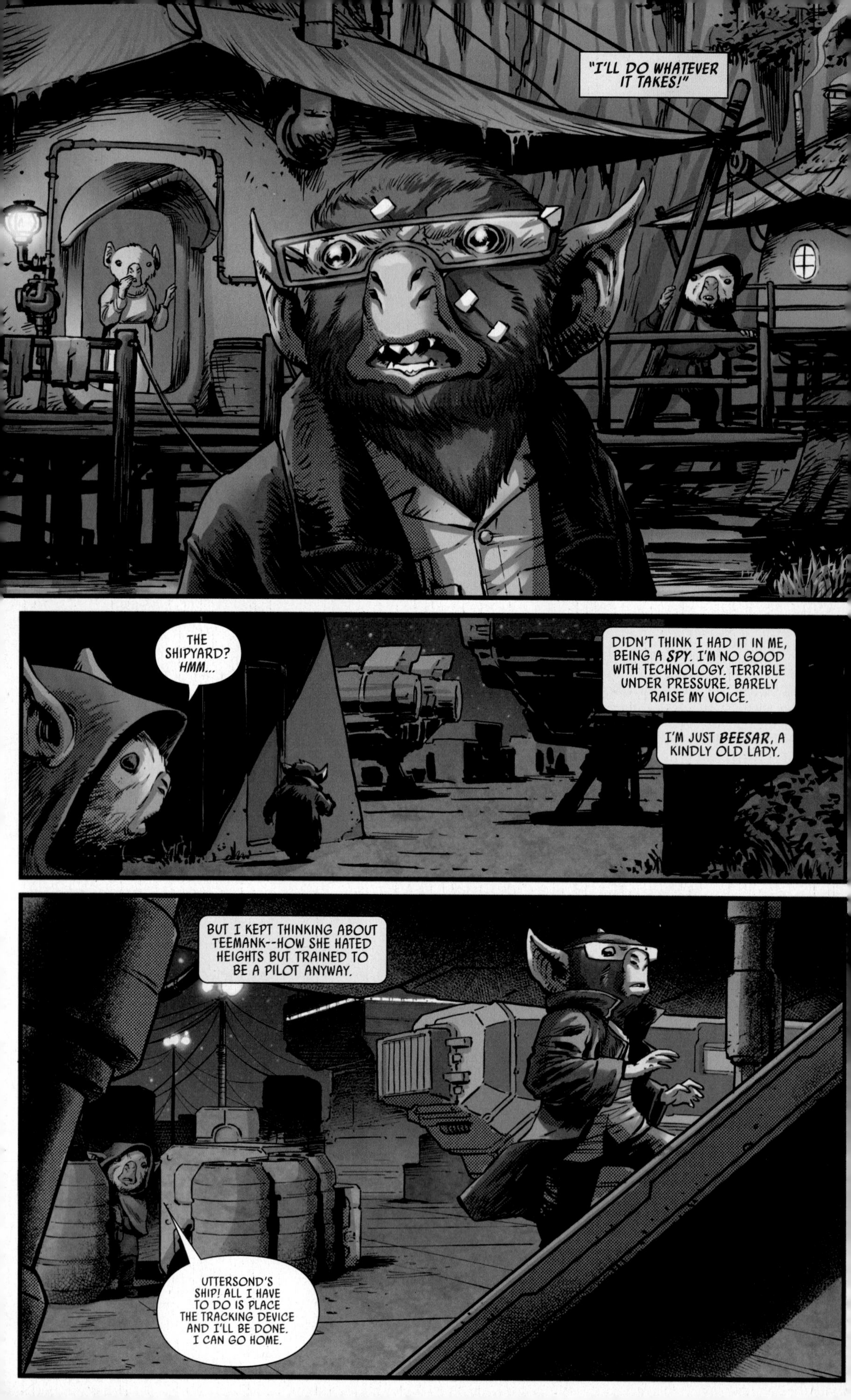
"I'LL DO WHATEVER IT TAKES!"
THE SHIPYARD? HMM...
DIDN'T THINK I HAD IT IN ME, BEING A SPY. I'M NO GOOD WITH TECHNOLOGY. TERRIBLE UNDER PRESSURE. BARELY RAISE MY VOICE.
I'M JUST BEESAR, A KINDLY OLD LADY.
BUT I KEPT THINKING ABOUT TEEMANK--HOW SHE HATED HEIGHTS BUT TRAINED TO BE A PILOT ANYWAY.
UTTERSOND'S SHIP! ALL I HAVE TO DO IS PLACE THE TRACKING DEVICE AND I'LL BE DONE. I CAN GO HOME.

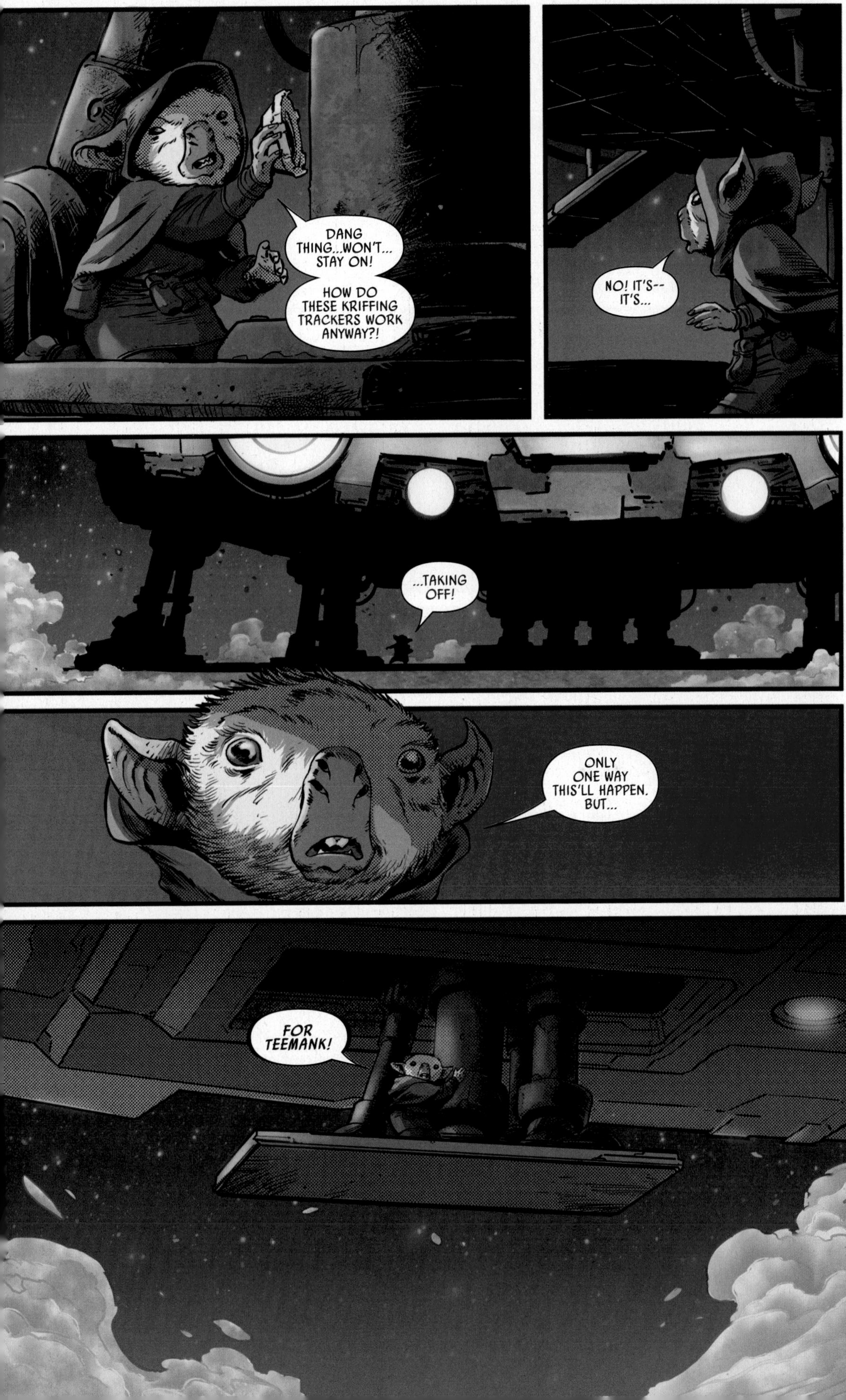
DANG THING...WON'T... STAY ON!
HOW DO THESE KRIFFING TRACKERS WORK ANYWAY?!
NO! IT'S-- IT'S...
...TAKING OFF!
ONLY ONE WAY THIS'LL HAPPEN. BUT...
FOR TEEMANK!

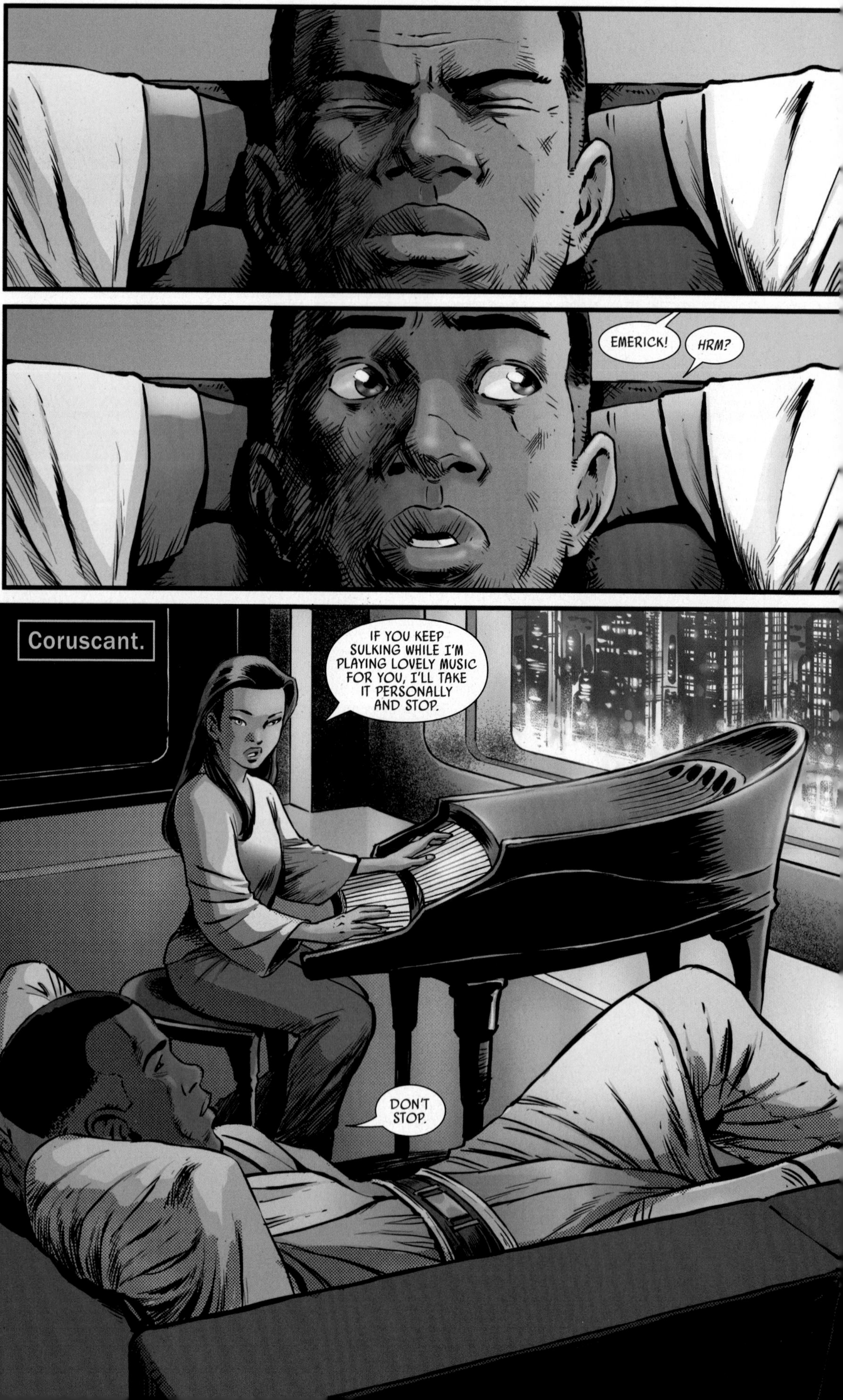
EMERICK!
HRM?
Coruscant.
IF YOU KEEP SULKING WHILE I'M PLAYING LOVELY MUSIC FOR YOU, I'LL TAKE IT PERSONALLY AND STOP.
DON'T STOP.

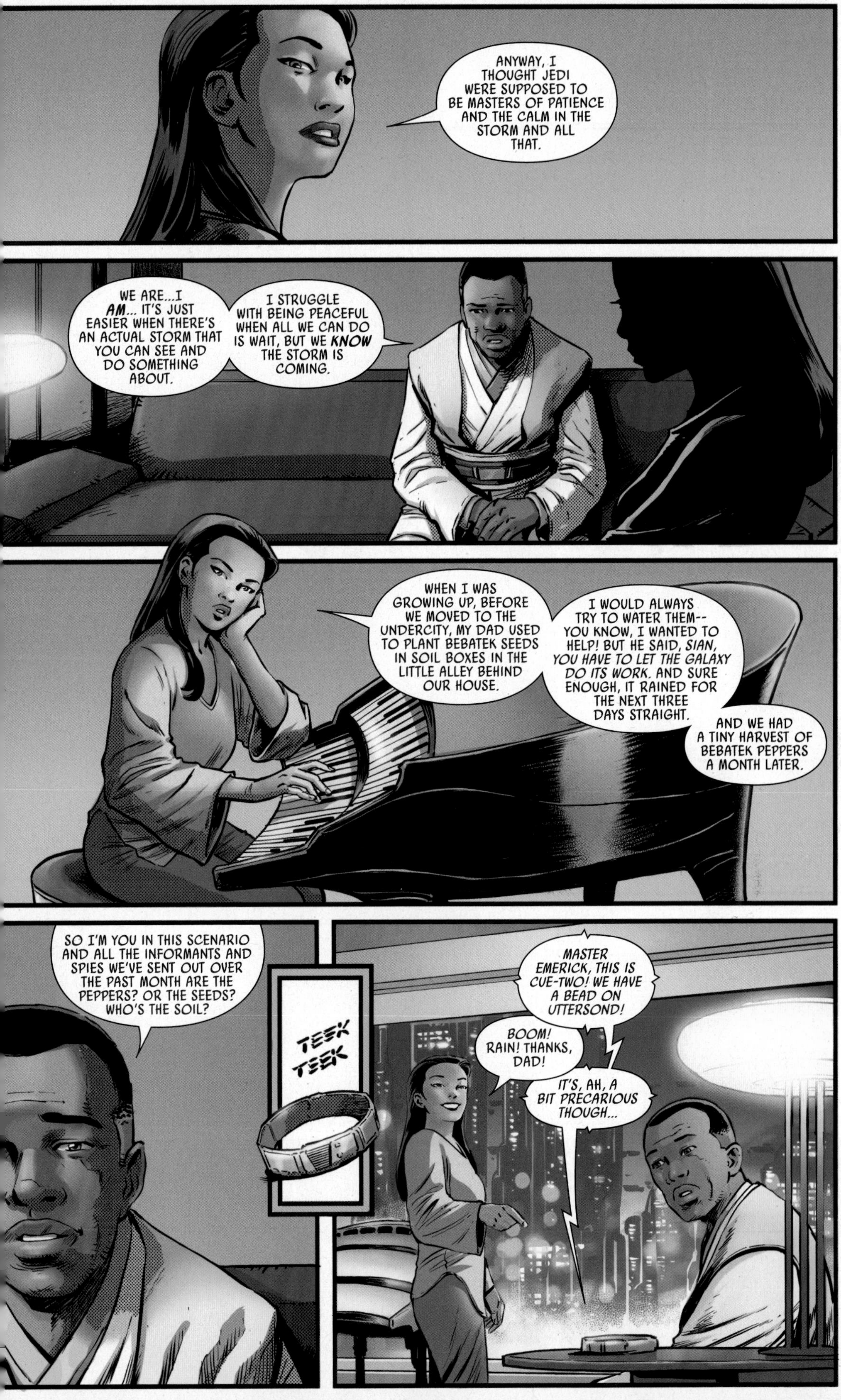
ANYWAY, I THOUGHT JEDI WERE SUPPOSED TO BE MASTERS OF PATIENCE AND THE CALM IN THE STORM AND ALL THAT.
WE ARE...I *AM*... IT'S JUST EASIER WHEN THERE'S AN ACTUAL STORM THAT YOU CAN SEE AND DO SOMETHING ABOUT.
I STRUGGLE WITH BEING PEACEFUL WHEN ALL WE CAN DO IS WAIT, BUT WE *KNOW* THE STORM IS COMING.
WHEN I WAS GROWING UP, BEFORE WE MOVED TO THE UNDERCITY, MY DAD USED TO PLANT BEBATEK SEEDS IN SOIL BOXES IN THE LITTLE ALLEY BEHIND OUR HOUSE.
I WOULD ALWAYS TRY TO WATER THEM-- YOU KNOW, I WANTED TO HELP! BUT HE SAID, *SIAN, YOU HAVE TO LET THE GALAXY DO ITS WORK.* AND SURE ENOUGH, IT RAINED FOR THE NEXT THREE DAYS STRAIGHT.
AND WE HAD A TINY HARVEST OF BEBATEK PEPPERS A MONTH LATER.
SO I'M YOU IN THIS SCENARIO AND ALL THE INFORMANTS AND SPIES WE'VE SENT OUT OVER THE PAST MONTH ARE THE PEPPERS? OR THE SEEDS? WHO'S THE SOIL?
TEEK TEEK
MASTER EMERICK, THIS IS CUE-TWO! WE HAVE A BEAD ON UTTERSOND!
BOOM! RAIN! THANKS, DAD!
IT'S, AH, A BIT PRECARIOUS THOUGH...

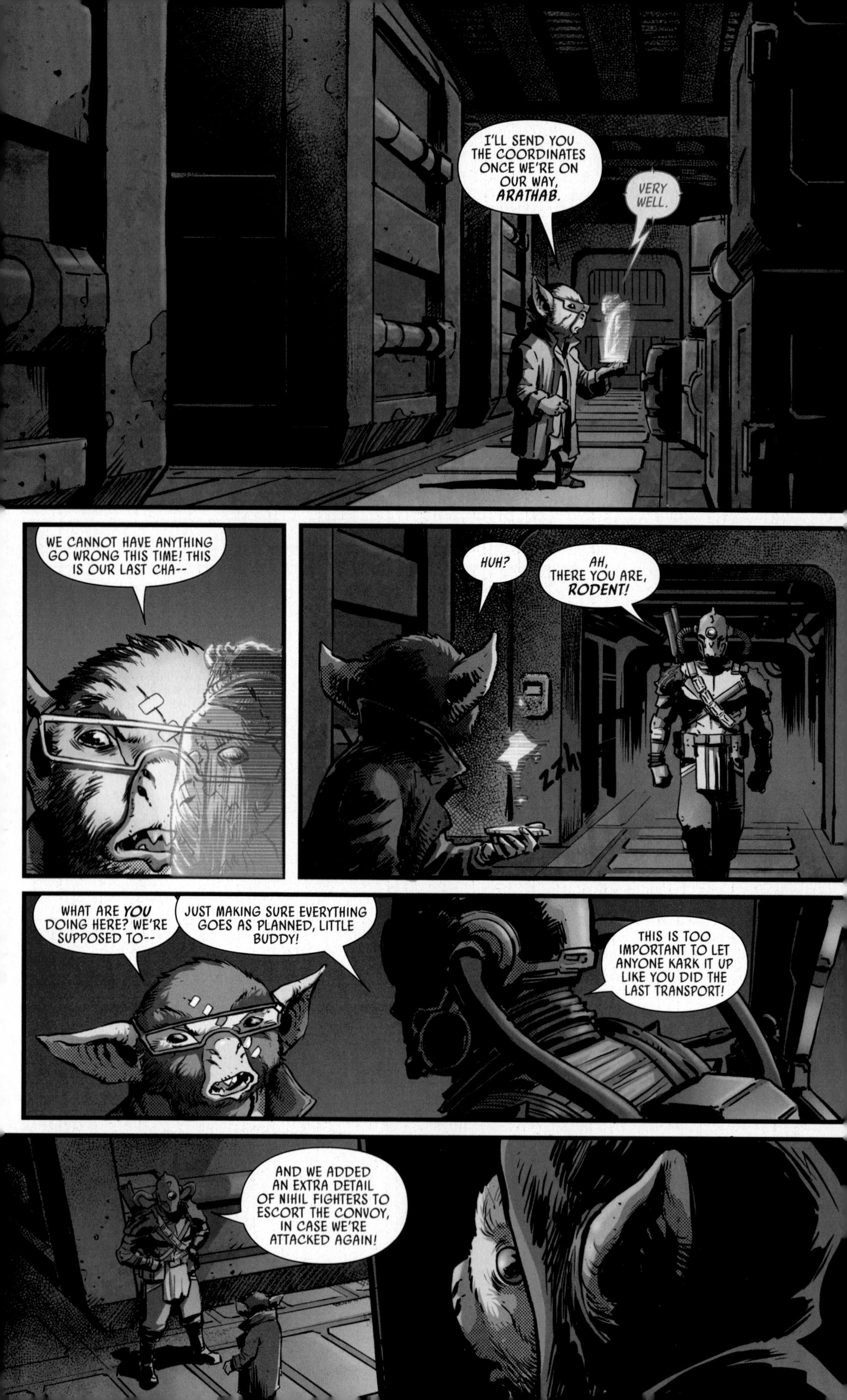
I'LL SEND YOU THE COORDINATES ONCE WE'RE ON OUR WAY, ARATHAB.
VERY WELL.
WE CANNOT HAVE ANYTHING GO WRONG THIS TIME! THIS IS OUR LAST CHA--
HUH?
AH, THERE YOU ARE, RODENT!
ZZH
WHAT ARE YOU DOING HERE? WE'RE SUPPOSED TO--
JUST MAKING SURE EVERYTHING GOES AS PLANNED, LITTLE BUDDY!
THIS IS TOO IMPORTANT TO LET ANYONE KARK IT UP LIKE YOU DID THE LAST TRANSPORT!
AND WE ADDED AN EXTRA DETAIL OF NIHIL FIGHTERS TO ESCORT THE CONVOY, IN CASE WE'RE ATTACKED AGAIN!

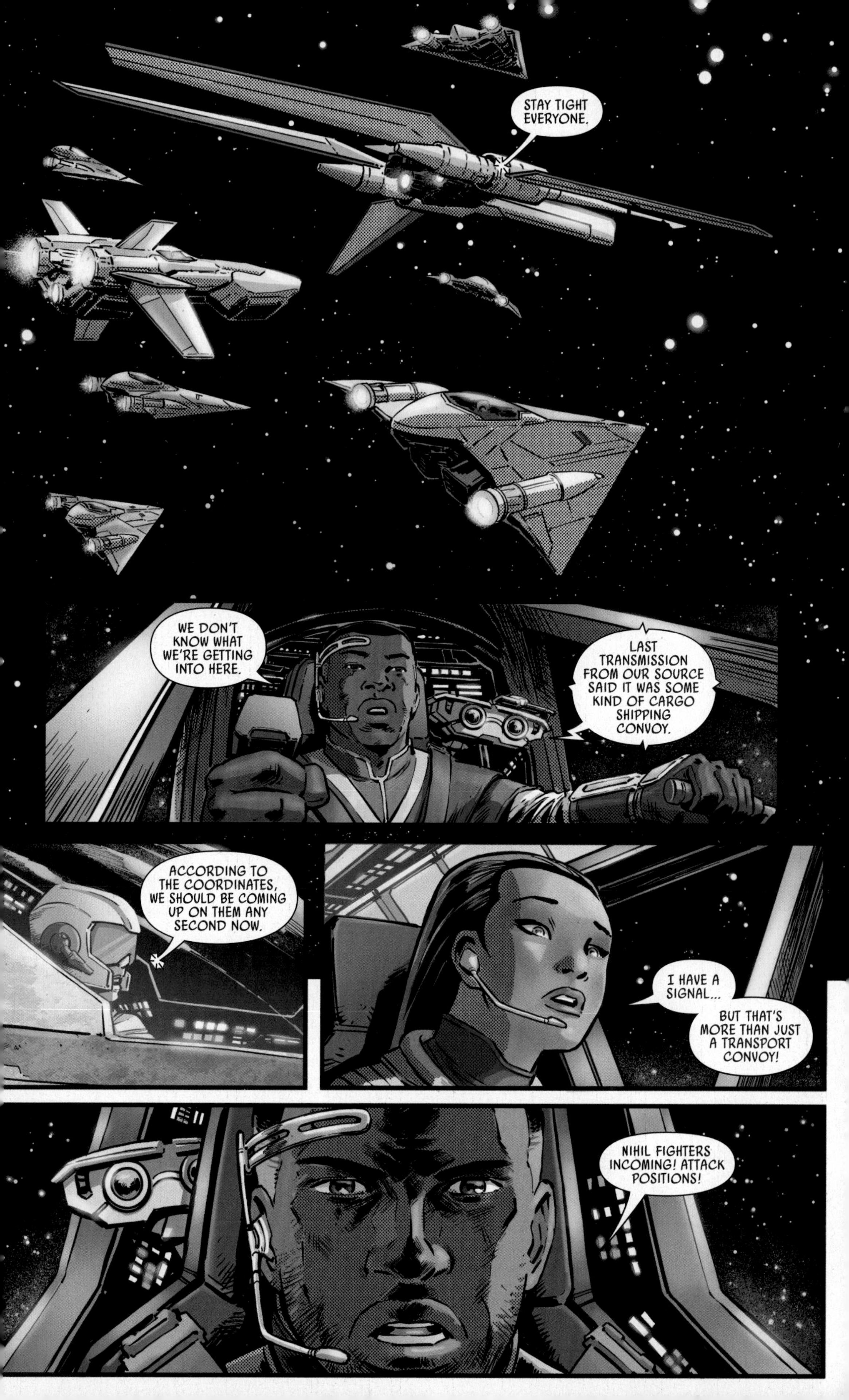
STAY TIGHT EVERYONE.
WE DON'T KNOW WHAT WE'RE GETTING INTO HERE.
LAST TRANSMISSION FROM OUR SOURCE SAID IT WAS SOME KIND OF CARGO SHIPPING CONVOY.
ACCORDING TO THE COORDINATES, WE SHOULD BE COMING UP ON THEM ANY SECOND NOW.
I HAVE A SIGNAL...
BUT THAT'S MORE THAN JUST A TRANSPORT CONVOY!
NIHIL FIGHTERS INCOMING! ATTACK POSITIONS!

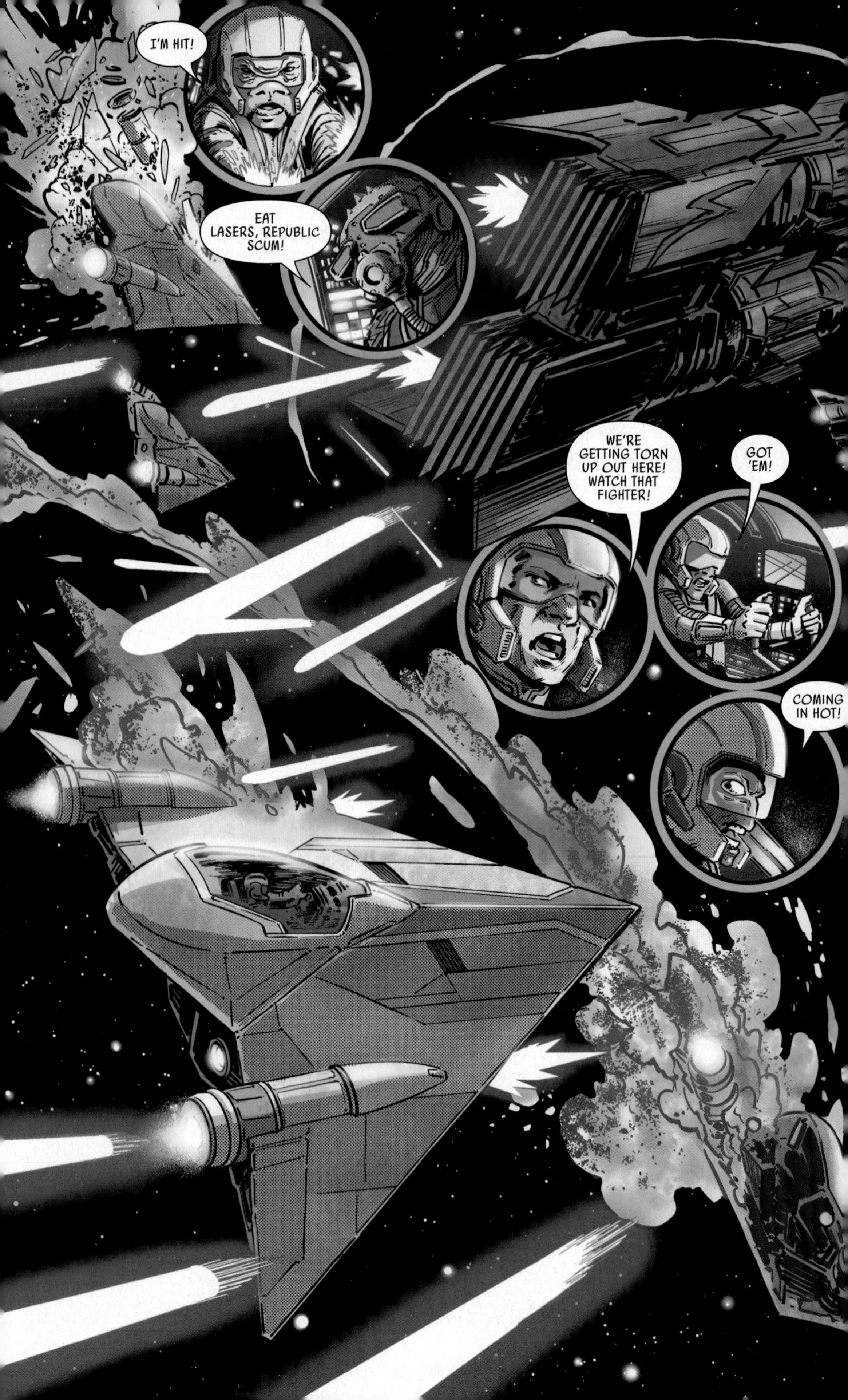
I'M HIT!
EAT LASERS, REPUBLIC SCUM!
WE'RE GETTING TORN UP OUT HERE! WATCH THAT FIGHTER!
GOT 'EM!
COMING IN HOT!

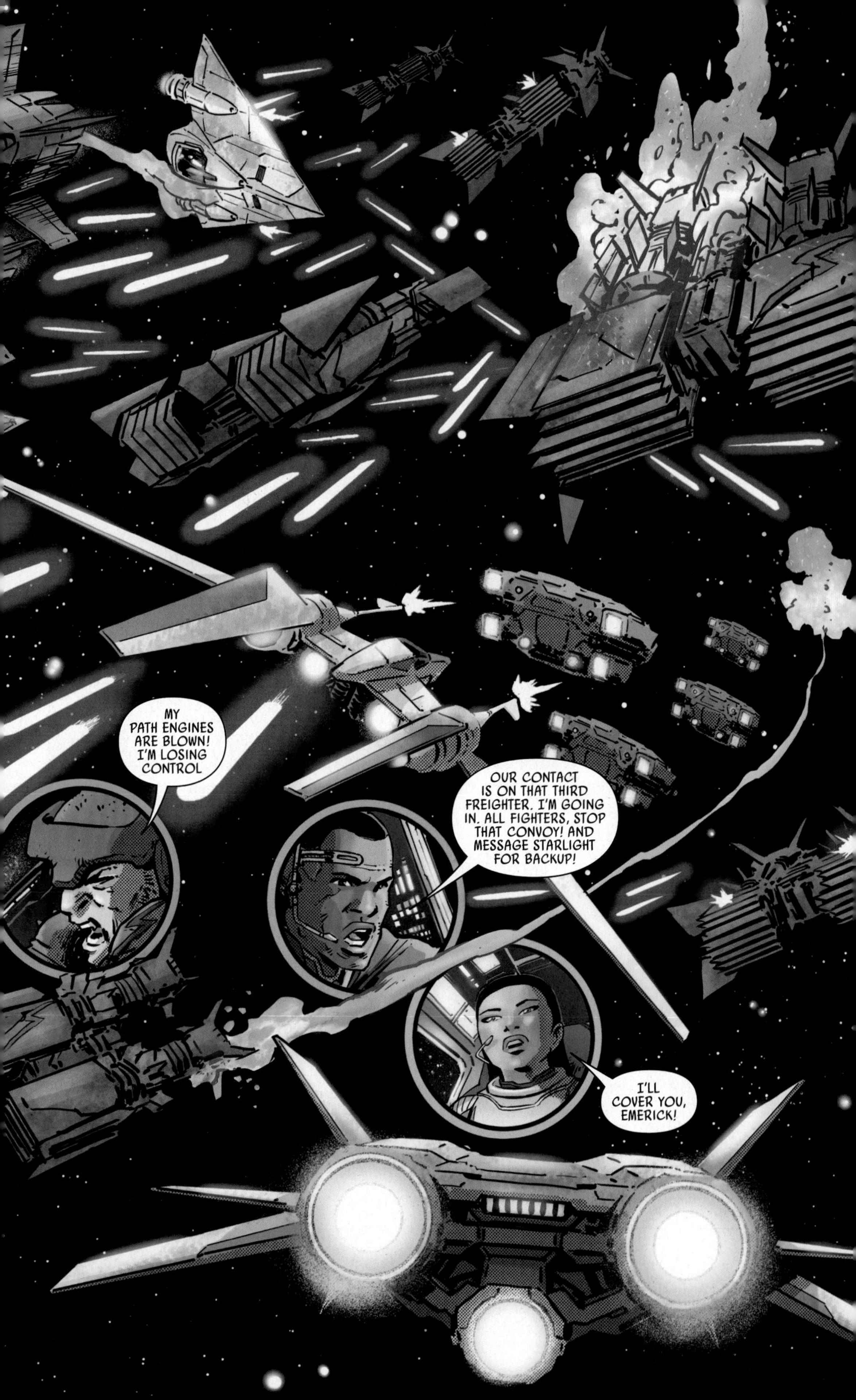
MY PATH ENGINES ARE BLOWN! I'M LOSING CONTROL
OUR CONTACT IS ON THAT THIRD FREIGHTER. I'M GOING IN. ALL FIGHTERS, STOP THAT CONVOY! AND MESSAGE STARLIGHT FOR BACKUP!
I'LL COVER YOU, EMERICK!

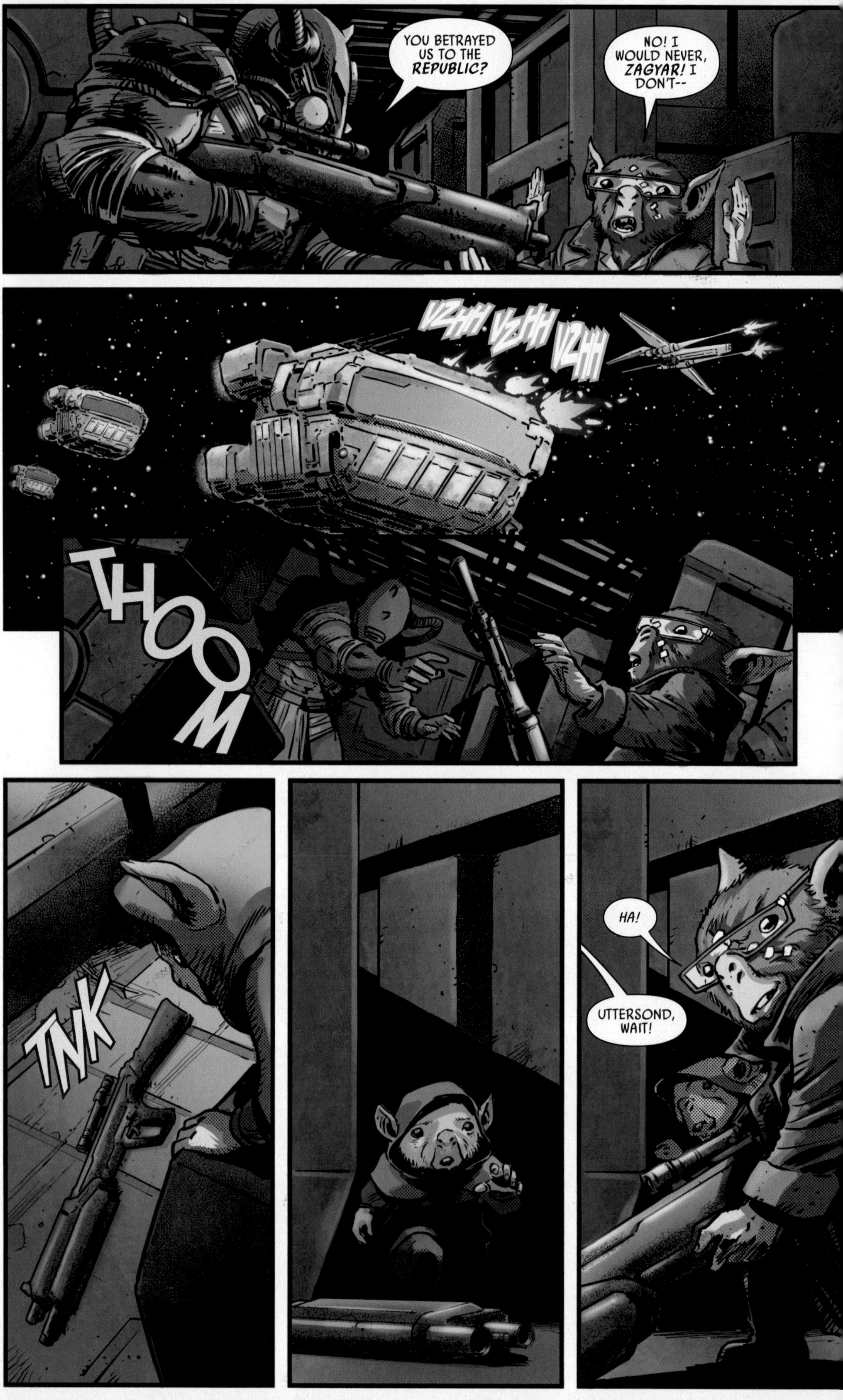
YOU BETRAYED US TO THE REPUBLIC?
NO! I WOULD NEVER, ZAGYAR! I DON'T--
VZHH VZHH VZHH
THOOM
TNK
HA!
UTTERSOND, WAIT!

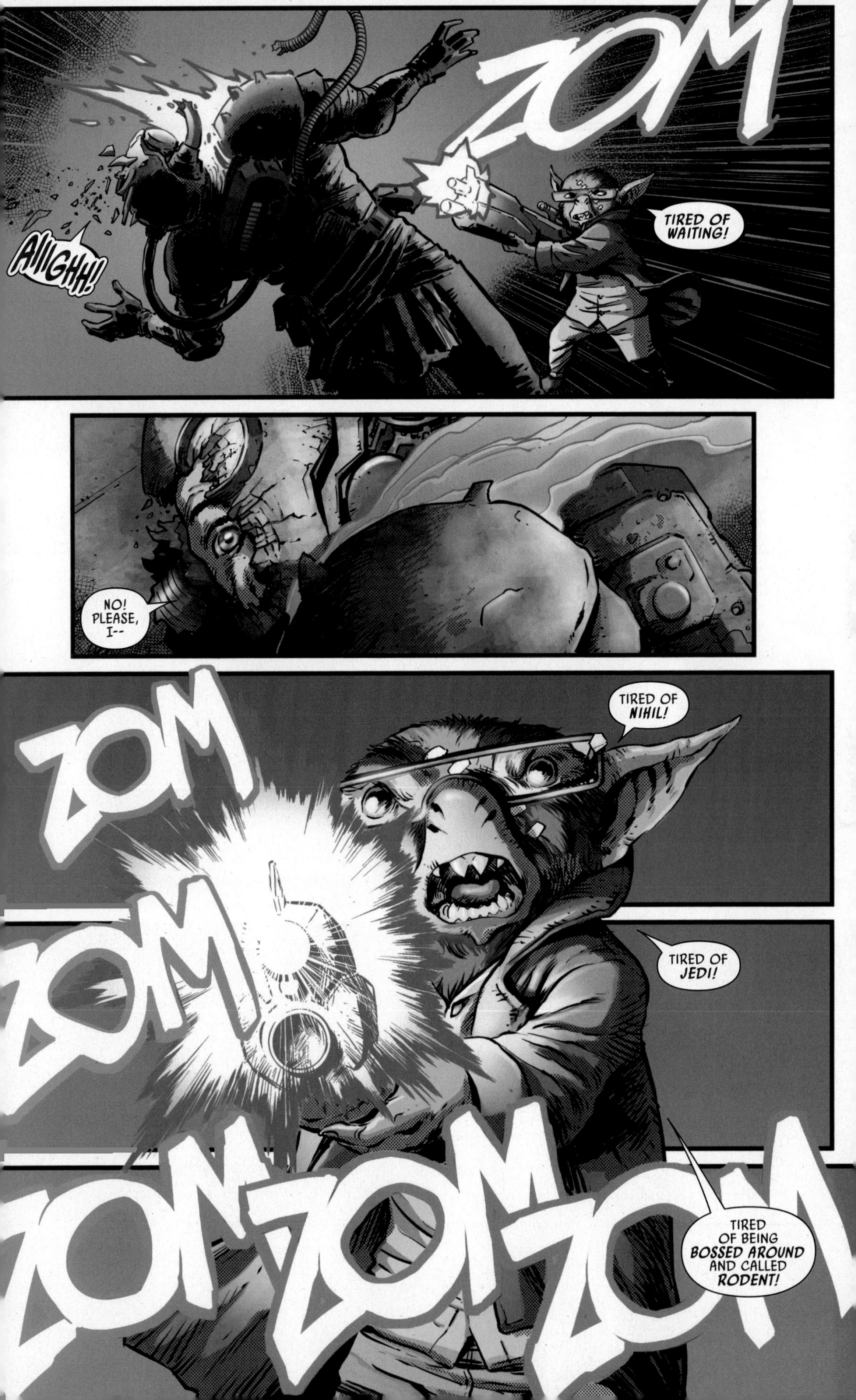
ZOM
TIRED OF WAITING!
AIIIGHH!
NO! PLEASE, I--
ZOM
TIRED OF NIHIL!
ZOM
TIRED OF JEDI!
ZOM ZOM ZOM
TIRED OF BEING BOSSED AROUND AND CALLED RODENT!

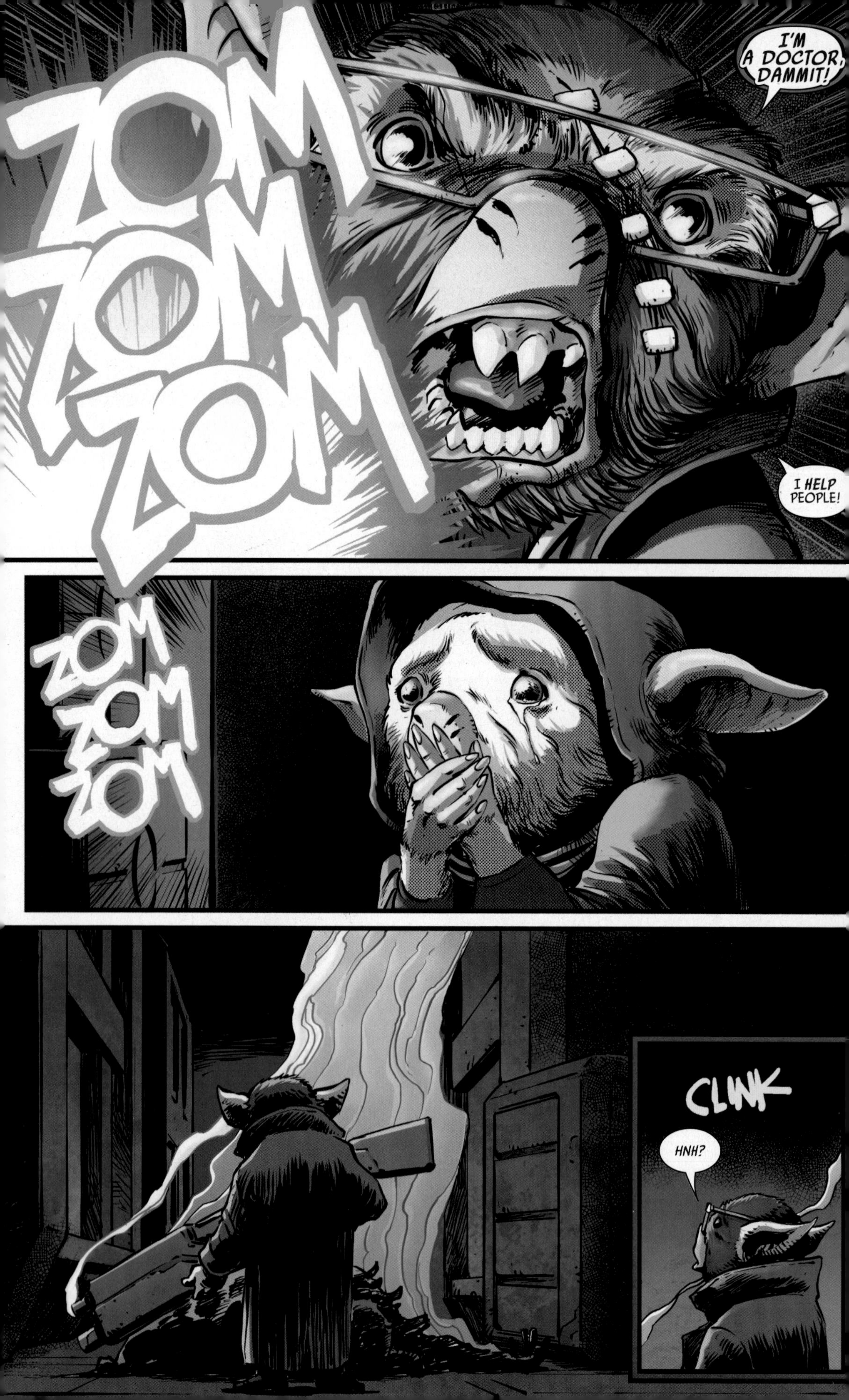
ZOM ZOM ZOM ZOM
I'M A DOCTOR, DAMMIT!
I HELP PEOPLE!
ZOM ZOM ZOM
CLINK
HNH?

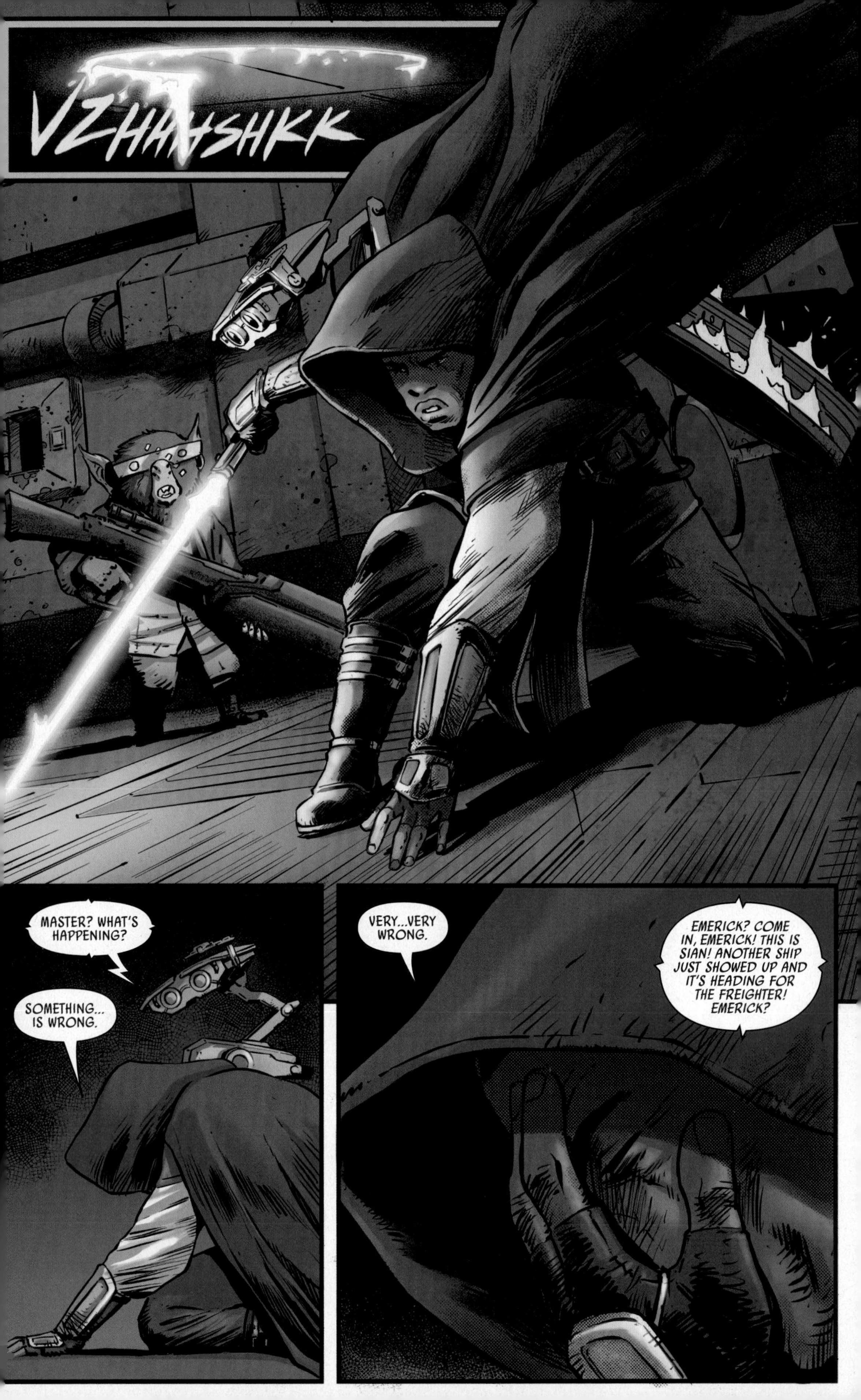
VZHHNSHKK
MASTER? WHAT'S HAPPENING?
SOMETHING... IS WRONG.
VERY...VERY WRONG.
EMERICK? COME IN, EMERICK! THIS IS SIAN! ANOTHER SHIP JUST SHOWED UP AND IT'S HEADING FOR THE FREIGHTER! EMERICK?

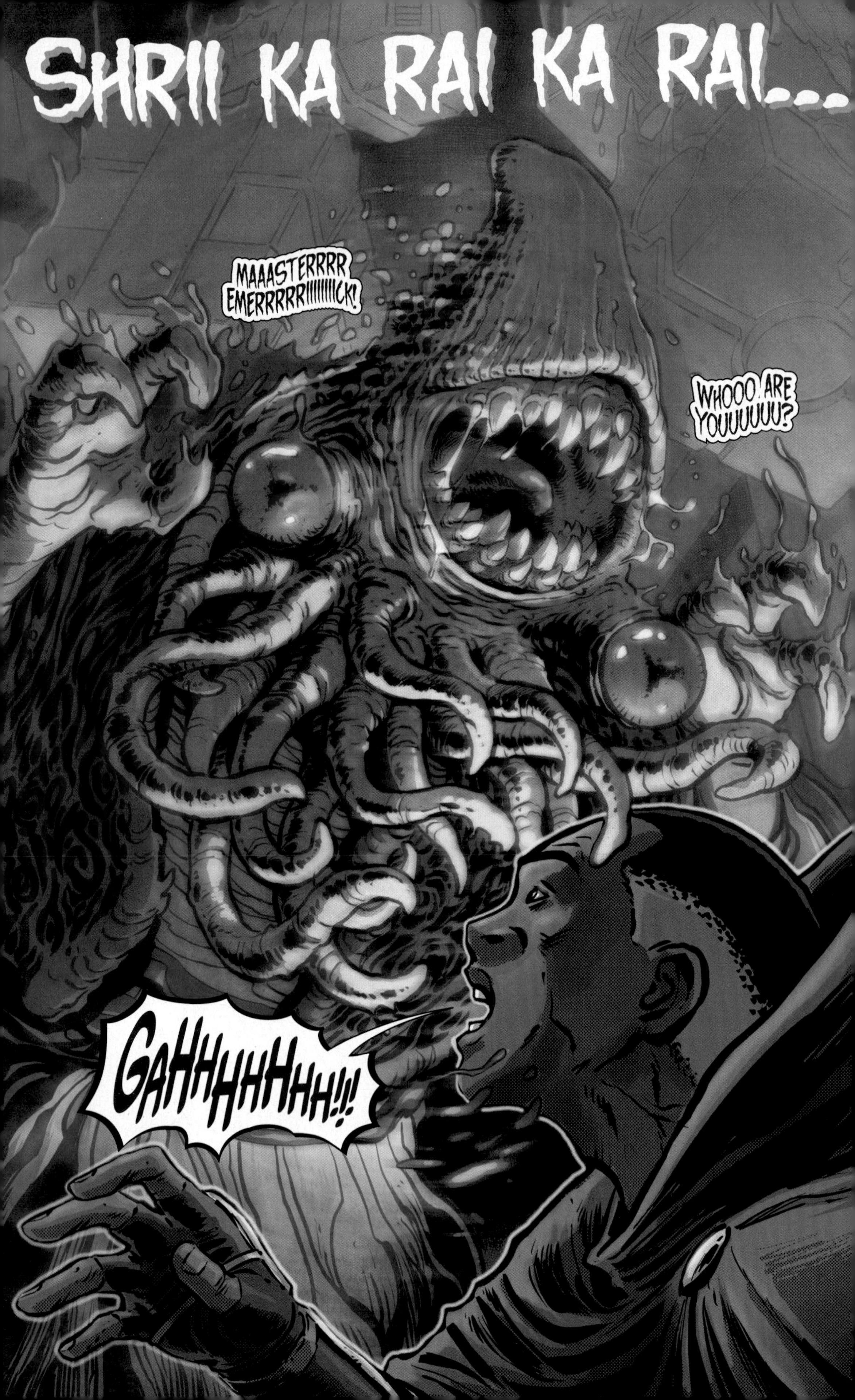
SHRII KA RAI KA RAI...
MAAASTERRRR EMERRRRR!!!!!!!!!CK!
WHOOO ARE YOUUUUUU?
GAHHHHHHH!!!

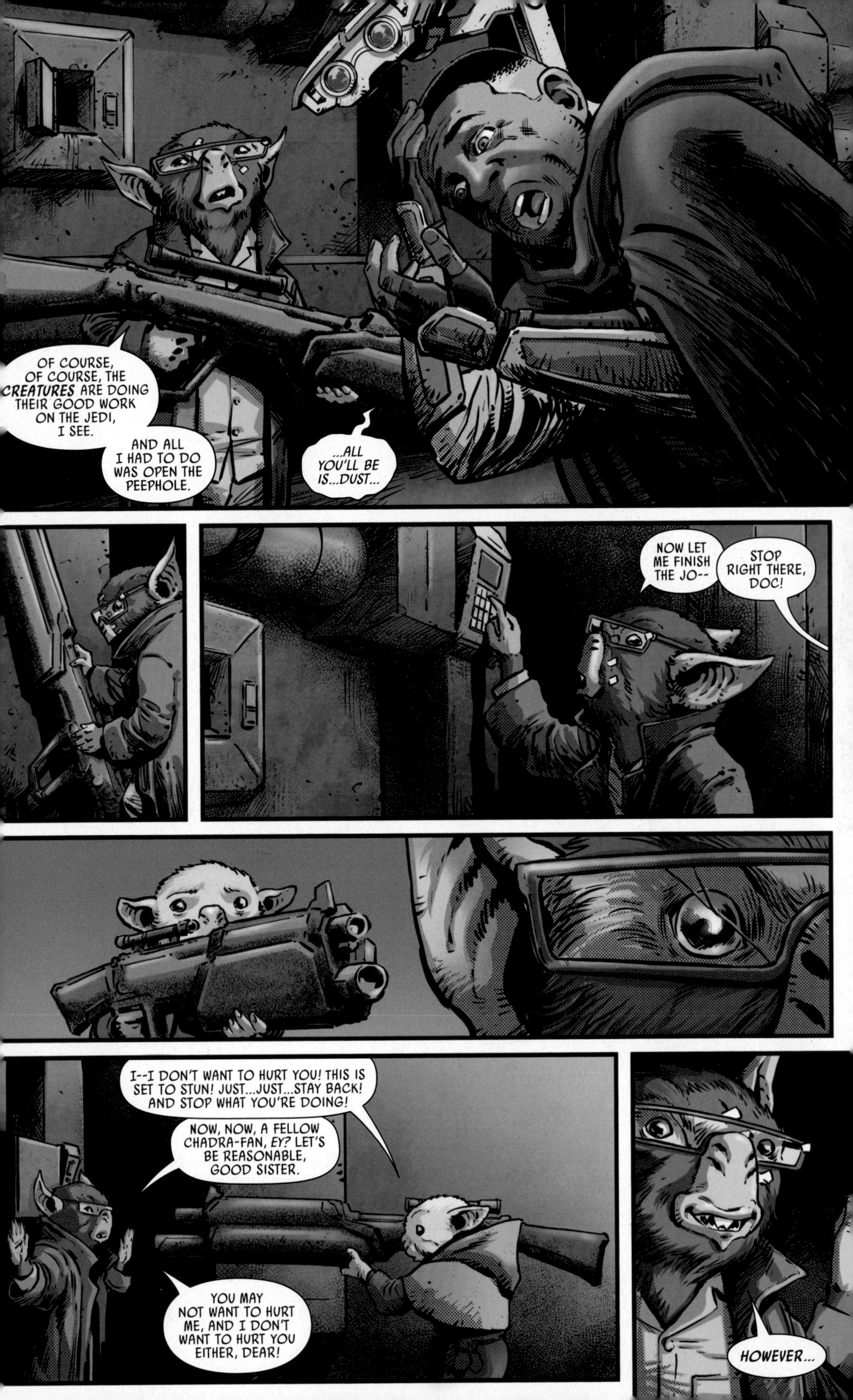
OF COURSE, OF COURSE, THE *CREATURES* ARE DOING THEIR GOOD WORK ON THE JEDI, I SEE.
AND ALL I HAD TO DO WAS OPEN THE PEEPHOLE.
...ALL YOU'LL BE IS...DUST...
NOW LET ME FINISH THE JO--
STOP RIGHT THERE, DOC!
I--I DON'T WANT TO HURT YOU! THIS IS SET TO STUN! JUST...JUST...STAY BACK! AND STOP WHAT YOU'RE DOING!
NOW, NOW, A FELLOW CHADRA-FAN, *EY?* LET'S BE REASONABLE, GOOD SISTER.
YOU MAY NOT WANT TO HURT ME, AND I DON'T WANT TO HURT YOU EITHER, DEAR!
HOWEVER...

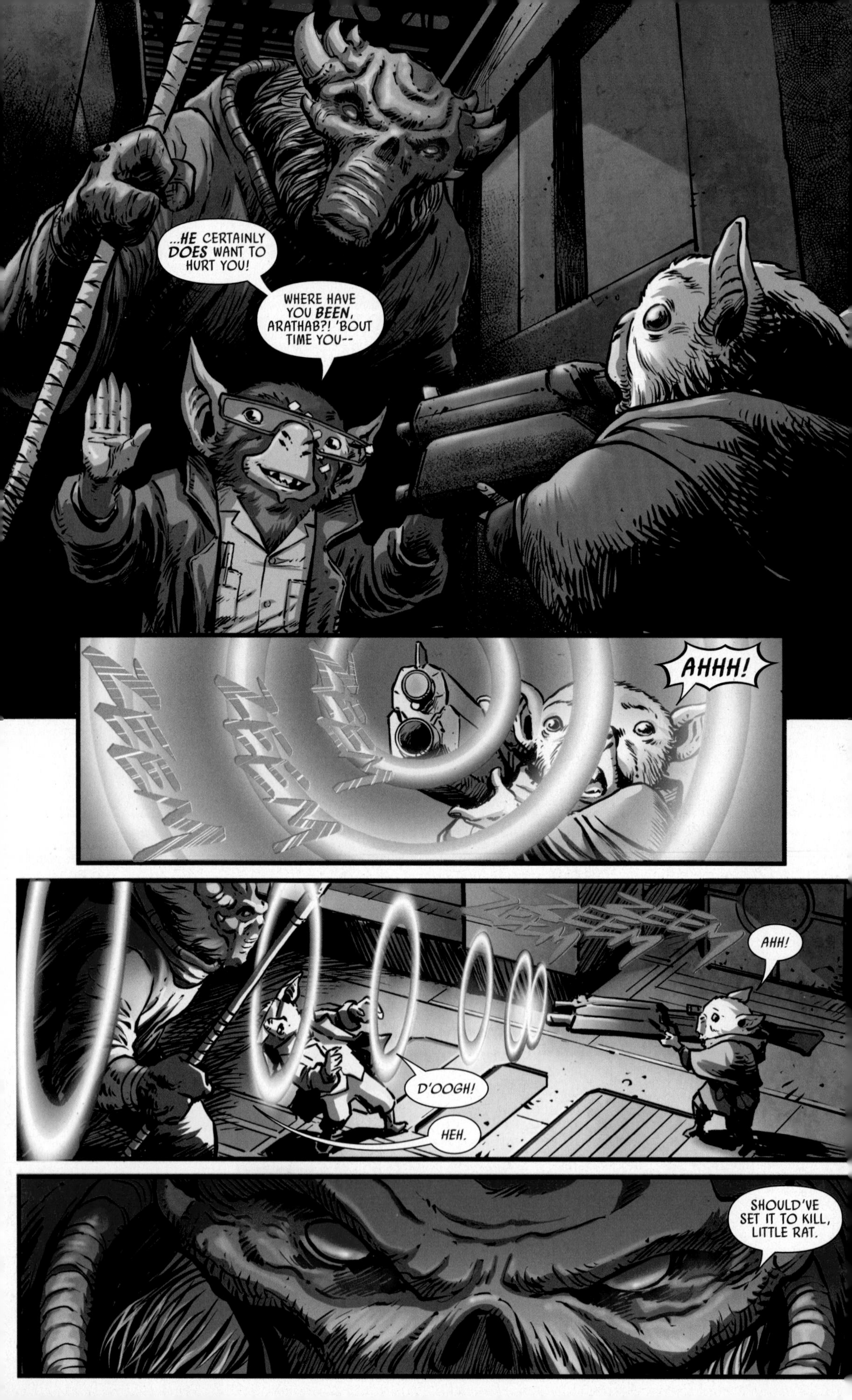
...HE CERTAINLY DOES WANT TO HURT YOU!
WHERE HAVE YOU BEEN, ARATHAB?! 'BOUT TIME YOU--
AHHH!
AHH!
D'OOGH!
HEH.
SHOULD'VE SET IT TO KILL, LITTLE RAT.

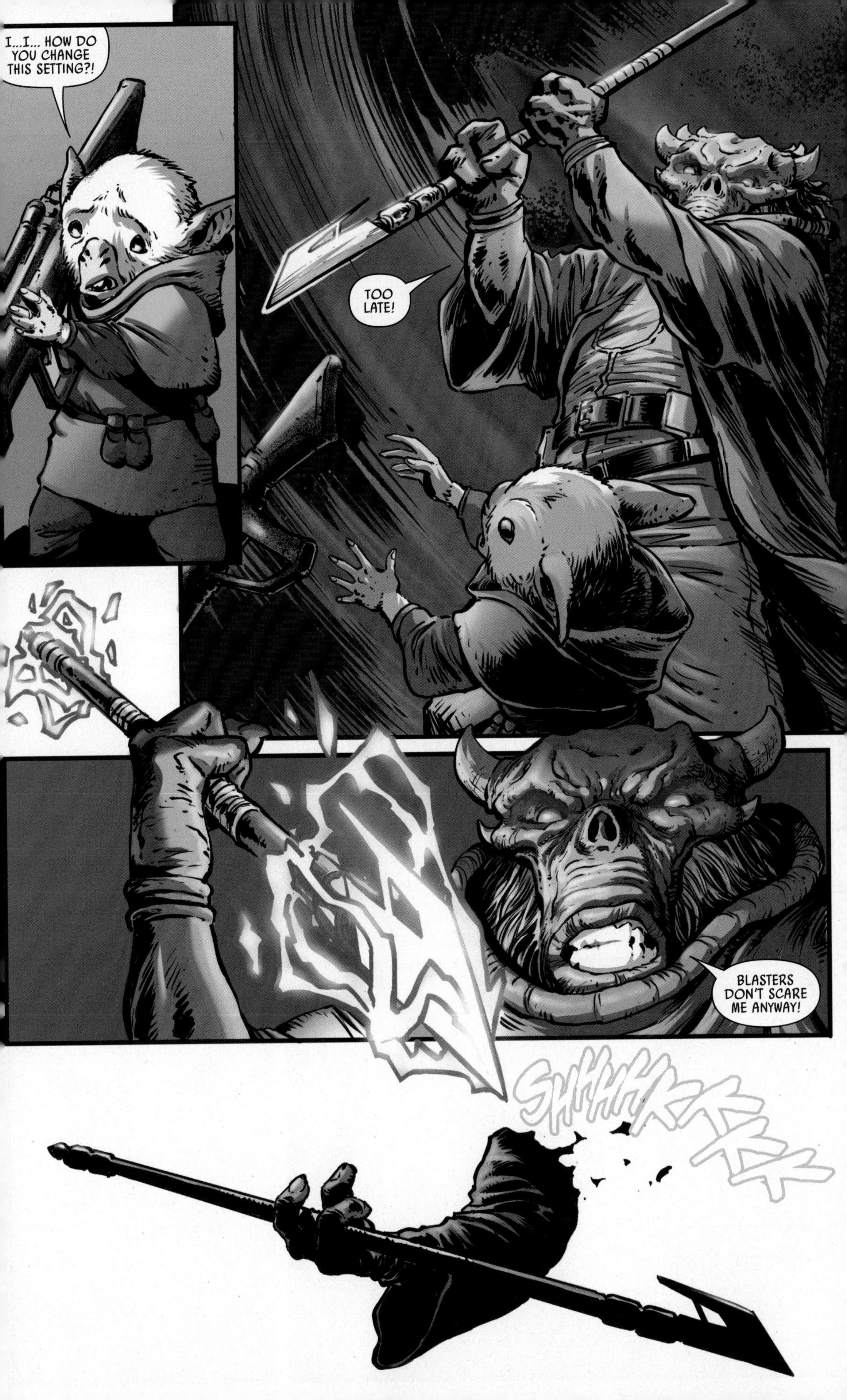
I...I... HOW DO YOU CHANGE THIS SETTING?!
TOO LATE!
BLASTERS DON'T SCARE ME ANYWAY!

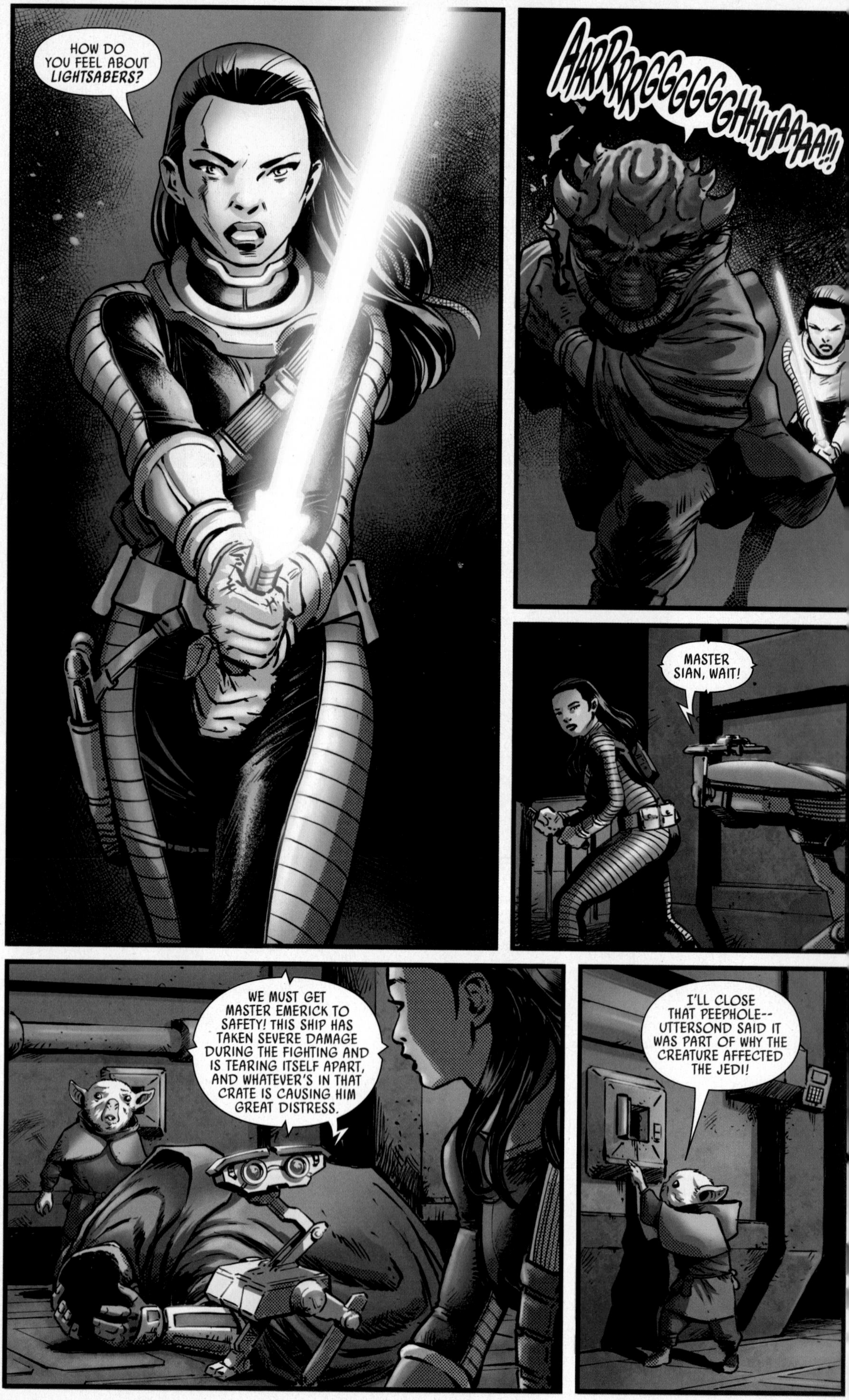

HOW DO YOU FEEL ABOUT LIGHTSABERS?
AARRRRGGGGGGHHHAAAA!!!
MASTER SIAN, WAIT!
WE MUST GET MASTER EMERICK TO SAFETY! THIS SHIP HAS TAKEN SEVERE DAMAGE DURING THE FIGHTING AND IS TEARING ITSELF APART, AND WHATEVER'S IN THAT CRATE IS CAUSING HIM GREAT DISTRESS.
I'LL CLOSE THAT PEEPHOLE-- UTTERSOND SAID IT WAS PART OF WHY THE CREATURE AFFECTED THE JEDI!

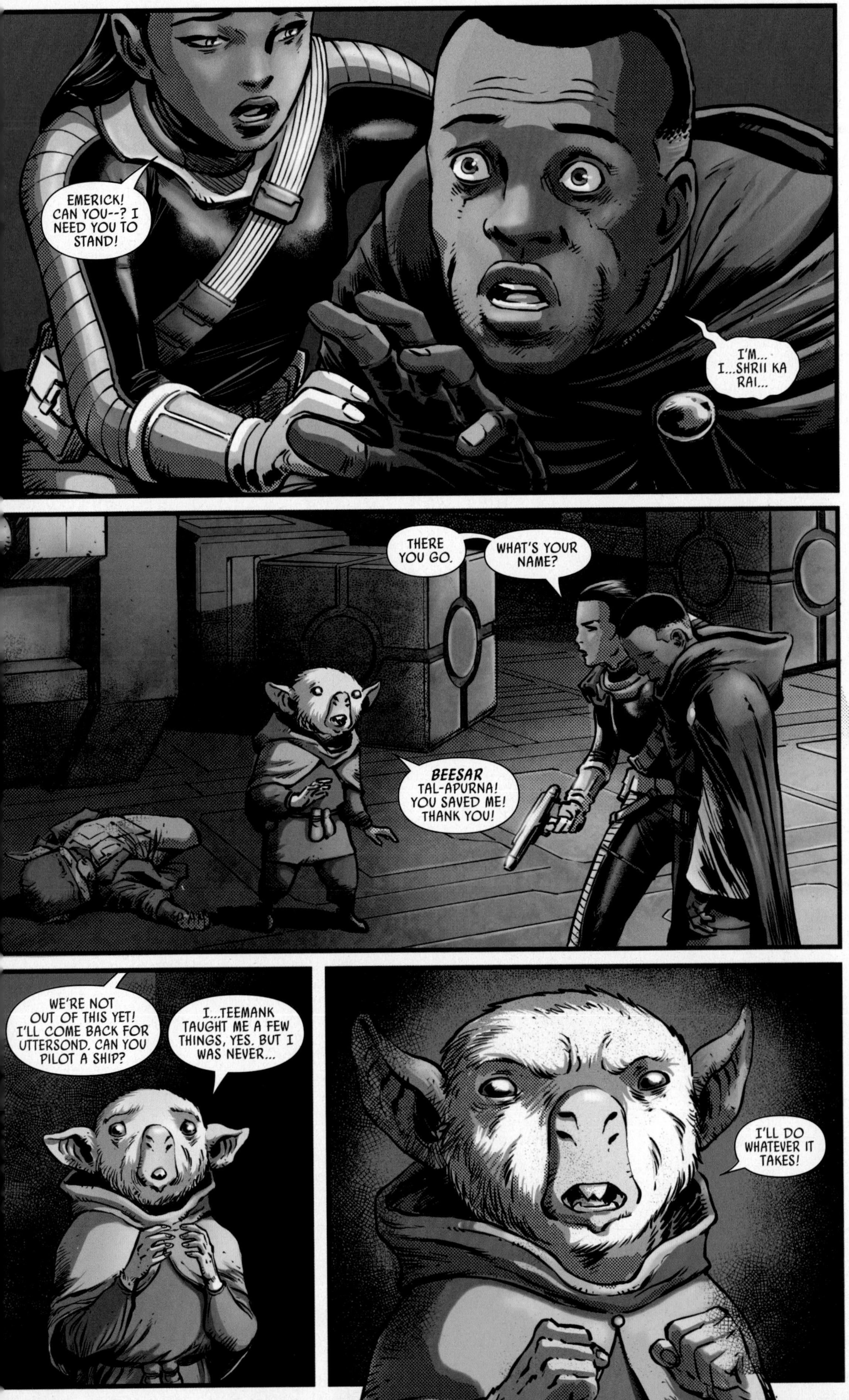
EMERICK! CAN YOU--? I NEED YOU TO STAND!
I'M... I...SHRII KA RAI...
THERE YOU GO.
WHAT'S YOUR NAME?
BEESAR TAL-APURNA! YOU SAVED ME! THANK YOU!
WE'RE NOT OUT OF THIS YET! I'LL COME BACK FOR UTTERSOND. CAN YOU PILOT A SHIP?
I...TEEMANK TAUGHT ME A FEW THINGS, YES. BUT I WAS NEVER...
I'LL DO WHATEVER IT TAKES!

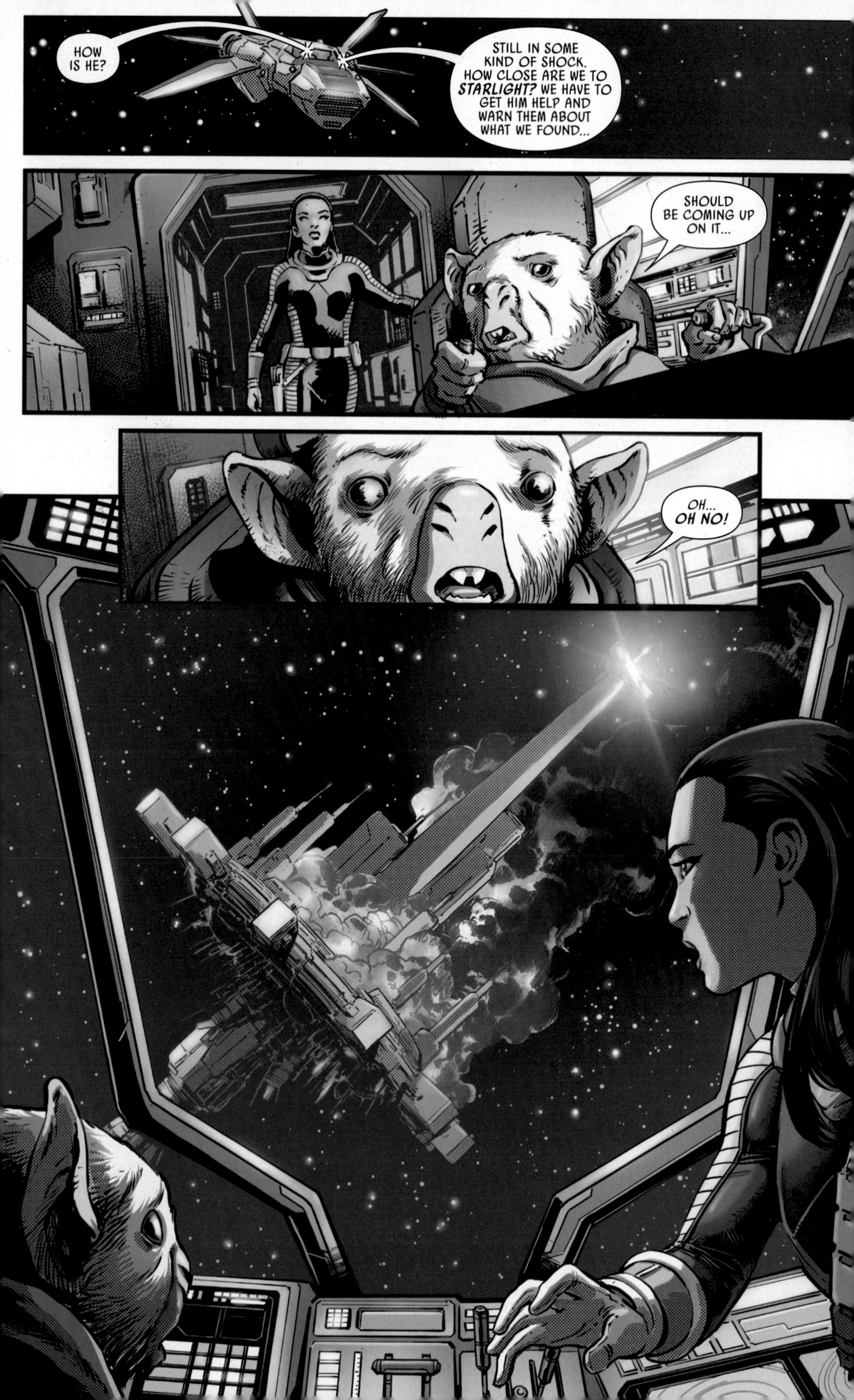
HOW IS HE?
STILL IN SOME KIND OF SHOCK. HOW CLOSE ARE WE TO STARLIGHT? WE HAVE TO GET HIM HELP AND WARN THEM ABOUT WHAT WE FOUND...
SHOULD BE COMING UP ON IT...
OH... OH NO!

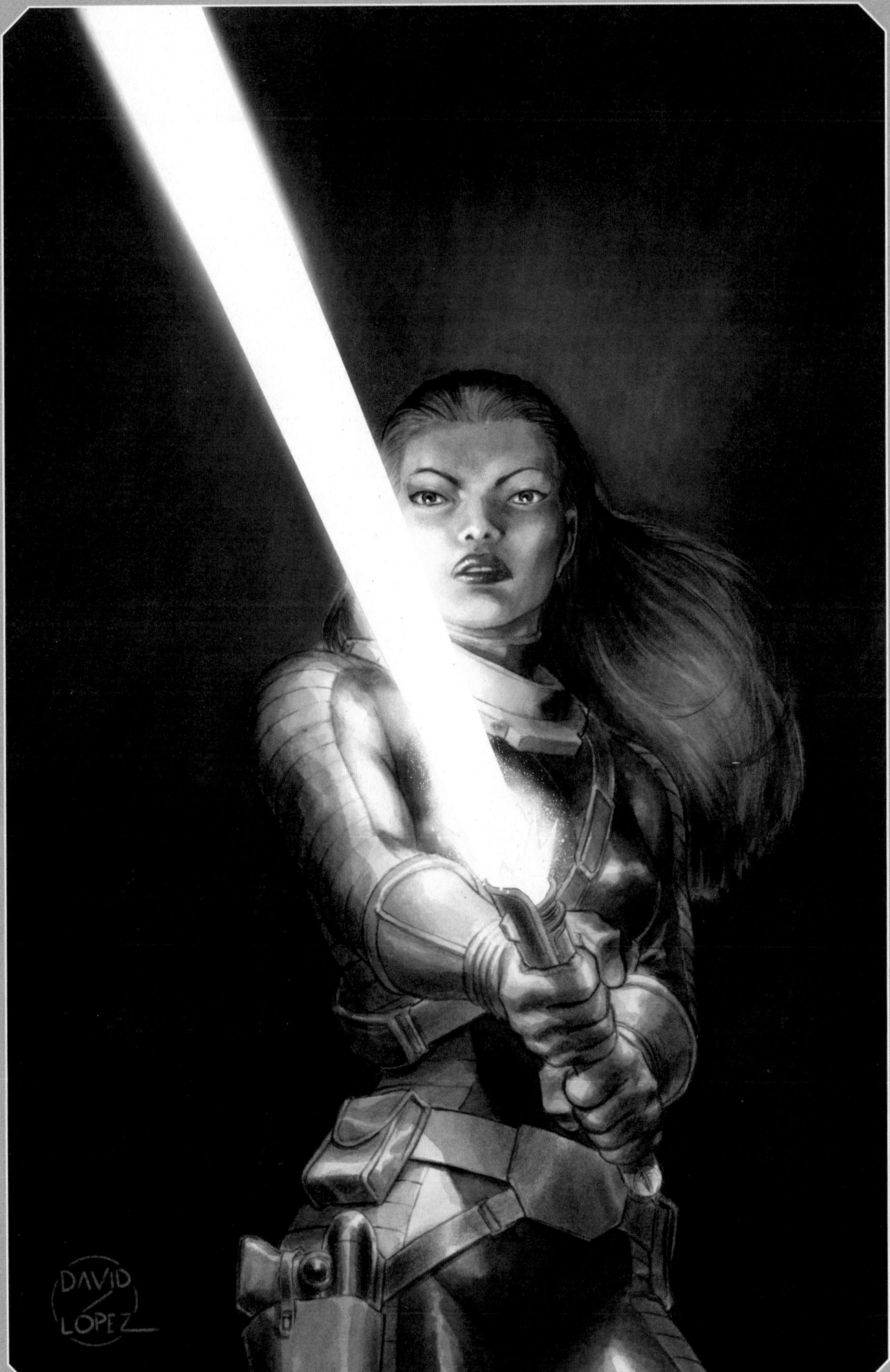
DAVID
LOPEZ

#5 Variant by
DAVID LOPEZ

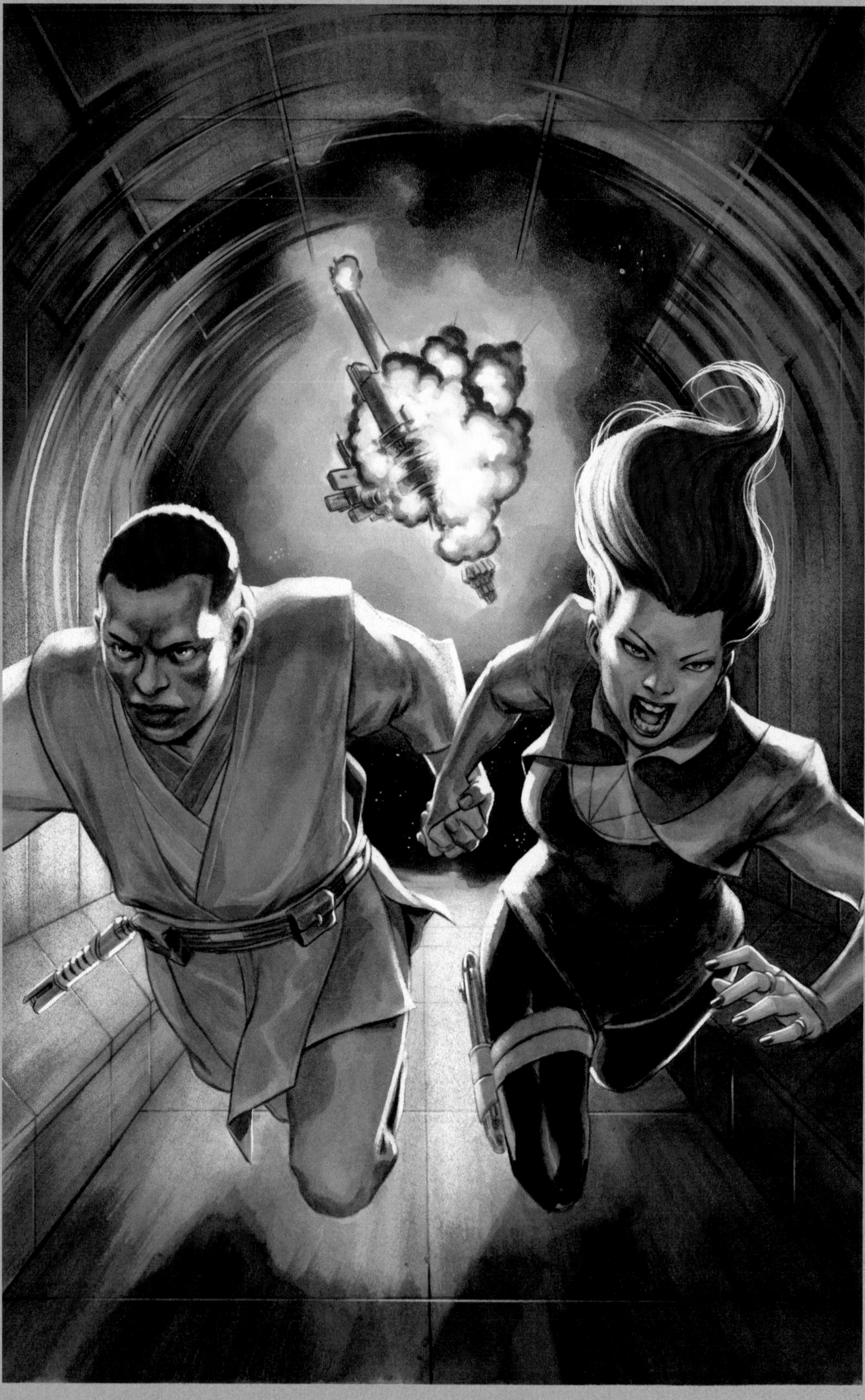

5 | DUST

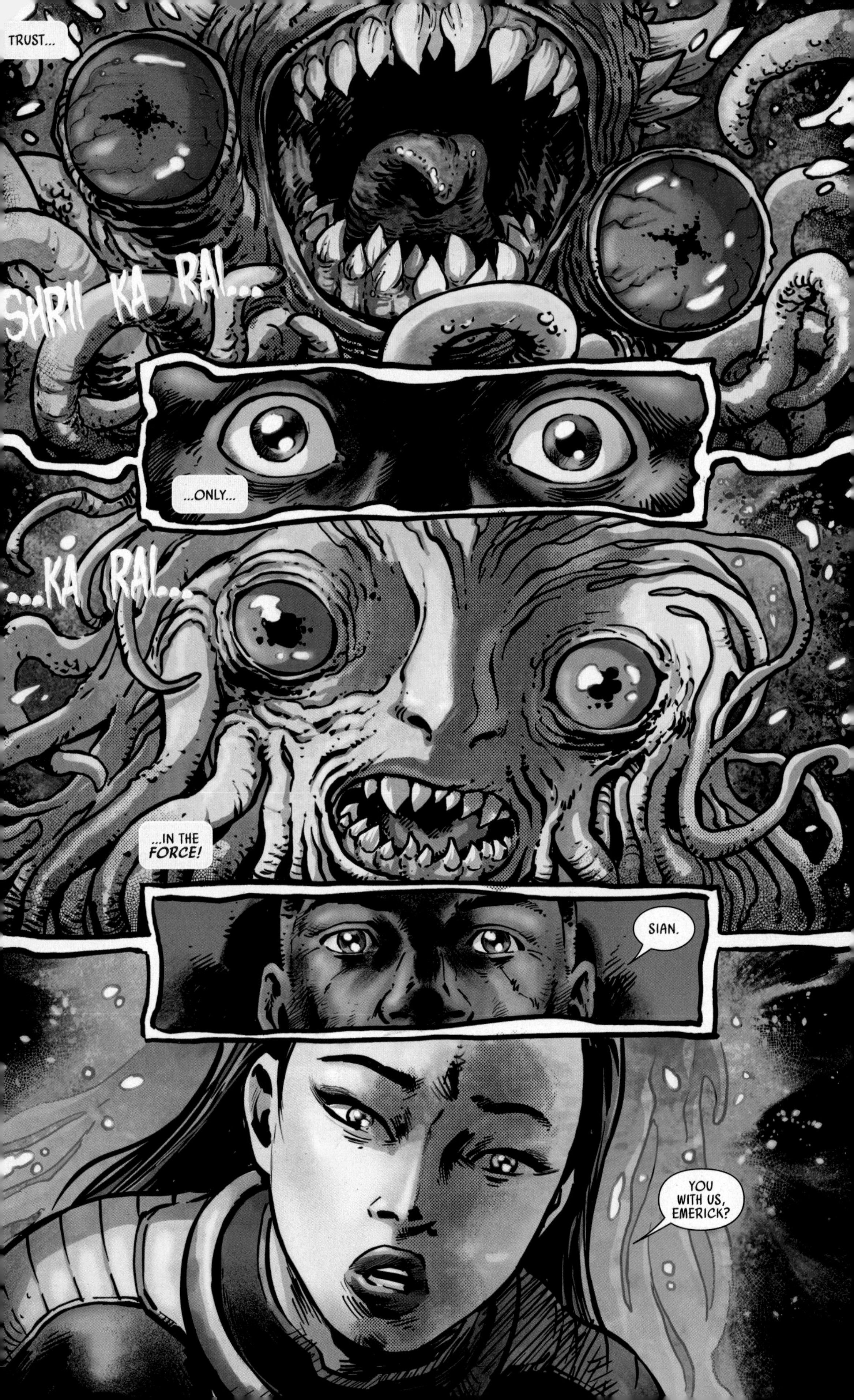
TRUST...
SHRII KA RAI...
...ONLY...
...KA RAI...
...IN THE FORCE!
SIAN.
YOU WITH US, EMERICK?

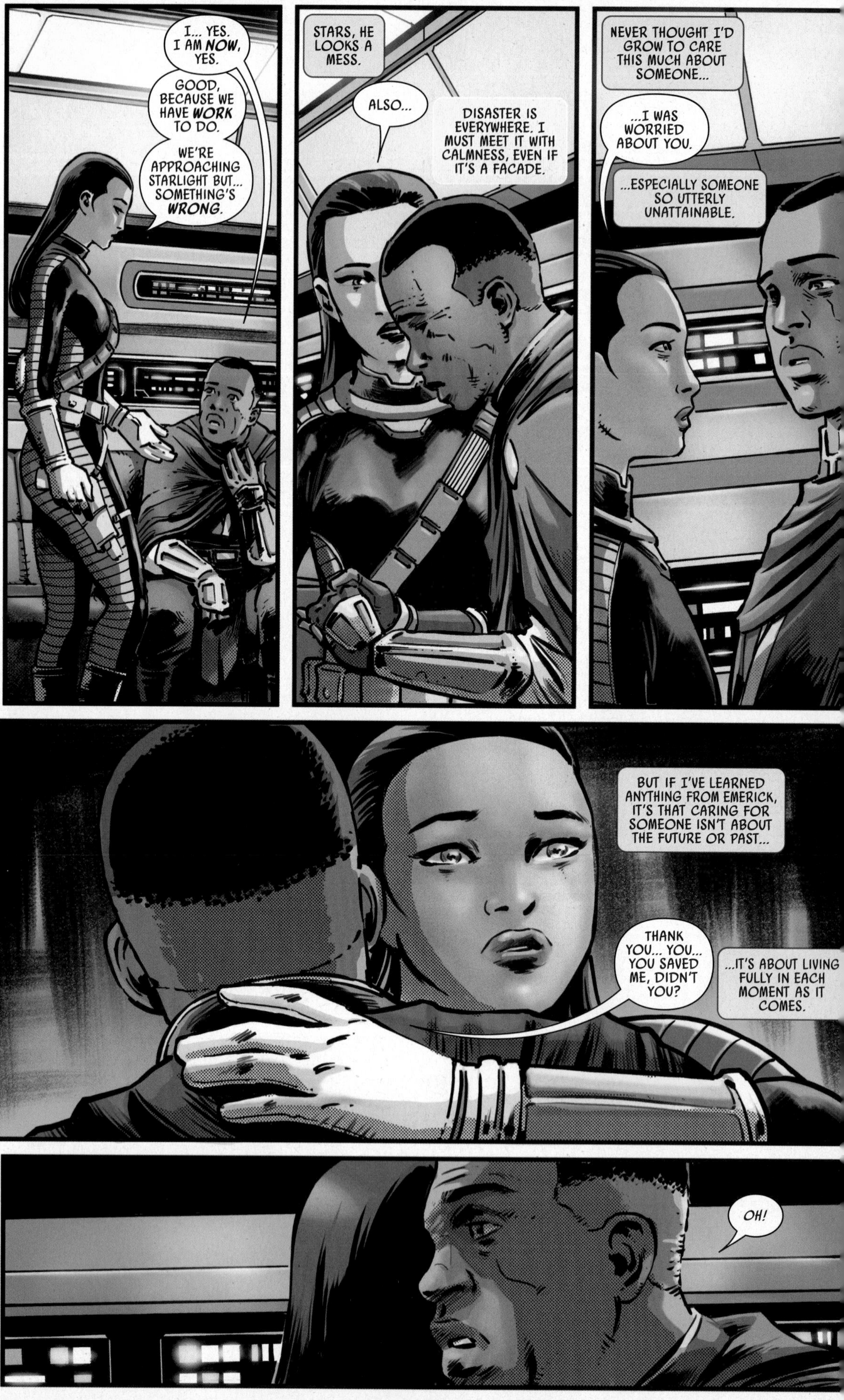
I... YES. I AM NOW, YES.
GOOD, BECAUSE WE HAVE WORK TO DO.
WE'RE APPROACHING STARLIGHT BUT... SOMETHING'S WRONG.
STARS, HE LOOKS A MESS.
ALSO...
DISASTER IS EVERYWHERE. I MUST MEET IT WITH CALMNESS, EVEN IF IT'S A FACADE.
NEVER THOUGHT I'D GROW TO CARE THIS MUCH ABOUT SOMEONE...
...I WAS WORRIED ABOUT YOU.
...ESPECIALLY SOMEONE SO UTTERLY UNATTAINABLE.
BUT IF I'VE LEARNED ANYTHING FROM EMERICK, IT'S THAT CARING FOR SOMEONE ISN'T ABOUT THE FUTURE OR PAST...
THANK YOU... YOU... YOU SAVED ME, DIDN'T YOU?
...IT'S ABOUT LIVING FULLY IN EACH MOMENT AS IT COMES.
OH!

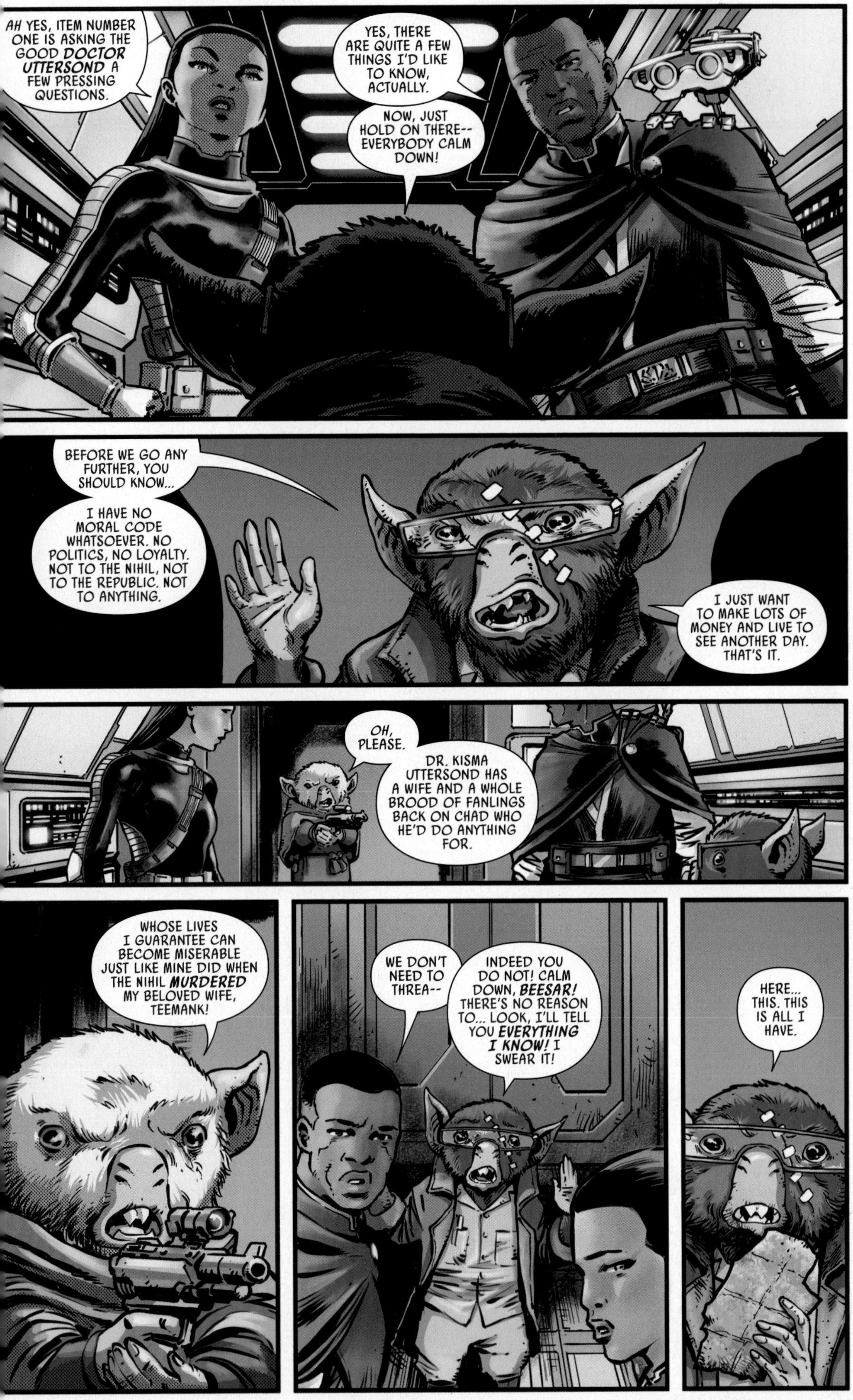
AH YES, ITEM NUMBER ONE IS ASKING THE GOOD DOCTOR UTTERSOND A FEW PRESSING QUESTIONS.
YES, THERE ARE QUITE A FEW THINGS I'D LIKE TO KNOW, ACTUALLY.
NOW, JUST HOLD ON THERE-- EVERYBODY CALM DOWN!
BEFORE WE GO ANY FURTHER, YOU SHOULD KNOW...
I HAVE NO MORAL CODE WHATSOEVER. NO POLITICS, NO LOYALTY. NOT TO THE NIHIL, NOT TO THE REPUBLIC. NOT TO ANYTHING.
I JUST WANT TO MAKE LOTS OF MONEY AND LIVE TO SEE ANOTHER DAY. THAT'S IT.
OH, PLEASE.
DR. KISMA UTTERSOND HAS A WIFE AND A WHOLE BROOD OF FANLINGS BACK ON CHAD WHO HE'D DO ANYTHING FOR.
WHOSE LIVES I GUARANTEE CAN BECOME MISERABLE JUST LIKE MINE DID WHEN THE NIHIL MURDERED MY BELOVED WIFE, TEEMANK!
WE DON'T NEED TO THREA--
INDEED YOU DO NOT! CALM DOWN, BEESAR! THERE'S NO REASON TO... LOOK, I'LL TELL YOU EVERYTHING I KNOW! I SWEAR IT!
HERE... THIS. THIS IS ALL I HAVE.

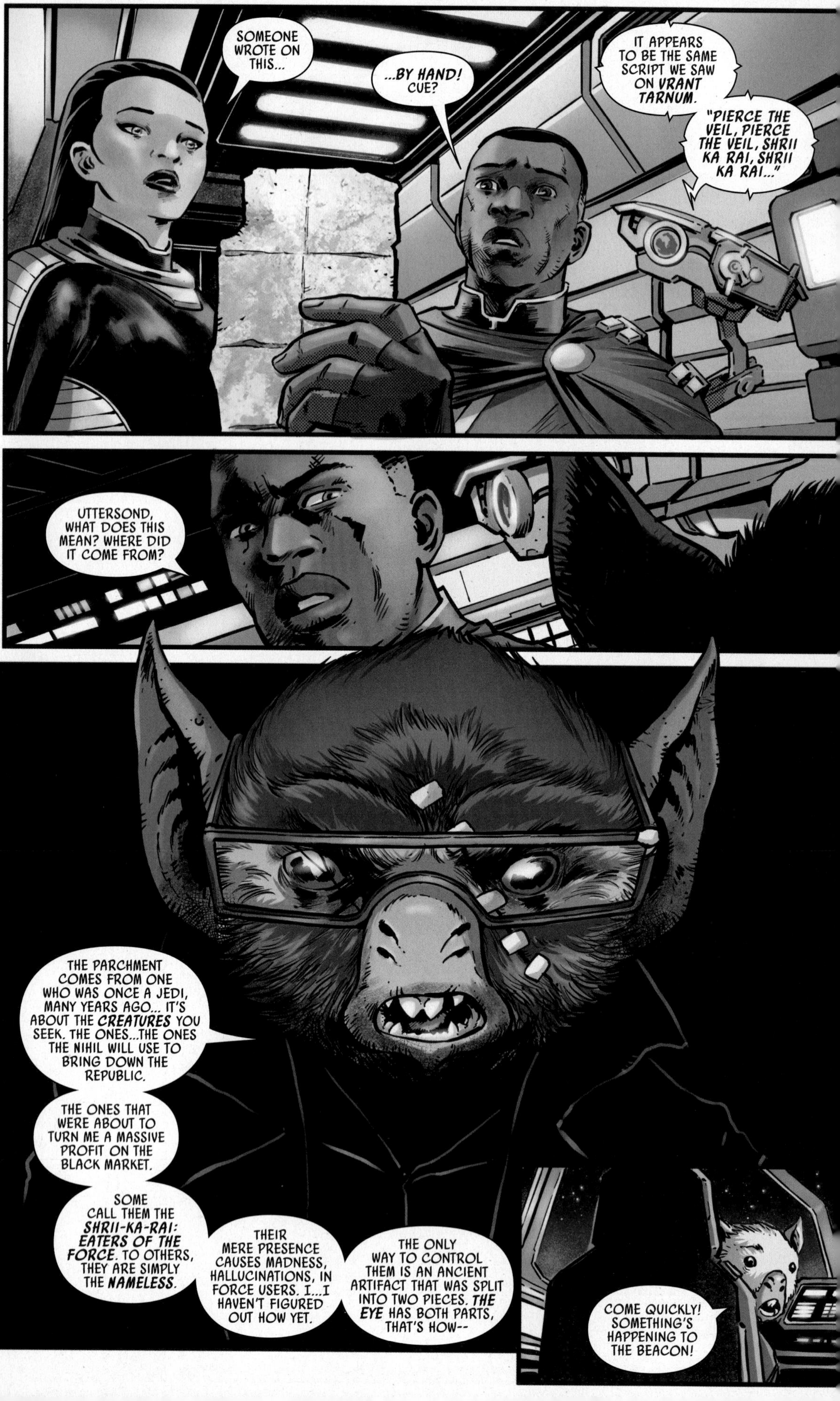
SOMEONE WROTE ON THIS...
...BY HAND! CUE?
IT APPEARS TO BE THE SAME SCRIPT WE SAW ON VRANT TARNUM.
"PIERCE THE VEIL, PIERCE THE VEIL, SHRII KA RAI, SHRII KA RAI..."
UTTERSOND, WHAT DOES THIS MEAN? WHERE DID IT COME FROM?
THE PARCHMENT COMES FROM ONE WHO WAS ONCE A JEDI, MANY YEARS AGO... IT'S ABOUT THE CREATURES YOU SEEK. THE ONES...THE ONES THE NIHIL WILL USE TO BRING DOWN THE REPUBLIC.
THE ONES THAT WERE ABOUT TO TURN ME A MASSIVE PROFIT ON THE BLACK MARKET.
SOME CALL THEM THE SHRII-KA-RAI: EATERS OF THE FORCE. TO OTHERS, THEY ARE SIMPLY THE NAMELESS.
THEIR MERE PRESENCE CAUSES MADNESS, HALLUCINATIONS, IN FORCE USERS. I...I HAVEN'T FIGURED OUT HOW YET.
THE ONLY WAY TO CONTROL THEM IS AN ANCIENT ARTIFACT THAT WAS SPLIT INTO TWO PIECES. THE EYE HAS BOTH PARTS, THAT'S HOW--
COME QUICKLY! SOMETHING'S HAPPENING TO THE BEACON!

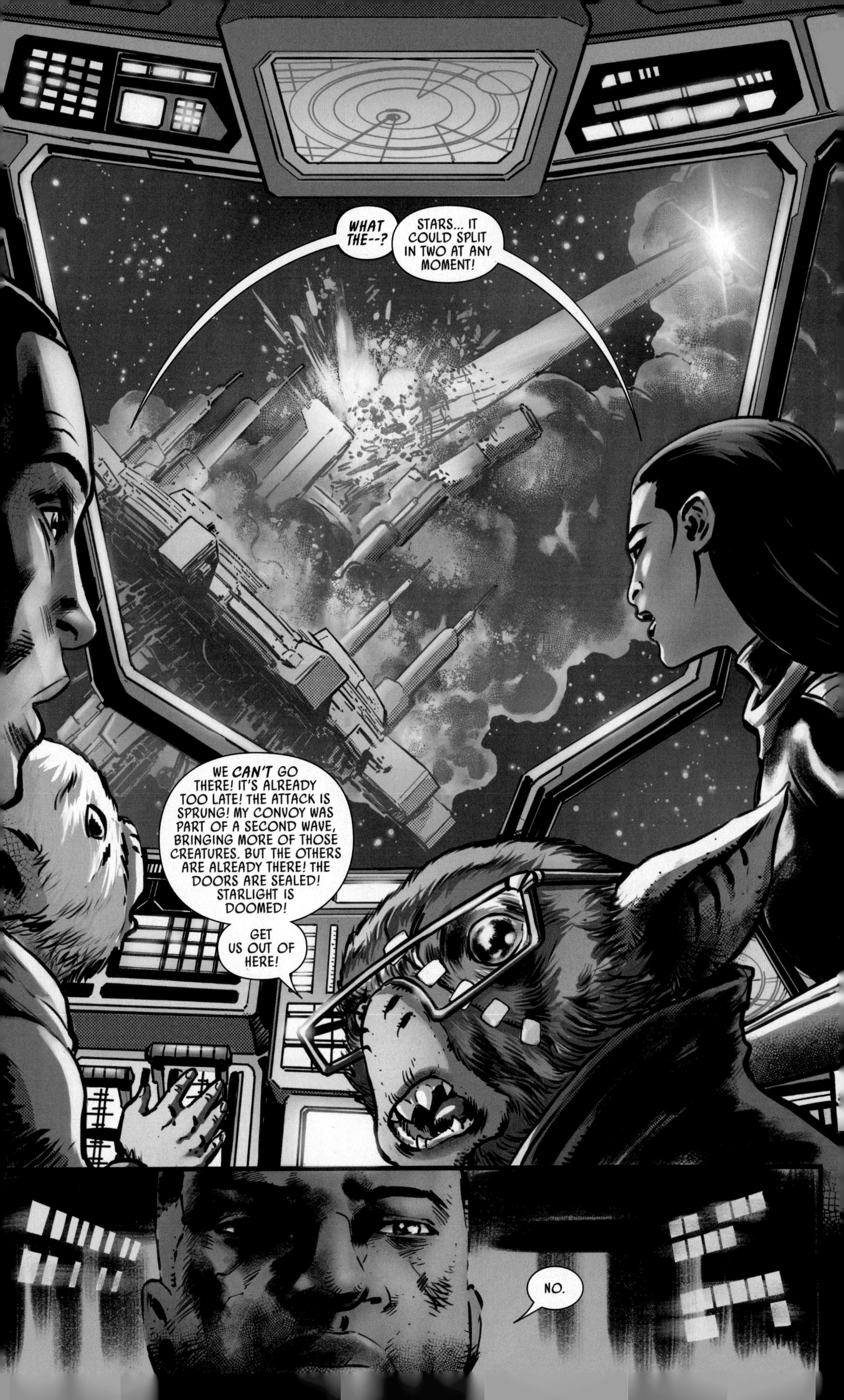
WHAT THE--?
STARS... IT COULD SPLIT IN TWO AT ANY MOMENT!
WE CAN'T GO THERE! IT'S ALREADY TOO LATE! THE ATTACK IS SPRUNG! MY CONVOY WAS PART OF A SECOND WAVE, BRINGING MORE OF THOSE CREATURES. BUT THE OTHERS ARE ALREADY THERE! THE DOORS ARE SEALED! STARLIGHT IS DOOMED!
GET US OUT OF HERE!
NO.

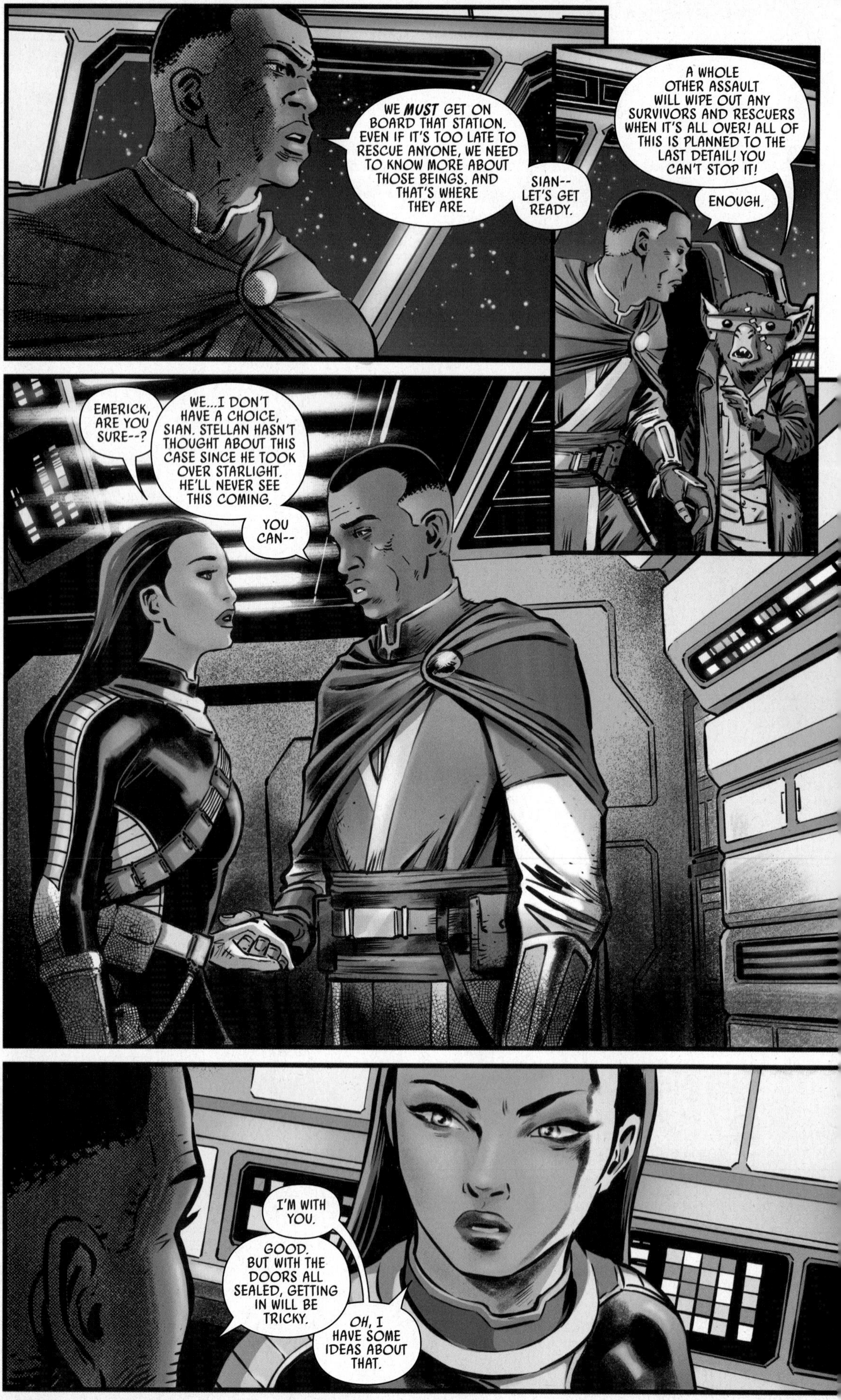
WE *MUST* GET ON BOARD THAT STATION. EVEN IF IT'S TOO LATE TO RESCUE ANYONE, WE NEED TO KNOW MORE ABOUT THOSE BEINGS. AND THAT'S WHERE THEY ARE.
SIAN-- LET'S GET READY.
A WHOLE OTHER ASSAULT WILL WIPE OUT ANY SURVIVORS AND RESCUERS WHEN IT'S ALL OVER! ALL OF THIS IS PLANNED TO THE LAST DETAIL! YOU CAN'T STOP IT!
ENOUGH.
EMERICK, ARE YOU SURE--?
WE...I DON'T HAVE A CHOICE, SIAN. STELLAN HASN'T THOUGHT ABOUT THIS CASE SINCE HE TOOK OVER STARLIGHT. HE'LL NEVER SEE THIS COMING.
YOU CAN--
I'M WITH YOU.
GOOD. BUT WITH THE DOORS ALL SEALED, GETTING IN WILL BE TRICKY.
OH, I HAVE SOME IDEAS ABOUT THAT.

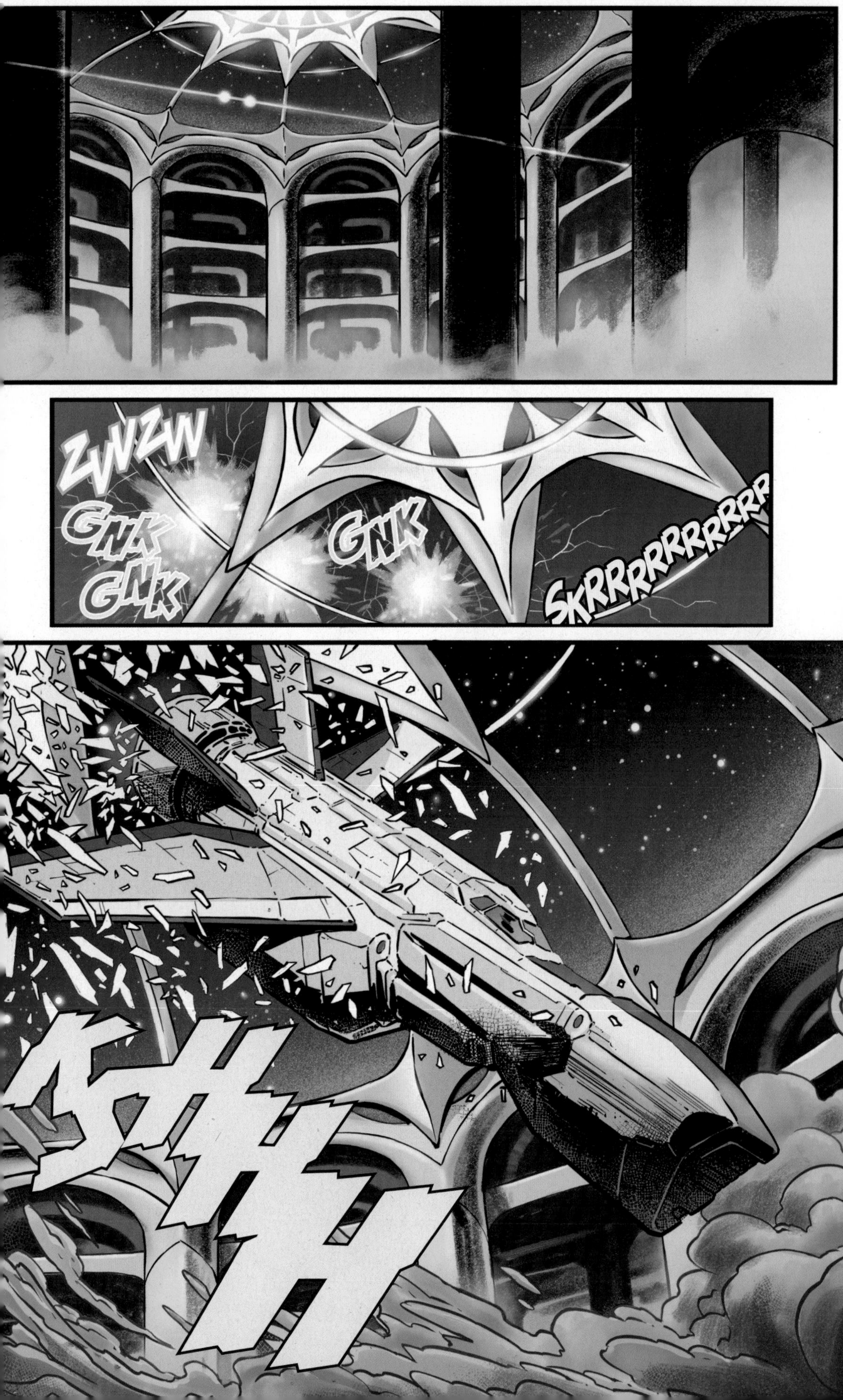
ZVVZVV
GNK
GNK
GNK
SKRRRRRRRRRR

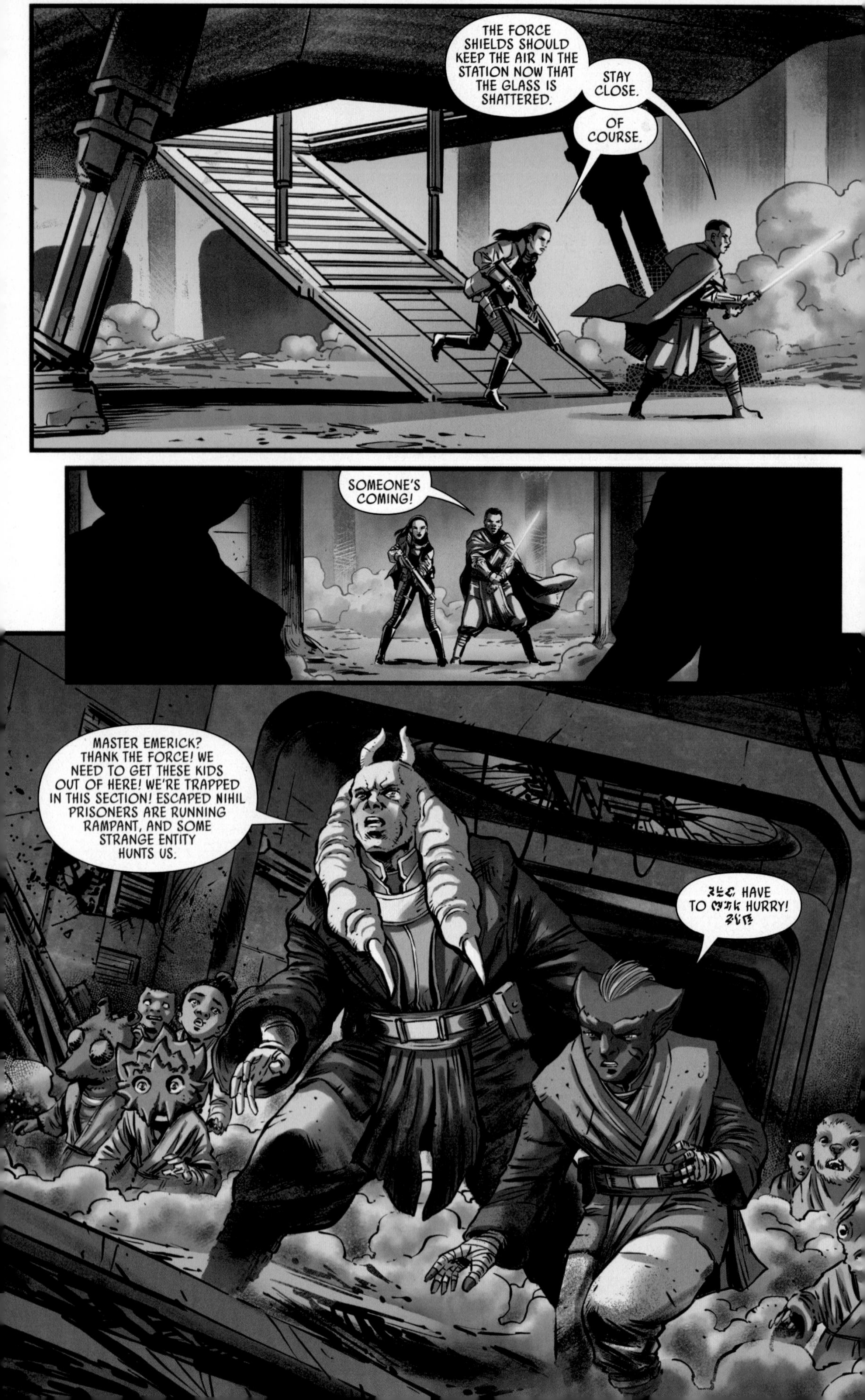
THE FORCE SHIELDS SHOULD KEEP THE AIR IN THE STATION NOW THAT THE GLASS IS SHATTERED.
STAY CLOSE.
OF COURSE.
SOMEONE'S COMING!
MASTER EMERICK? THANK THE FORCE! WE NEED TO GET THESE KIDS OUT OF HERE! WE'RE TRAPPED IN THIS SECTION! ESCAPED NIHIL PRISONERS ARE RUNNING RAMPANT, AND SOME STRANGE ENTITY HUNTS US.
HAVE TO HURRY!

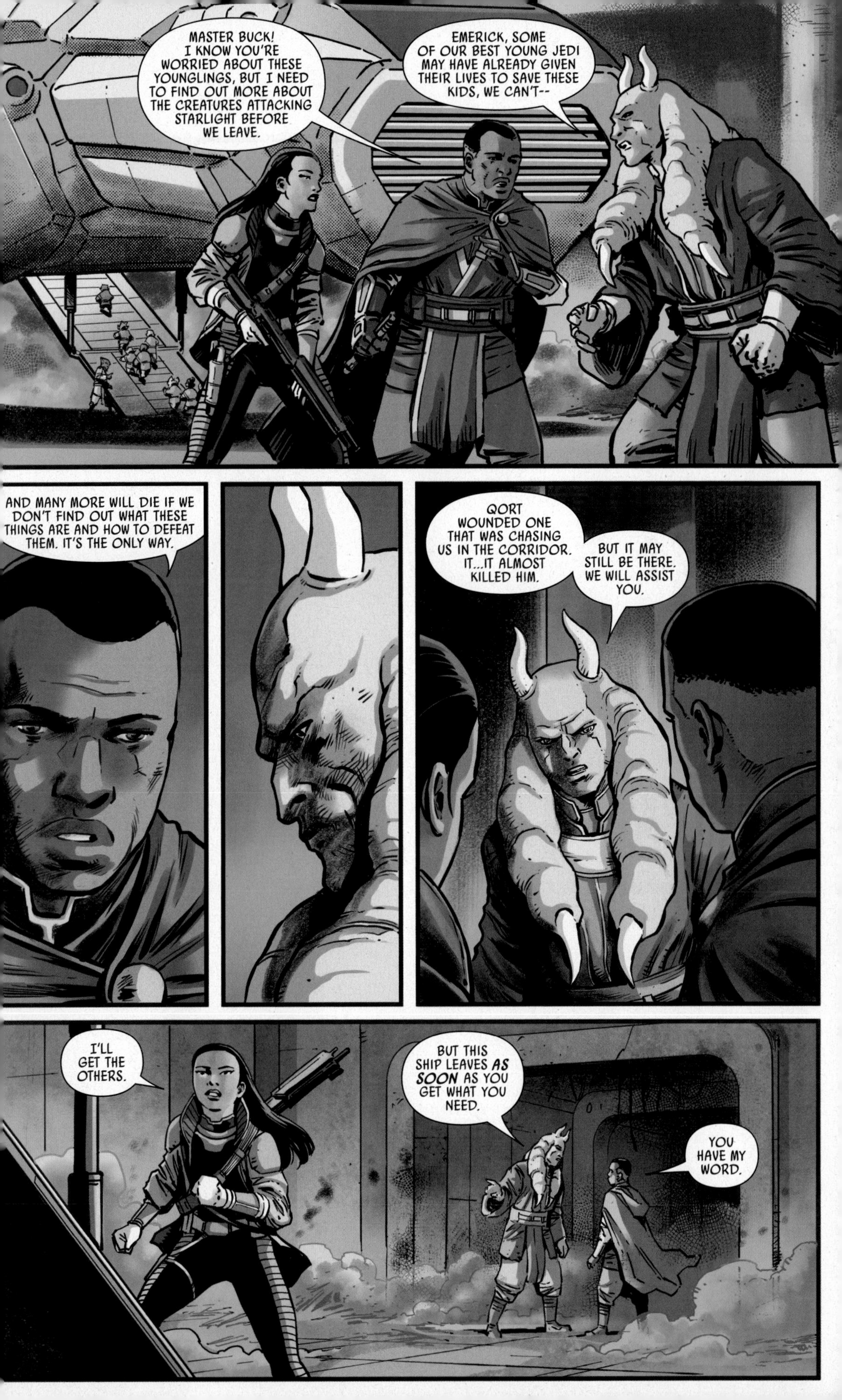
MASTER BUCK! I KNOW YOU'RE WORRIED ABOUT THESE YOUNGLINGS, BUT I NEED TO FIND OUT MORE ABOUT THE CREATURES ATTACKING STARLIGHT BEFORE WE LEAVE.
EMERICK, SOME OF OUR BEST YOUNG JEDI MAY HAVE ALREADY GIVEN THEIR LIVES TO SAVE THESE KIDS, WE CAN'T--
AND MANY MORE WILL DIE IF WE DON'T FIND OUT WHAT THESE THINGS ARE AND HOW TO DEFEAT THEM. IT'S THE ONLY WAY.
QORT WOUNDED ONE THAT WAS CHASING US IN THE CORRIDOR. IT...IT ALMOST KILLED HIM.
BUT IT MAY STILL BE THERE. WE WILL ASSIST YOU.
I'LL GET THE OTHERS.
BUT THIS SHIP LEAVES AS SOON AS YOU GET WHAT YOU NEED.
YOU HAVE MY WORD.

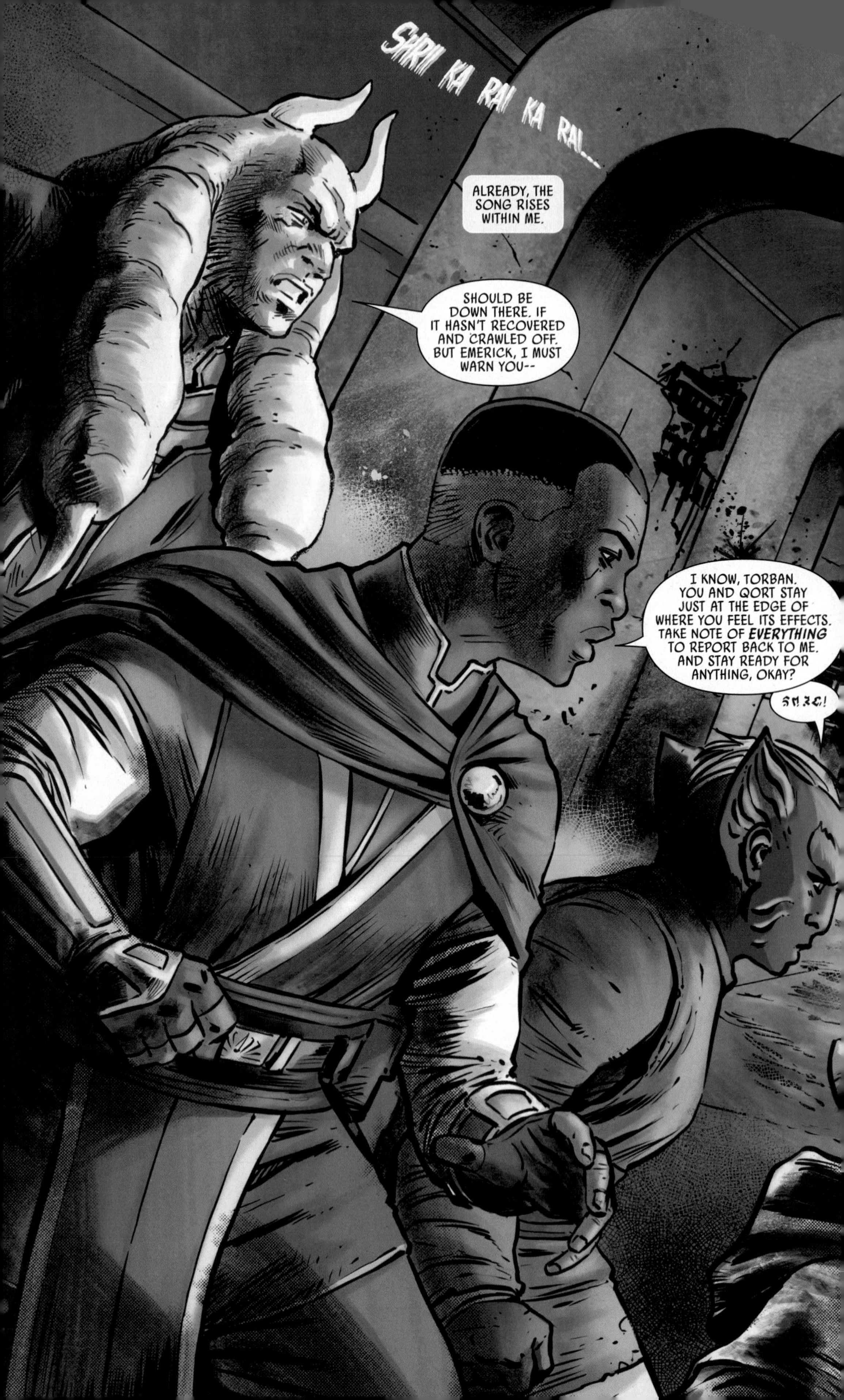
SHRII KA RAI KA RAI...
ALREADY, THE SONG RISES WITHIN ME.
SHOULD BE DOWN THERE. IF IT HASN'T RECOVERED AND CRAWLED OFF. BUT EMERICK, I MUST WARN YOU--
I KNOW, TORBAN. YOU AND QORT STAY JUST AT THE EDGE OF WHERE YOU FEEL ITS EFFECTS. TAKE NOTE OF *EVERYTHING* TO REPORT BACK TO ME. AND STAY READY FOR ANYTHING, OKAY?

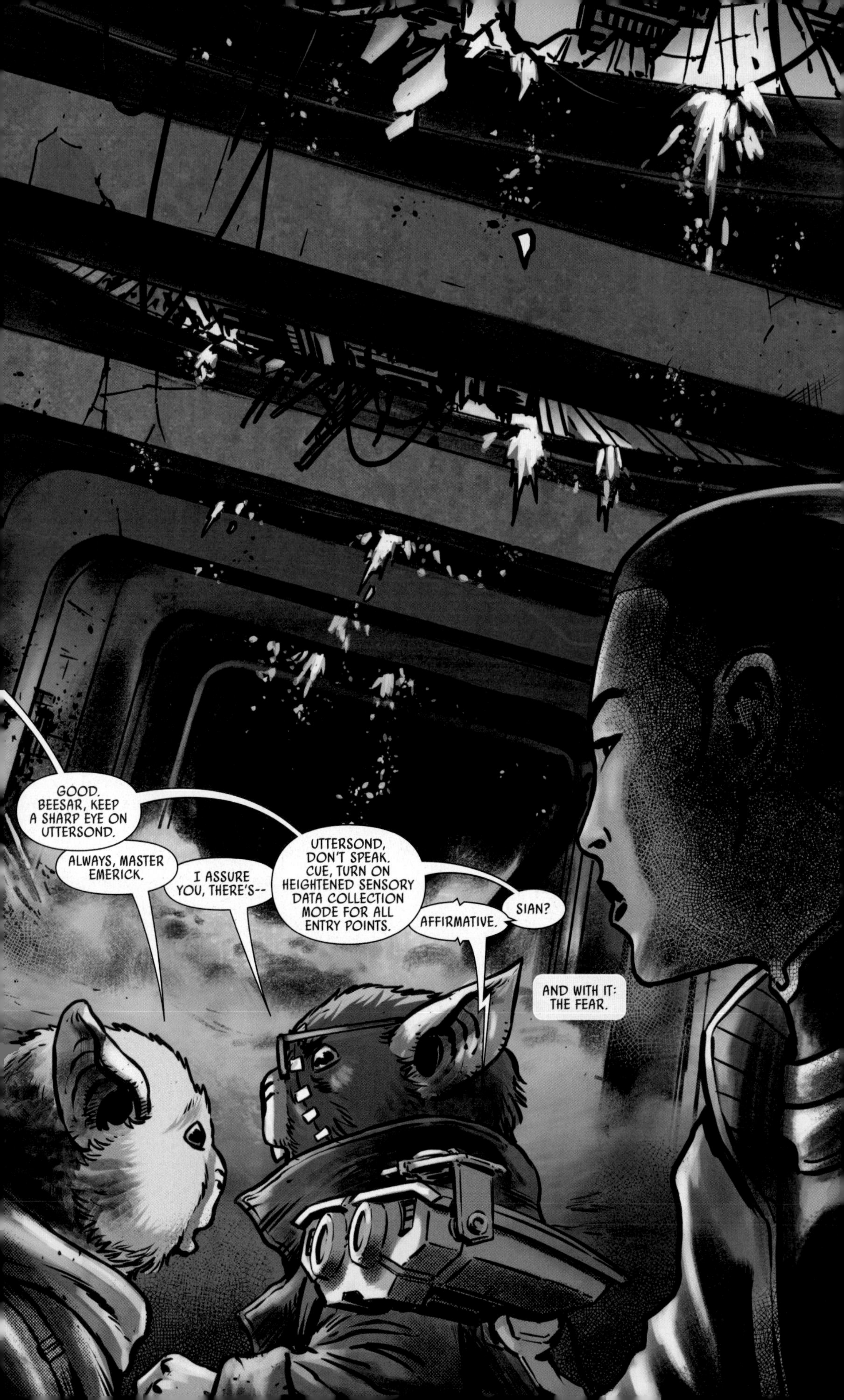
GOOD. BEESAR, KEEP A SHARP EYE ON UTTERSOND.
ALWAYS, MASTER EMERICK.
I ASSURE YOU, THERE'S--
UTTERSOND, DON'T SPEAK. CUE, TURN ON HEIGHTENED SENSORY DATA COLLECTION MODE FOR ALL ENTRY POINTS.
SIAN?
AFFIRMATIVE.
AND WITH IT: THE FEAR.

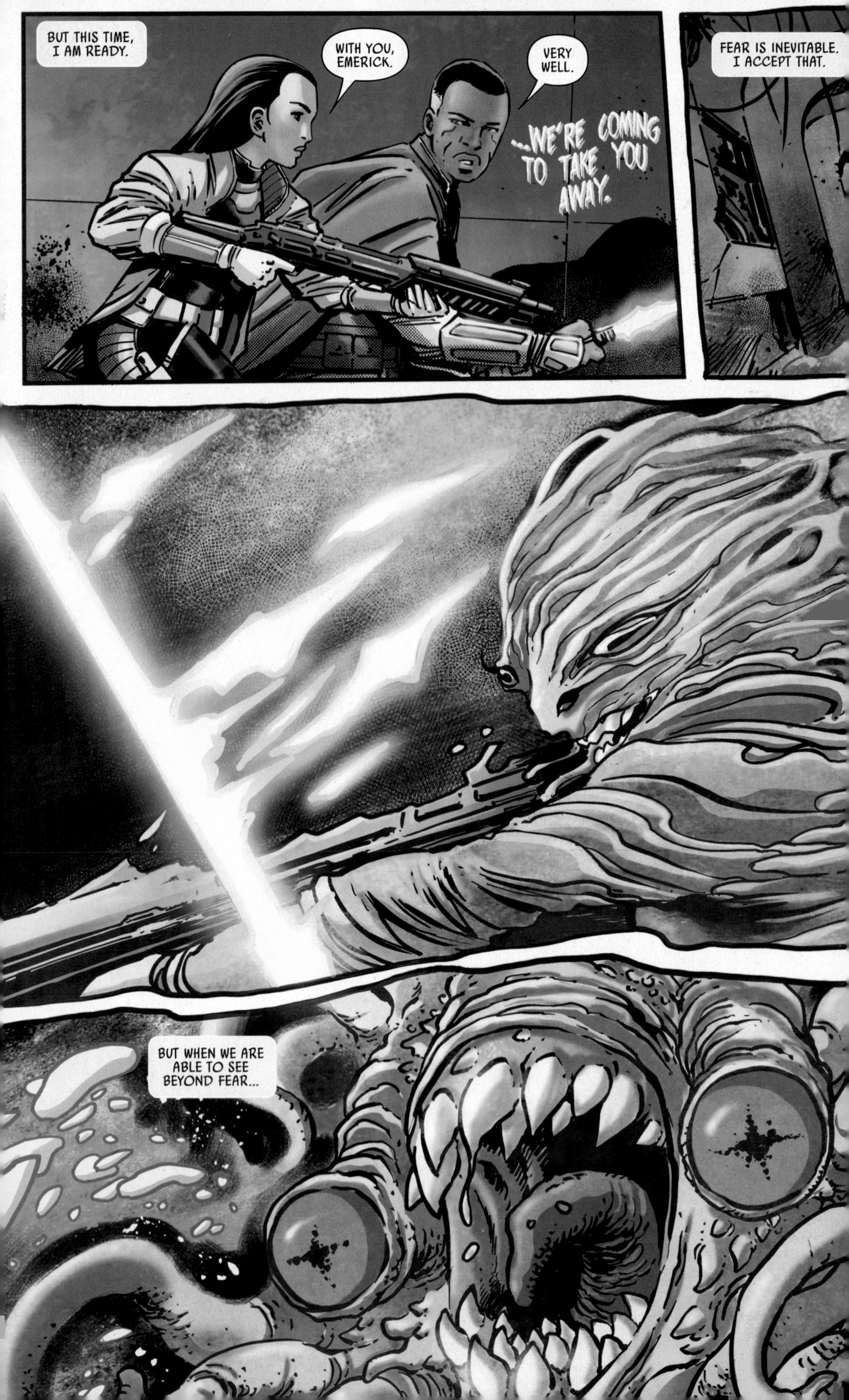
BUT THIS TIME, I AM READY.
WITH YOU, EMERICK.
VERY WELL.
...WE'RE COMING TO TAKE YOU AWAY.
FEAR IS INEVITABLE. I ACCEPT THAT.
BUT WHEN WE ARE ABLE TO SEE BEYOND FEAR...

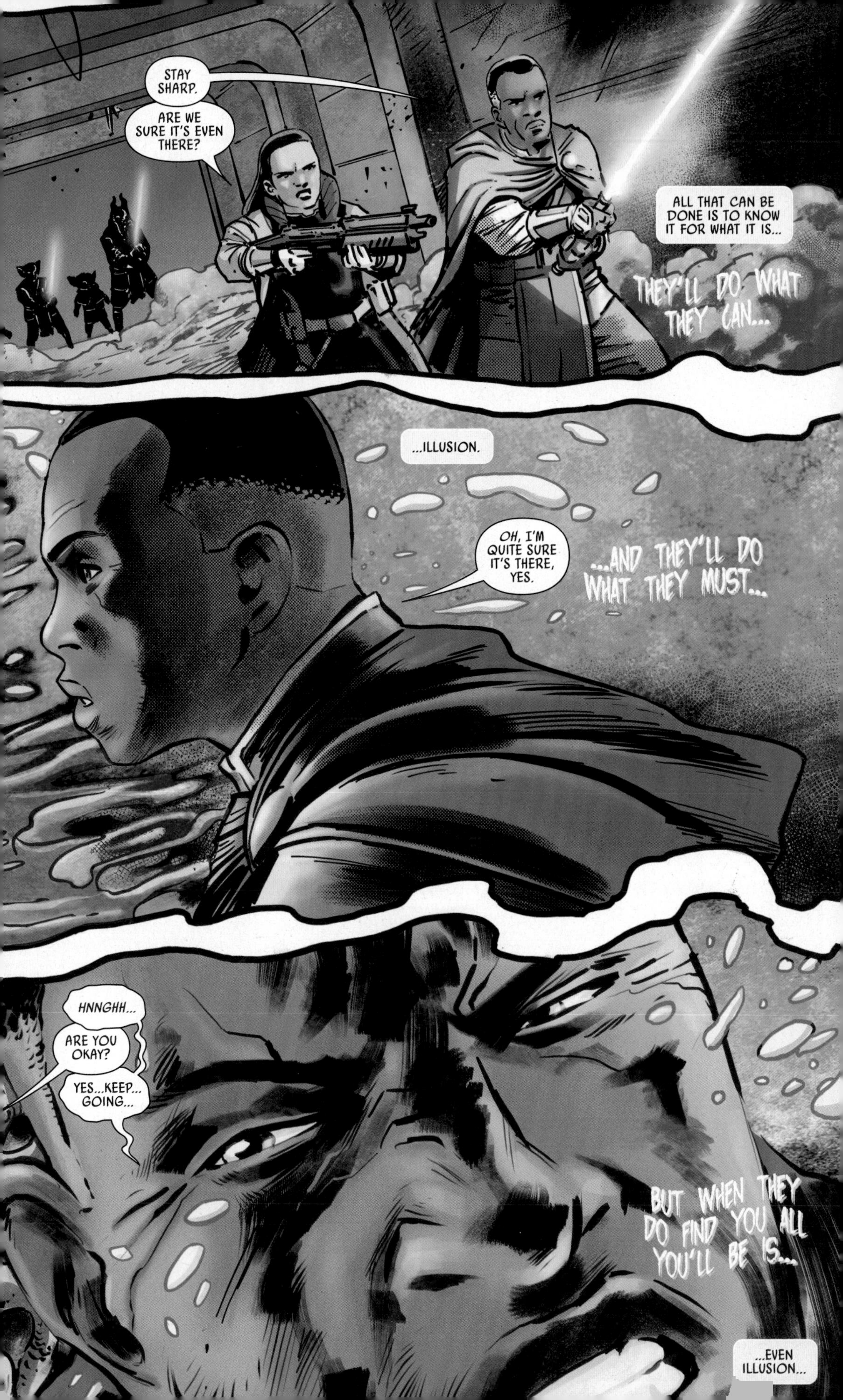
STAY SHARP.
ARE WE SURE IT'S EVEN THERE?
ALL THAT CAN BE DONE IS TO KNOW IT FOR WHAT IT IS...
THEY'LL DO WHAT THEY CAN...
...ILLUSION.
OH, I'M QUITE SURE IT'S THERE, YES.
...AND THEY'LL DO WHAT THEY MUST...
HNNGHH...
ARE YOU OKAY?
YES...KEEP... GOING...
BUT WHEN THEY DO FIND YOU ALL YOU'LL BE IS...
...EVEN ILLUSION...

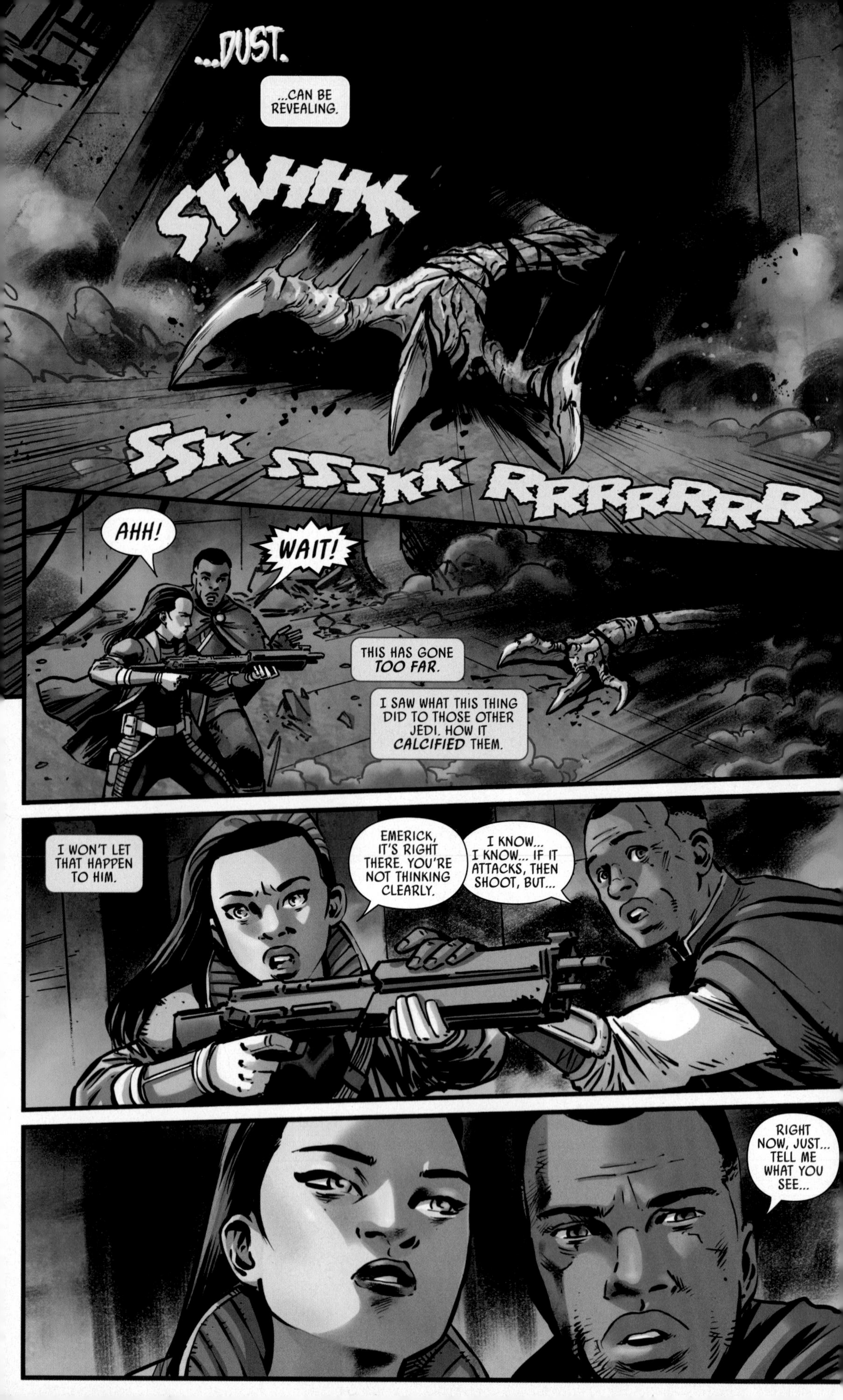

...DUST.
...CAN BE REVEALING.
SHHHK
SSK SSSKK RRRRRRRR
AHH!
WAIT!
THIS HAS GONE *TOO FAR*.
I SAW WHAT THIS THING DID TO THOSE OTHER JEDI. HOW IT *CALCIFIED* THEM.
I WON'T LET THAT HAPPEN TO HIM.
EMERICK, IT'S RIGHT THERE. YOU'RE NOT THINKING CLEARLY.
I KNOW... I KNOW... IF IT ATTACKS, THEN SHOOT, BUT...
RIGHT NOW, JUST... TELL ME WHAT YOU SEE...

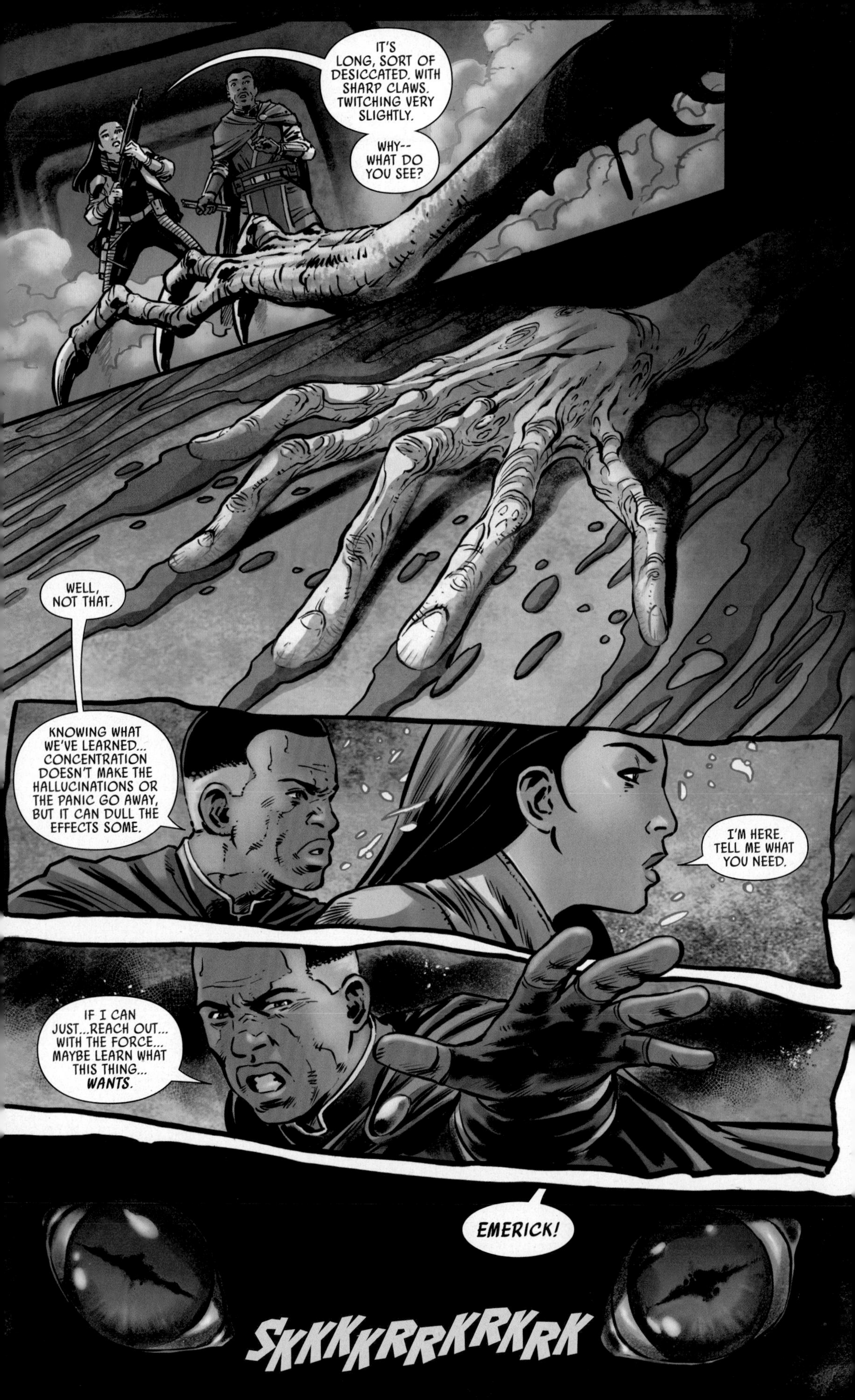
IT'S LONG, SORT OF DESICCATED. WITH SHARP CLAWS. TWITCHING VERY SLIGHTLY.
WHY-- WHAT DO YOU SEE?
WELL, NOT THAT.
KNOWING WHAT WE'VE LEARNED... CONCENTRATION DOESN'T MAKE THE HALLUCINATIONS OR THE PANIC GO AWAY, BUT IT CAN DULL THE EFFECTS SOME.
I'M HERE. TELL ME WHAT YOU NEED.
IF I CAN JUST...REACH OUT... WITH THE FORCE... MAYBE LEARN WHAT THIS THING... *WANTS*.
EMERICK!
SKKKKRRKRKRK

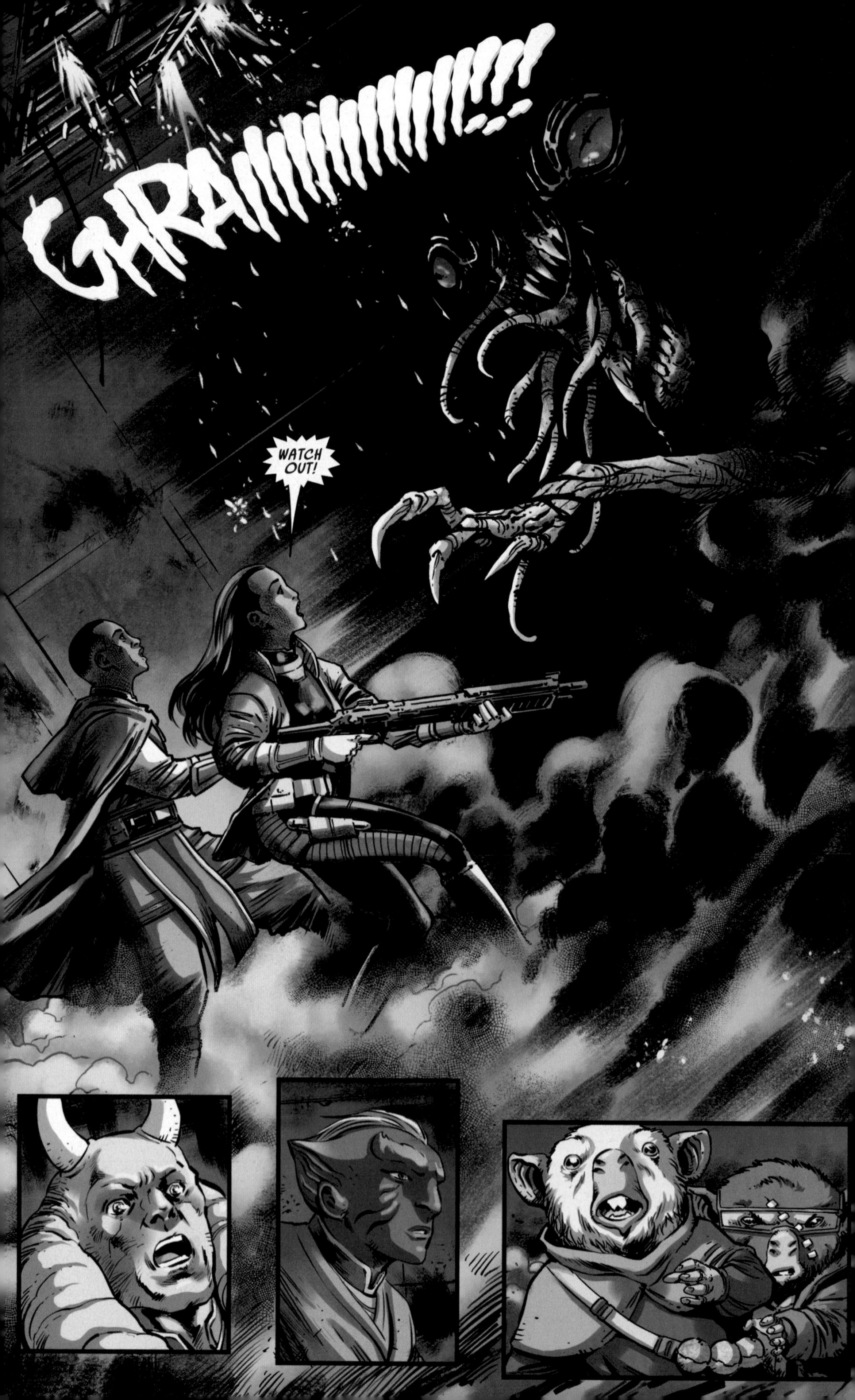
GHRAIIIIIIIIIII!!!
WATCH OUT!

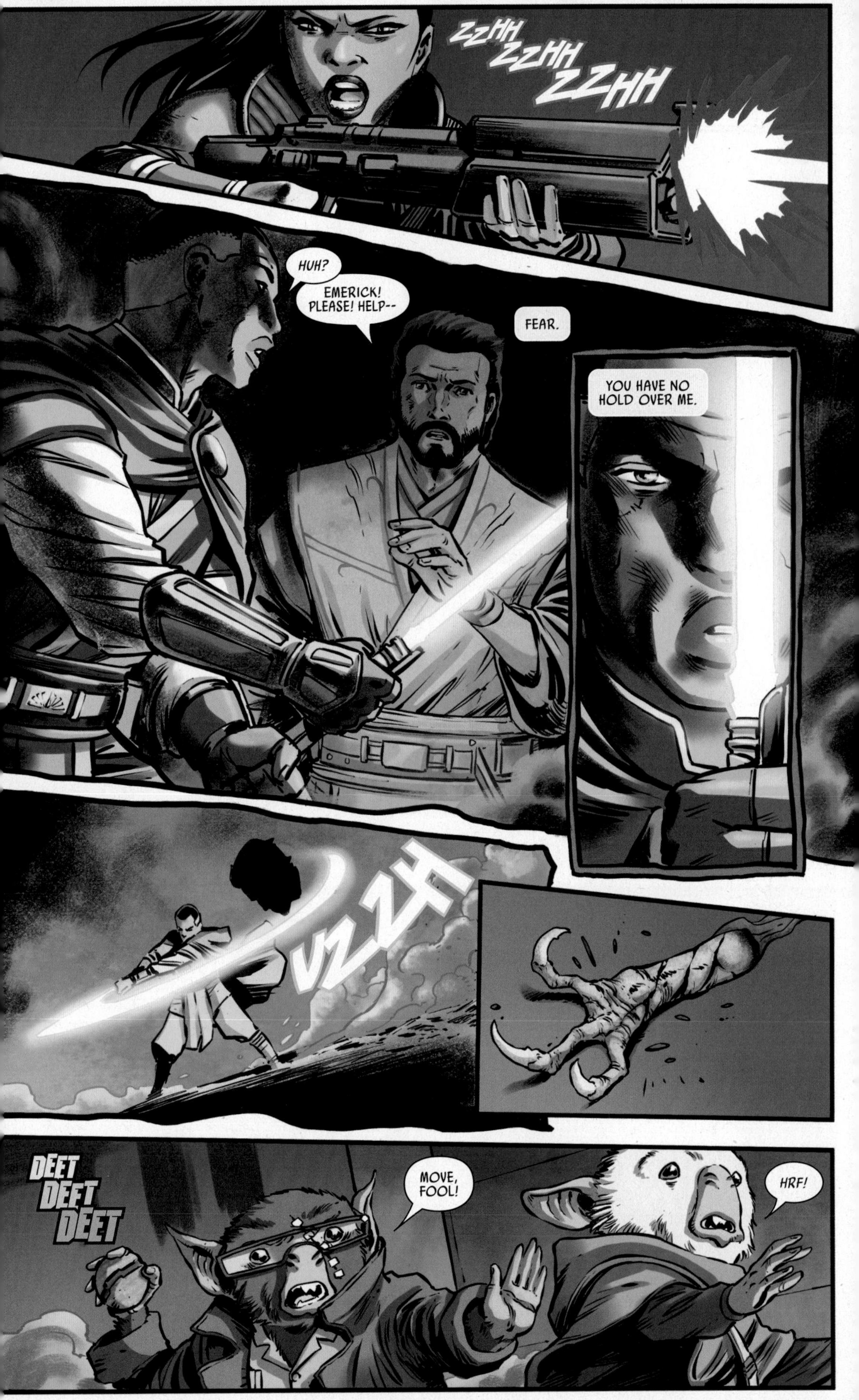
ZZHH
ZZHH
ZZHH
HUH?
EMERICK! PLEASE! HELP--
FEAR.
YOU HAVE NO HOLD OVER ME.
VZZH
DEET
DEET
DEET
MOVE, FOOL!
HRF!

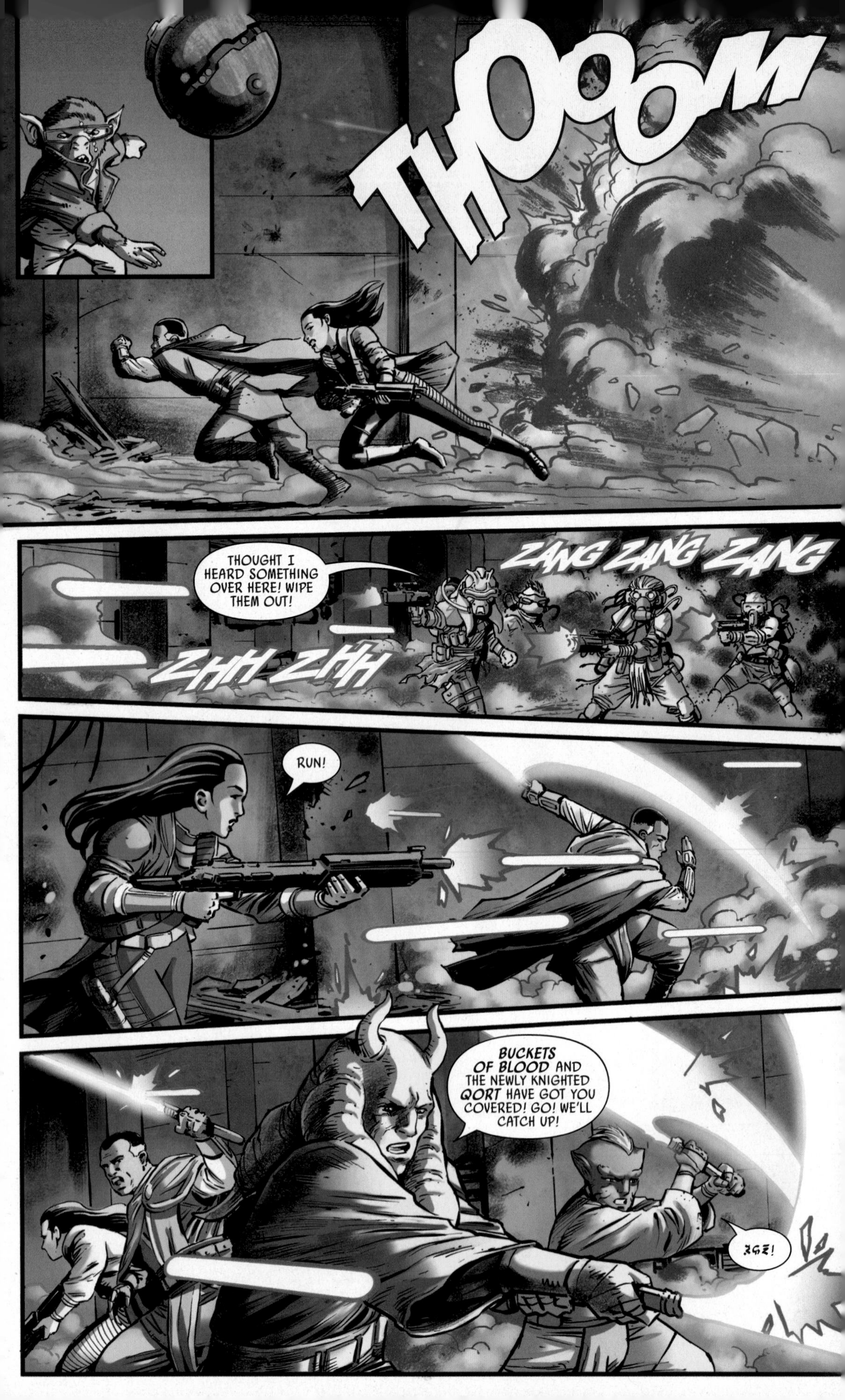
THOOOOM
THOUGHT I HEARD SOMETHING OVER HERE! WIPE THEM OUT!
ZANG ZANG ZANG
ZHH ZHH
RUN!
BUCKETS OF BLOOD AND THE NEWLY KNIGHTED QORT HAVE GOT YOU COVERED! GO! WE'LL CATCH UP!

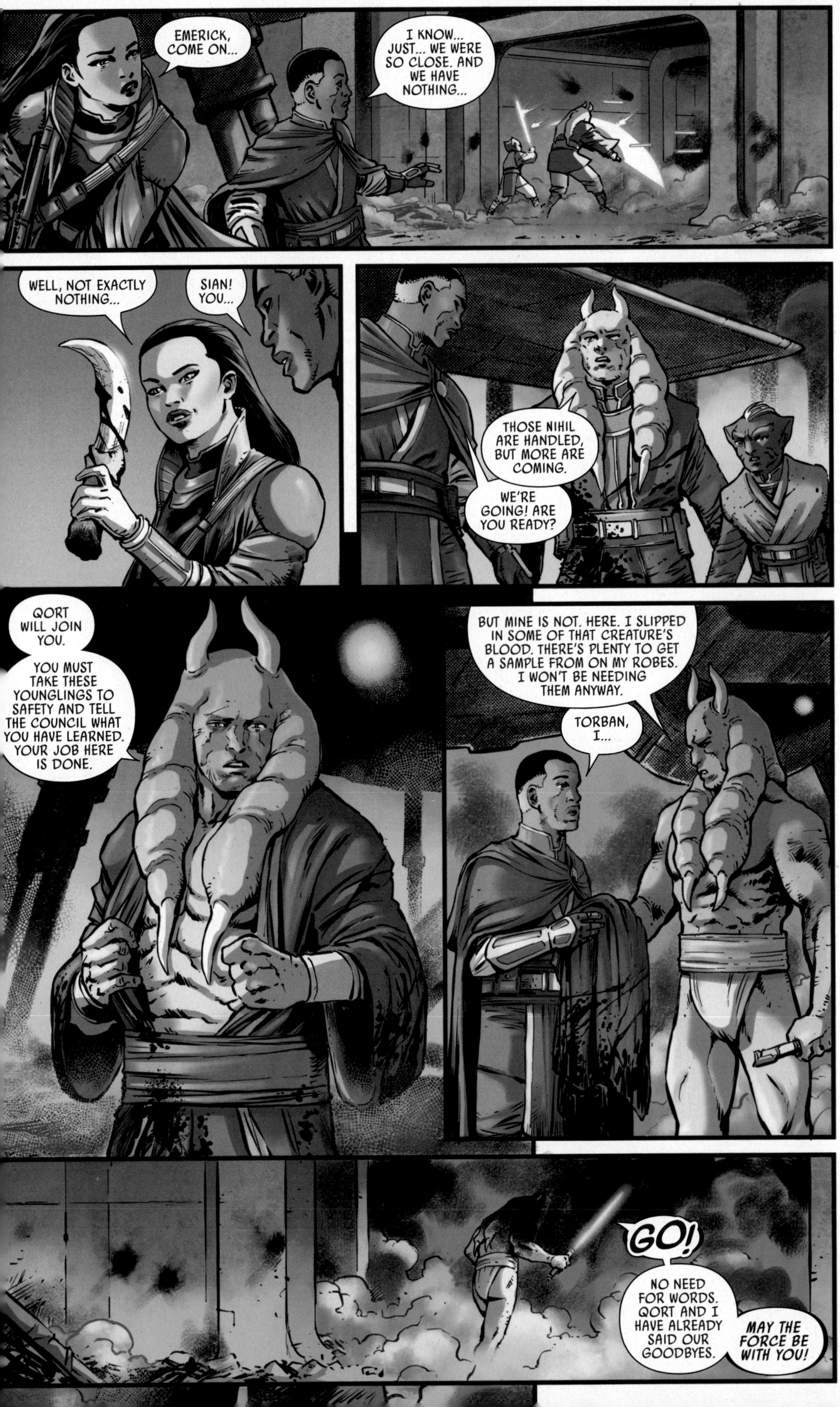
EMERICK, COME ON...
I KNOW... JUST... WE WERE SO CLOSE. AND WE HAVE NOTHING...
WELL, NOT EXACTLY NOTHING...
SIAN! YOU...
THOSE NIHIL ARE HANDLED, BUT MORE ARE COMING.
WE'RE GOING! ARE YOU READY?
QORT WILL JOIN YOU.
YOU MUST TAKE THESE YOUNGLINGS TO SAFETY AND TELL THE COUNCIL WHAT YOU HAVE LEARNED. YOUR JOB HERE IS DONE.
BUT MINE IS NOT. HERE. I SLIPPED IN SOME OF THAT CREATURE'S BLOOD. THERE'S PLENTY TO GET A SAMPLE FROM ON MY ROBES. I WON'T BE NEEDING THEM ANYWAY.
TORBAN, I...
GO!
NO NEED FOR WORDS. QORT AND I HAVE ALREADY SAID OUR GOODBYES.
MAY THE FORCE BE WITH YOU!

STARLIGHT IS DOWN. THE GALAXY HAS CHANGED FOREVER.

SO MANY LIVES LOST. MORE THAN WE CAN EVEN GRASP. THE NIHIL TRIUMPHANT. AND UTTERSOND SLIPPED AWAY IN THE CHAOS--DEAD PERHAPS. DEVOURED BY THE VERY CREATURES HE TRIED TO SELL ON THE BLACK MARKET.

WHO'S TO SAY?

STILL...

BEGIN DATA ANALYSIS, CUE. EVERYTHING IS--

--SOMETHING. I KNOW, MASTER. ALREADY IN PROGRESS.

...WE FOLLOWED THIS PATH INTO THE GAPING JAWS OF TERROR...

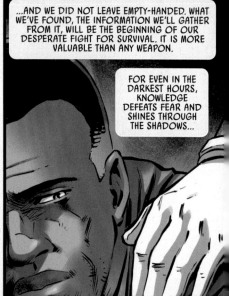

...AND WE DID NOT LEAVE EMPTY-HANDED. WHAT WE'VE FOUND, THE INFORMATION WE'LL GATHER FROM IT, WILL BE THE BEGINNING OF OUR DESPERATE FIGHT FOR SURVIVAL. IT IS MORE VALUABLE THAN ANY WEAPON.

FOR EVEN IN THE DARKEST HOURS, KNOWLEDGE DEFEATS FEAR AND SHINES THROUGH THE SHADOWS...

...TO SHOW US THE PATH BACK TO THE *LIGHT*.

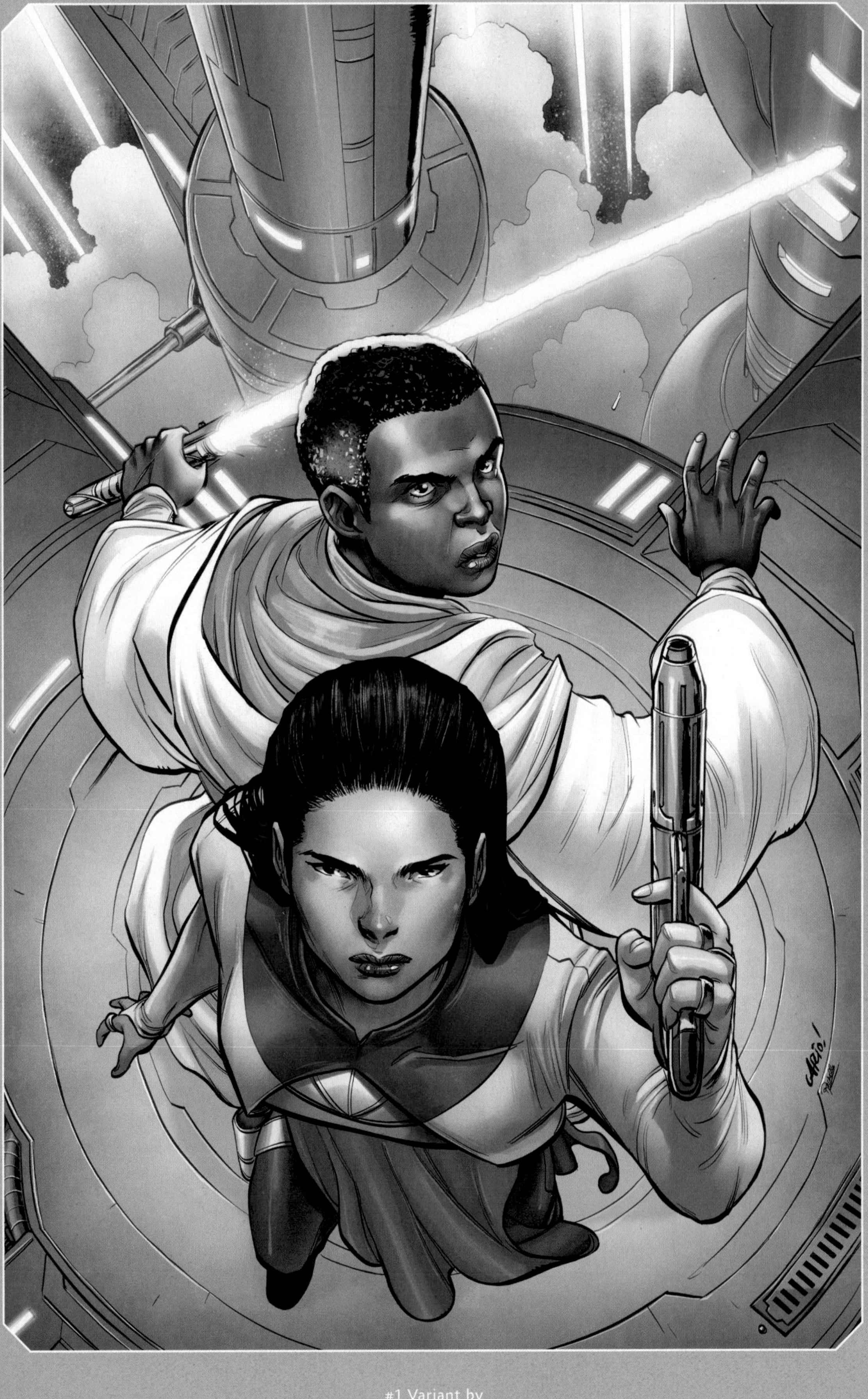

#1 Variant by
ARIO ANINDITO & RACHELLE ROSENBERG

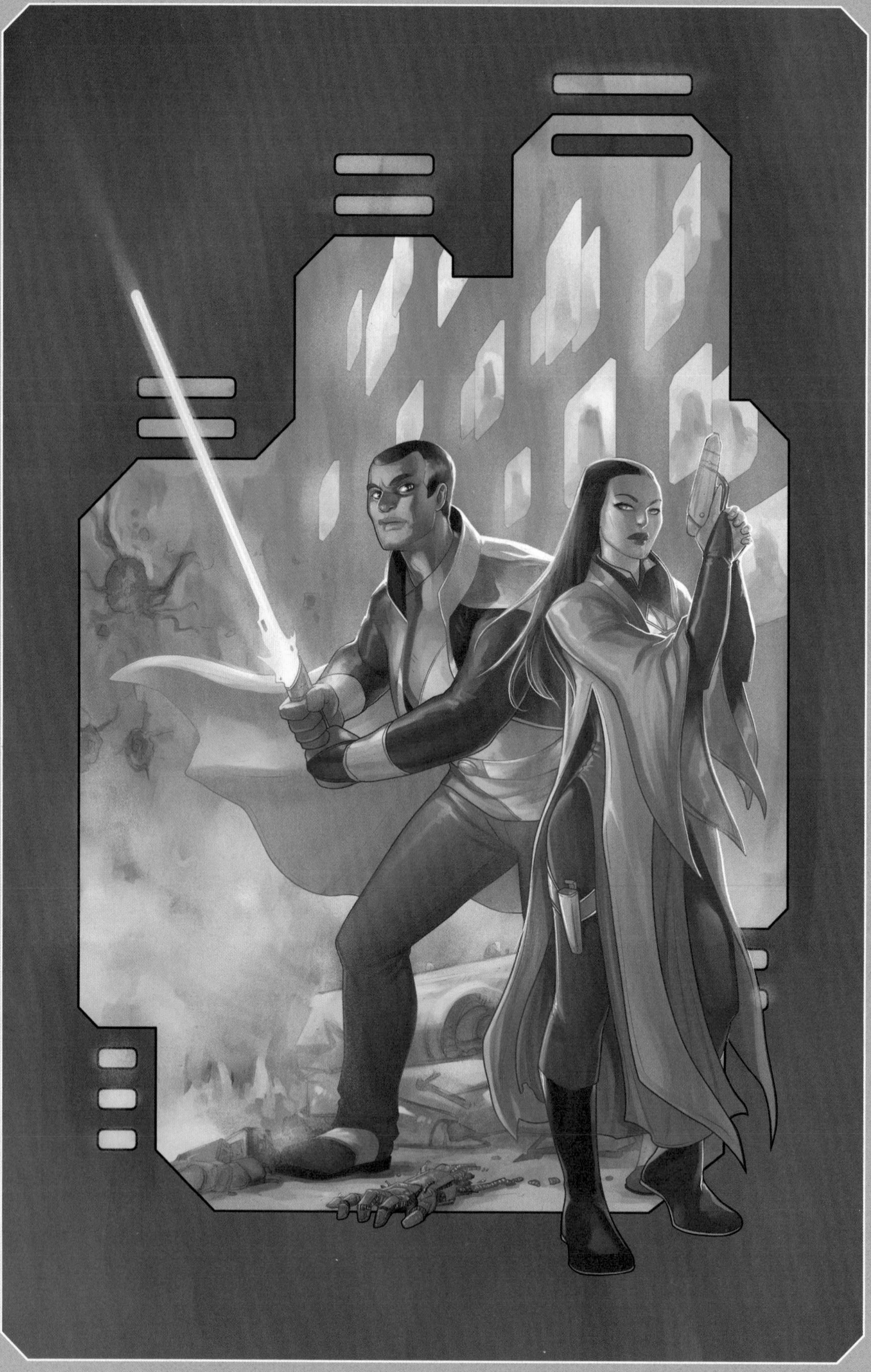

#2 Variant by
MEGHAN HETRICK

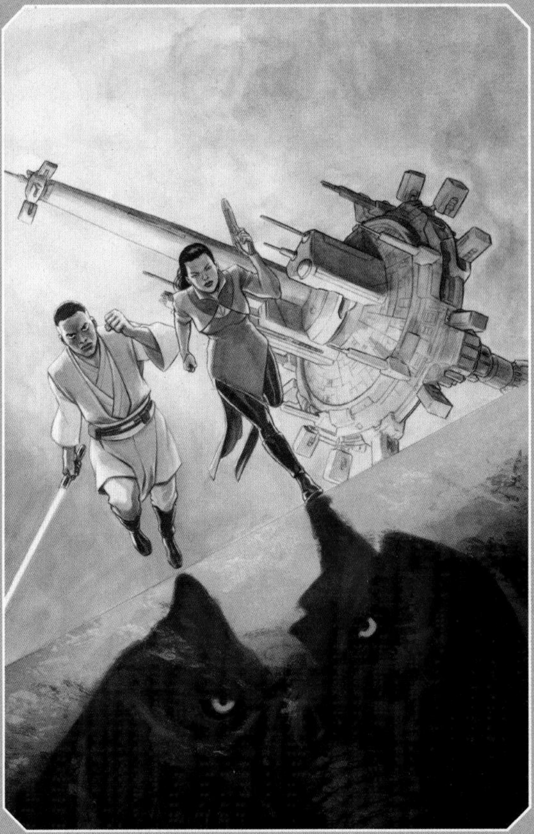

#2 Variant by
DAVID LOPEZ

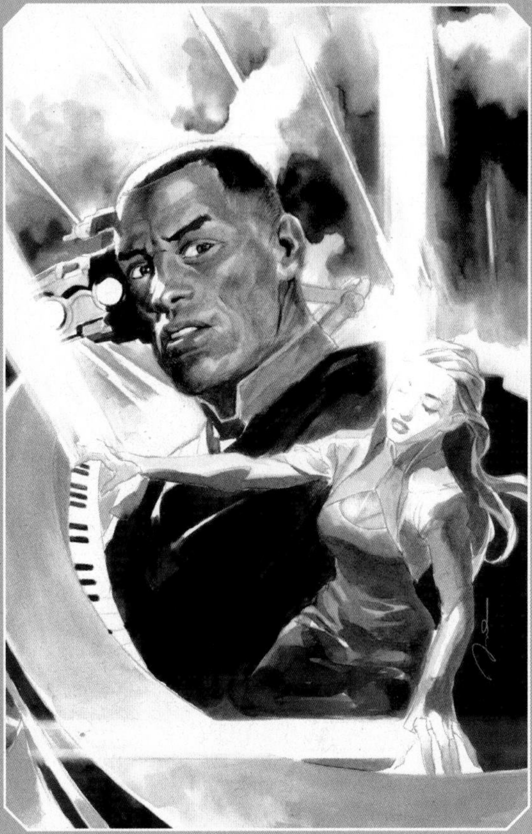

#3 Variant by
GERALD PAREL

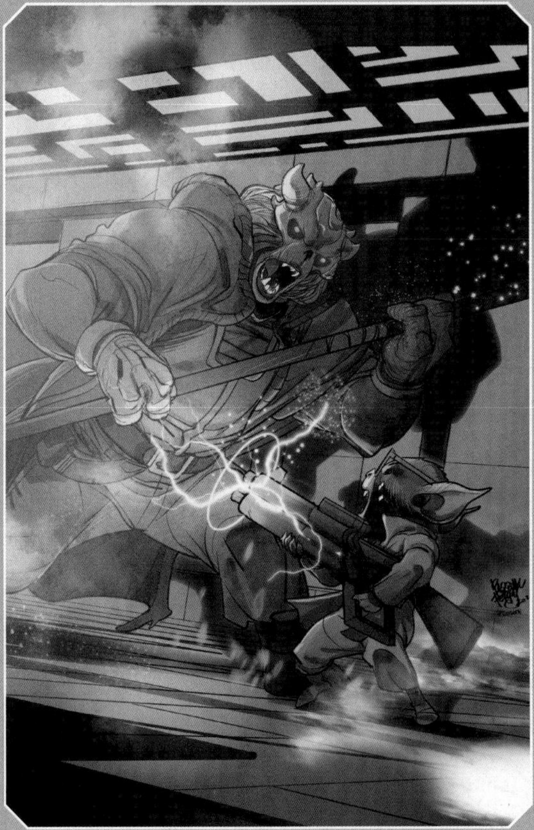

#4 Variant by
PASQUAL FERRY & MATT HOLLINGSWORTH

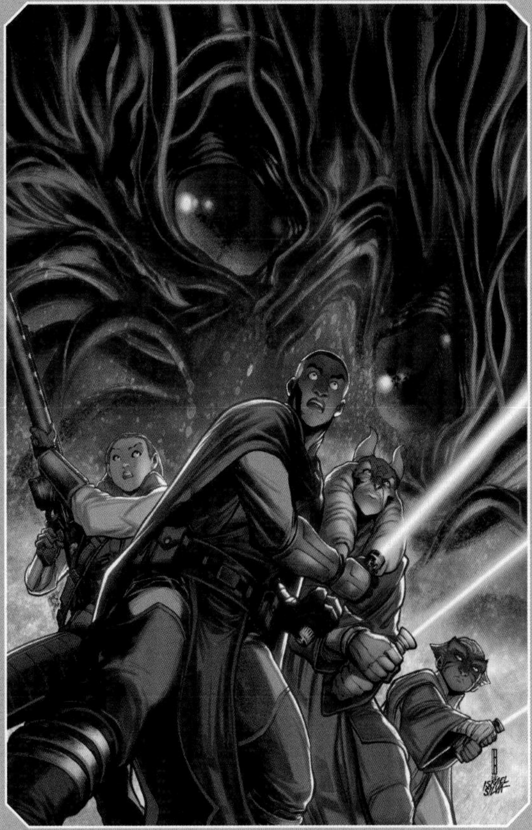

#5 Variant by
DAVID BALDEÓN & ISRAEL SILVA

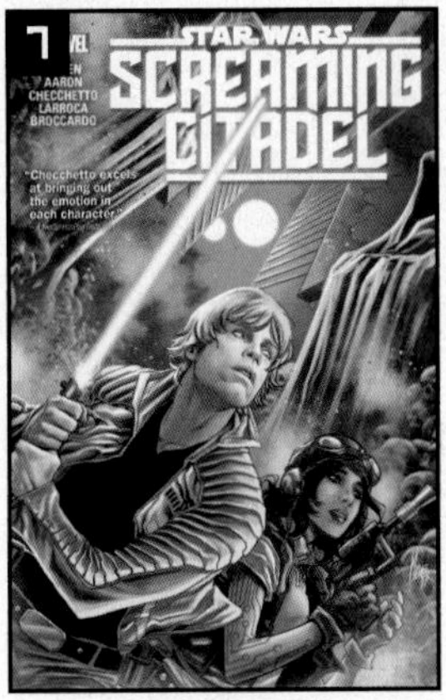
7
STAR WARS
SCREAMING CITADEL

Star Wars:
The Screaming Citadel
ISBN 978-1-302-90678-8

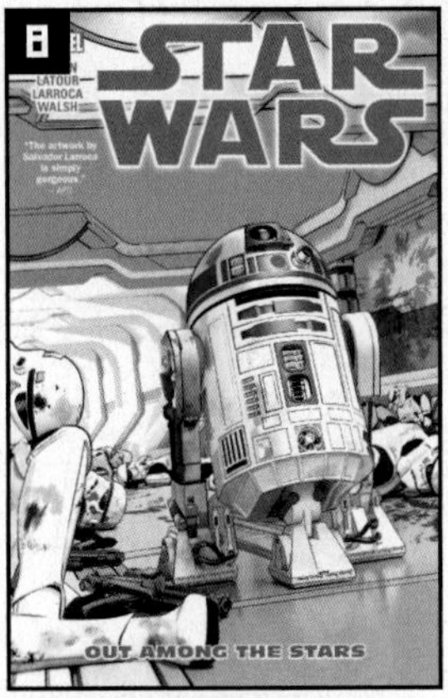
8
LATOUR
LARROCA
WALSH
STAR WARS
OUT AMONG THE STARS

Star Wars Vol. 6:
Out Among the Stars
ISBN 978-1-302-90553-8

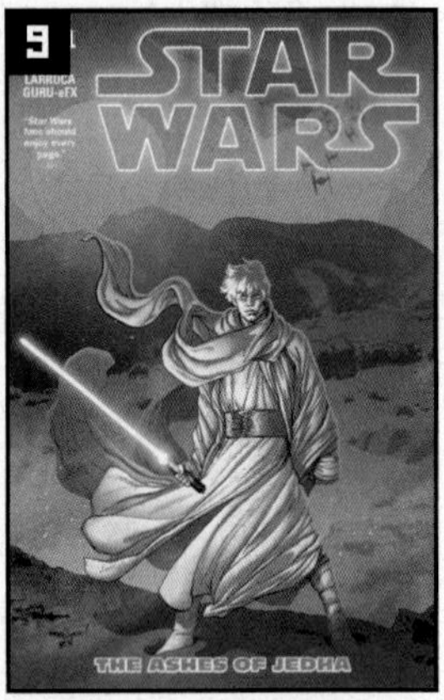
9
LARROCA
GURU-eFX
STAR WARS
THE ASHES OF JEDHA

Star Wars Vol. 7:
The Ashes of Jedha
ISBN 978-1-302-91052-5

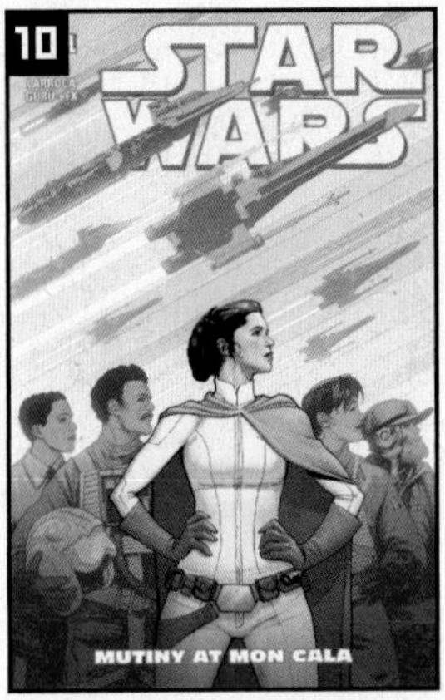
10
STAR WARS
MUTINY AT MON CALA

Star Wars Vol. 8:
Mutiny at Mon Cala
ISBN 978-1-302-91053-2

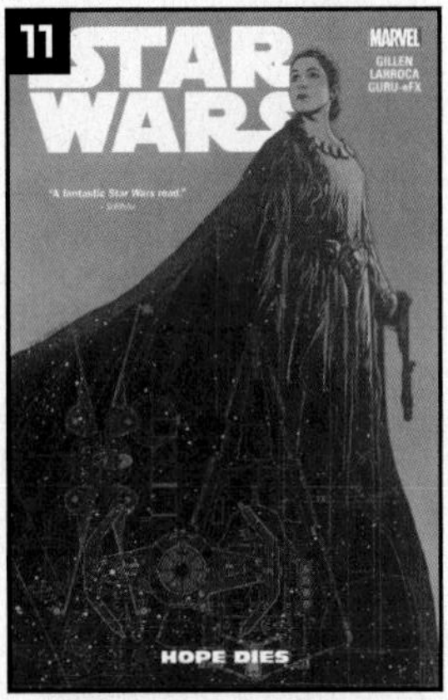
11
STAR WARS
MARVEL
GILLEN
LARROCA
GURU-eFX
"A fantastic Star Wars read."
HOPE DIES

Star Wars Vol. 9:
Hope Dies
ISBN 978-1-302-91054-9

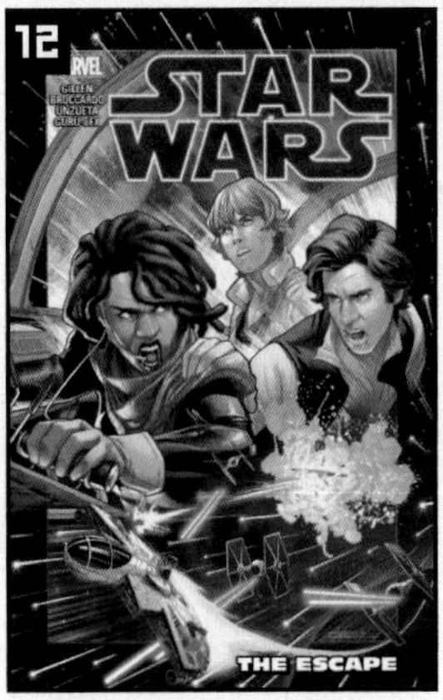
12
STAR WARS
THE ESCAPE

Star Wars Vol. 10:
The Escape
ISBN 978-1-302-91449-3

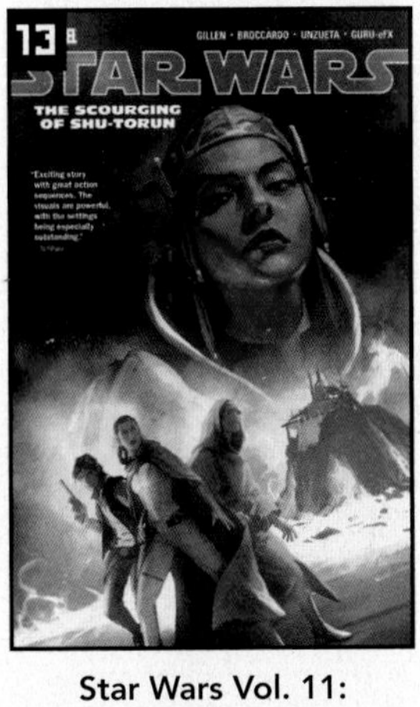
13
GILLEN · BROCCARDO · UNZUETA · GURU-eFX
STAR WARS
THE SCOURGING OF SHU-TORUN

Star Wars Vol. 11:
The Scourging of Shu-Torun
ISBN 978-1-302-91450-9

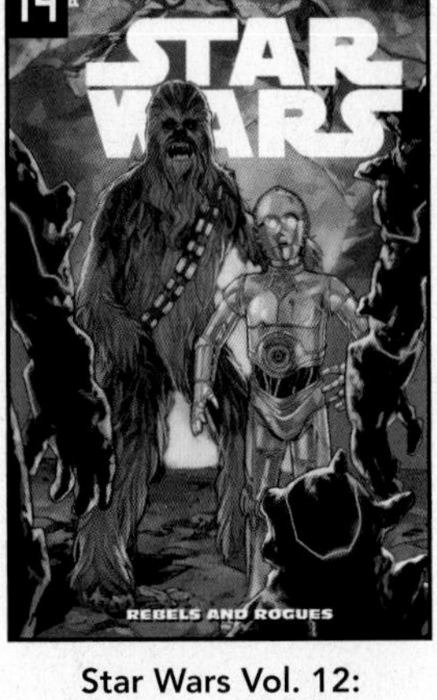
14
STAR WARS
REBELS AND ROGUES

Star Wars Vol. 12:
Rebels and Rogues
ISBN 978-1-302-91451-6

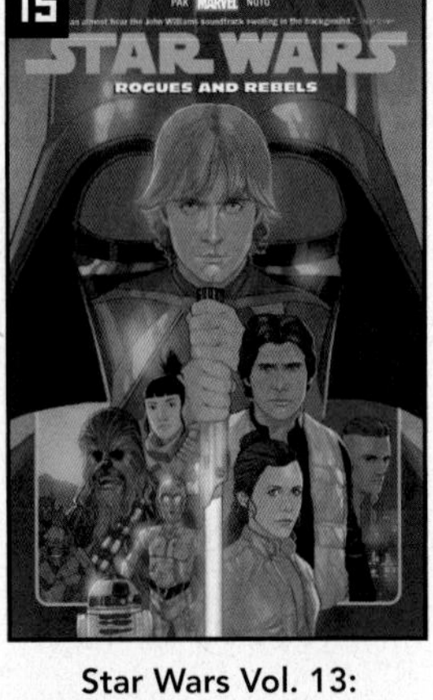
15
PAK
MARVEL
NOTO
STAR WARS
ROGUES AND REBELS

Star Wars Vol. 13:
Rogues and Rebels
ISBN 978-1-302-91450-9

Centuries before the Skywalker saga, a new adventure begins....

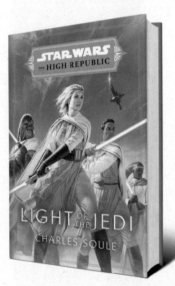

Books, Comics, ebooks, and Audiobooks Available Now!

Visit StarWars.com/TheHighRepublic for the latest news

© & TM 2021 Lucasfilm Ltd.